A SMALL, GOOD THING

A SMALL, GOOD THING

Stories of Children with HIV and

Those Who Care for Them

ANNE HUNSAKER HAWKINS

W. W. NORTON & COMPANY

NEW YORK · LONDON

For information about permission to reproduce selections from this book,
write to Permissions, W. W. Norton & Company, Inc.,
500 Fifth Avenue, New York, NY 10110

The text of this book is composed in Electra with the display set in Copperplate Gothic
Composition by Carol Desnoes
Manufacturing by The Maple-Vail Book Manufacturing Group
Book design by JAM design

Library of Congress Cataloging-in-Publication Data

Hawkins, Anne Hunsaker, 1944–
A small, good thing : stories of children with HIV
and those who care for them / Anne Hunsaker Hawkins.
p.   cm.
Includes bibliographical references.
ISBN 0-393-04944-2
1. AIDS (Disease) in children—Patients—Biography. 2. AIDS (Disease)
in children—Popular works. I. Title.

RJ387.A25 H39 2000
362.1'98929792—dc21   00-027018

W. W. Norton & Company, Inc., 500 Fifth Avenue, New York, N.Y. 10110
www.wwnorton.com

W. W. Norton & Company Ltd., 10 Coptic Street, London WC1A 1PU

1 2 3 4 5 6 7 8 9 0

When I think about having HIV I wonder why the HIV has to bother everybody ~~everybody~~ everyone is different. some have different skin colors some have different acents. HIV is not a scary thing. Seienst, doctor and nurses around the world are trying to find cures. People that have HIV will get worse if they dont have heart. People dont lose hope a cure will come and if you have faith and the cure doesnt come you will know that youve lived life to the fullest. HIV may have your body but it doesnt have your heart.

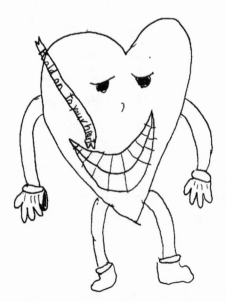

JAMAL ANDERSON
Age Twelve

The frontispiece is by Jamal Anderson, one of several children whose stories I was unable to include. Jamal, now twelve, has advanced HIV infection. Hospitalized a dozen times in early childhood, he has undergone a long series of life-threatening opportunistic infections and drastic treatments. For several years, he was on home ventilator support. Like many children with HIV, Jamal has suffered beyond his disease. His mother was unable to care for him, and his father, an IV drug user, was frequently in prison. Jamal was placed in foster care at the age of two. His foster mother subsequently took in three other HIV-infected children, including Jamal's sister. But this was before the advent of lifesaving HIV medications, and unfortunately these children died.

By the age of six Jamal was having trouble controlling his anger, both at home and in school. Ritalin seemed to help, but two years later his behavior turned violent. He set fires and repeatedly threatened his foster mother. This escalated until, at age ten, he was placed in the institution where he now lives. Today Jamal has adjusted to institutional life and is doing well in school (early on he was identified as academically gifted). He is hoping for another foster family, though this does not seem likely given his age, his illness, and his history. His medical future is a race between his disease and the development of new, effective medications. But Jamal believes in self-healing and the power of his mind. He has hope — and he has heart.

To the Children

In the eye of a hurricane the sky is blue and birds can fly there without suffering harm. The eye of the hurricane is in the very middle of destructive power, and that power is always near, surrounding that blue beauty and threatening to invade it. . . .

In a world of moral hurricanes some people can and do carve out rather large ethical spaces. In a natural world and a social world swirling in cruelty and love we can make room. We who are not pure ethical beings can push away the choking circle of brute force that is around and within us. We may not be able to push it far . . . , but when we have made as much room as we can, we may know a blue peace that the storm does not know.

—PHILIP HALLIE
Tales of Good and Evil

We are all responsible to all for all.

—FYODOR DOSTOEVSKY
The Brothers Karamazov

CONTENTS

ACKNOWLEDGMENTS

FIRST, I want to give special thanks to the families at our hospital's HIV clinic, both those I write about and those I do not. These people allowed me to witness, and sometimes to share, their hopes, fears, and struggles, their moments of happiness and of discouragement.

I owe much to the members of the clinic staff, who made me feel a part of "the team." I am especially grateful to the physician I call Dr. Bennett, who has been generous in so many ways: welcoming me to his clinic, endorsing the idea of such a book and helping me win the approval of our Institutional Review Board, talking with me at length about his values and background as well as his experience as a physician, and, perhaps most important, giving the project his full support while knowing that I intended to write candidly about him and his work.

I am very grateful to family members, friends, and colleagues who read and commented on early versions of the manuscript: Debra and Rob Chwast, Margie Ehmann, Seth and Kelly Hawkins, Gale Kase, Marilyn McEntyre, and especially my daughter, Katherine Hawkins. As Katy read through the manuscript chapter by chapter, at my request (or insistence), she offered me invaluable, if not always welcome, advice. We are always grateful to those who enable us to see and feel beyond our own personal boundaries and confines; such gratitude is mixed with pride when this person is one's own child.

My chairman and others at the medical college affiliated with the hospital I refer to as St. Luke's granted me a sabbatical leave to write this book. During those ten months I immersed myself in the lives of the clinic families, read widely among the works of such authors as Dickens, Dostoevsky, and Sophocles, and spent long and hard hours writing and revising the manucript. This would not have been possible without the protected time provided by a sabbatical.

My debts to literary authors are too numerous to mention. Most I have found a way to mention, however briefly, in the text of the book. An exception is the author and psychiatrist Robert Coles. My motives for writing my book happened to coincide exactly with Coles's urging that academic knowledge be used in the service of practical needs. Coles's *Call of Service* has been especially helpful in his description of the rewards and difficulties (and the benefits and limitations) of an ethic of service and in helping me interrogate my own personal "call of service."

The title of my book is also the title of a short story by Raymond Carver. While I do not intend any allusion to Carver's fictional story, there are some similarities to my book of real-life stories, since Carver's story is about a child's death, the suffering of the child's parents, and the new communities that take shape around that suffering.

I want to thank Starling Lawrence and Tabitha Griffin of W. W. Norton & Company, my publisher. I am impressed by Norton's generosity in donating a substantial part of its proceeds from the sale of this book to the Elizabeth Glaser Pediatric AIDS Foundation.

As sources on pediatric HIV and its treatment, I used articles by Andrew Wiznia et al. and by James Oleske, books by Philip Pizzo and Catherine Wilfert and by Gerald Stine, and reports from the CDC. These are cited in the bibliography. "Dr. Bennett" at my request verified the accuracy of all medical references and explanations in the book.

Other mentors, colleagues, and friends (categories now often indistinguishable) to whom I am grateful and whom I have not mentioned before include Rosanne Ayala, David Barnard, Joanne Trautmann Banks, Rita Charon, Philip Hallie, Catherine Morrison, Carmen Prophet, Oliver Sacks, Stephanie Shuey, Howard Spiro, and Tammy Walmers.

Lastly, there is my husband, Sherman, "*min runwita ond min rædbora.*" Without his patience, generosity, and support I could never have undertaken this project, much less completed it.

INTRODUCTION

ONE April morning in 1996 I decided to take up Dr. Bennett's invitation to attend his HIV clinic for children at the hospital in southern Ohio that I call St. Luke's. St. Luke's is a tertiary care medical center associated with a highly respected medical school that, in any given year, provides clinical training for some five hundred students in medicine, nursing, and pastoral care. The complex consists of a cluster of massive concrete and glass structures that house hospital units, research labs, classrooms, and outpatient facilities. Situated as it is in the heartland of America, it looks out on cornfields to the west and cows grazing in a big meadow to the south. Despite this rural setting, there are several moderate-size cities close by.

St. Luke's is relatively new, dating back to the late 1960s. From its earliest beginnings it was an institution with a vision. The founding dean wanted this vision incorporated into the architectural design of the building. Huge windows with fabulous views of the surrounding countryside spanned all seven stories of the medical complex. The intent was not so much aesthetic as didactic: to remind medical staff and students to focus outward on the community they served. The concrete and glass building was designed in the shape of a crescent, meant to suggest open arms that embrace and comfort those who enter its halls. One side of the building houses the hospital and the other side, the college. And the college includes a department of humanities, the first in the country. In between hospital and college is the library, which brings together knowledge drawn from the sciences and wisdom from the humanities, both considered vital to medical practice and medical education.

But all things must change, and with the passage of time the realization of this vision became somewhat compromised. Jokes were made that the crescent shape symbolized not comfort and compassion but the greed of the institution, its arms outstretched to demand money for services rendered. Gradually, as the goals of the institution shifted away from serving the community and toward excellence in biomedical research, the huge picture windows, though still visible from the outside of the building, were shut off from view within by the offices of administrators and department chairpersons and the laboratories of researchers. Now, these windows with their spectacular views are to be found inside the building only in lobbies and in waiting rooms.

Although the institution is different now, the original humanistic vision, like the original shape of the embracing crescent, is still present. It survives in the dedication of many doctors to humanistic values that transcend making money or advancing one's career; it is evident in the sympathy for a worried parent that compels a pediatrician to give out his or her home phone number, or the devotion to research that keeps a clinician or a scientist up late at night in the lab, or the interest in students that drives a busy physician to spend time talking with them and, perhaps even more important, listening.

After coming to St. Luke's in 1990 as a member of the humanities department, I tried to acquire firsthand knowledge of medical education and medical practice. I studied gross anatomy alongside my students. Like them, I steeled myself for the very first cut of the scalpel and flinched when I had to look at our cadaver's face; like them, I was filled with wonder at the incredible intricacies of nerves, veins, and arteries; and like many of them, I gave up eating meat for the duration of the course. I then moved from cadavers to living persons, taking the course in interviewing techniques, in which students are expected to develop and hone their listening skills while filtering a patient's story through diagnostic acronyms. And all along, I have watched doctors at work. The days I spent in the surgical suite were among the most memorable: seeing a heart (which was smaller than I would have thought) beating inside a woman's chest cavity; watching an elderly gentleman's arthroscopic laser surgery; standing for hours at the side of a plastic surgeon as he performed a painstakingly delicate parotidectomy on a middle-aged man. I shadowed doctors in a family practice outpatient clinic, I spent a harrowing month on the intensive care unit, and for several days I floated in the otherworldly atmosphere of the hospital's neonatal ICU.

But of all these forays into the world of medicine, the morning I spent in the pediatric HIV clinic affected me most powerfully. It is tertiary care medical centers like St. Luke's that, for the most part, provide treatment for children who are HIV-infected or who are born to HIV-infected mothers. As will become evident, the hospital does not always make the right decisions about clinic organization and staffing, and the clinic is not without its faults and limitations. But it remains true that children with HIV tend to receive more comprehensive and up-to-date treatment at an institution such as St. Luke's than at community hospitals and clinics. Moreover, treatment of these children can be extremely difficult. Every month, every week, every day research reveals a new drug, a major drawback in some particular treatment, more refined tests, or fresh information about the relation of certain symptoms to the progression of the disease. Not only must physicians be well informed about therapeutic regimens, but they must have a great deal of firsthand experience with patients to interpret the meaning of a cough, a stomachache, eyestrain, or fever. For example, all children have colds and coughs, but pneumonia is a common opportunistic infection for individuals with HIV. Should an infected child with a cough just be sent home or should the child be given chest X rays and maybe hospitalized? How should one interpret

stomach pain, a common childhood complaint? Is it caused by
constipation, or a virus, or a reluctance to go to school, or could it
be a symptom of pancreatitis caused by an HIV medication or a
clinical manifestation of *Cryptosporidium?* These are questions
that can be difficult for even the most experienced and most informed specialist.

Another factor in treating children with HIV is the range of problems that attend on this disease. Academic medical centers, because of their many resources, are uniquely able to provide the
comprehensive medical care such patients need. These children
are vulnerable to a variety of opportunistic infections, which could
lodge in any part of the body. In a tertiary care hospital specialists
can be brought in to share decisions about treatment. In addition,
there are services these children require for other, nonmedical
problems arising from their HIV infections—problems with
schools or day care centers, difficulties in navigating our complicated welfare system, situations in which the biological family does
not seem to be able to care for the child—or simpler issues like
finding an interpreter for a family that does not speak English or arranging transportation for a family unable to get to the clinic on its
own. Of course all this costs money. Most of the children in St.
Luke's HIV clinic are on welfare, and hospitals tend to lose money
on welfare patients. Cost-cutting measures introduced through
managed care make this a problem for all medical institutions, but
it is even more a problem for teaching hospitals, which must also
absorb the costs of medical education.

Too often we think of big tertiary care hospitals as impersonal,
research-oriented, geared toward training future doctors, and indifferent to the nonmedical needs of patients and families. This is not
true. The kind of care I have witnessed at our children's HIV clinic
seems comprehensive and exemplary. My hunch is that what is offered our young patients at St. Luke's is typical of what is provided
at pediatric HIV clinics at other tertiary care centers throughout the
country. However, all this can change. Institutions like St. Luke's
may seem as permanent and impervious to societal change as their

concrete and cinder block construction. But there are enormous institutional pressures to conform to business ethics. These pressures are growing all the time.

The present goal of reducing or at least containing health care costs in the United States is sensible, timely, and long overdue, but in the process our health care system nationwide is being seriously undermined. Academic medical centers are especially affected by these changes since the marketplace mentality that now dominates our medical system is not concerned with educating future doctors or with medical research. Not only are medical schools and the hospitals affiliated with them scrambling to remain solvent, often jettisoning other concerns in doing so, but the most fundamental ideal of the profession—providing care for patients that is both compassionate and competent—is likely to become a matter of individual choice rather than institutional commitment. I want others to know about the kind of care our young HIV patients are receiving at St. Luke's clinic. I want to do this before it is too late to prevent damage to this and other medical centers, damage that will inevitably result if health care delivery becomes little else than a business enterprise.

It is now nearly four years since my first visit to the pediatric HIV clinic, and many of my recollections of the people I met that day have faded. But I do remember vividly two particular patients. One was a nine-year-old girl whose face, hands, and arms were covered with hundreds of warts. She kept her face down most of the time, and she would not smile. Her name, I was told, was Angelina. What a beautiful name, I thought, and what an unhappy child. When Dr. Bennett told me about her history of life-threatening pneumonias, abandonment, and psychotic episodes, I felt a deep and complicated sadness that has stayed with me ever since.

The second child was an extremely sick African-American boy, about seven years old. Kofi was emaciated. His eyes were glazed, focused out somewhere in the middle distance. He never spoke. Dr. Bennett examined him, talking gently to the boy as he did so. Then he turned to the child's foster mother, a dignified older woman with gray hair done up in a bun. I could tell that she was trying hard not to break down and cry. Dr. Bennett's voice was steady and even, as though to offer her strength. I don't remember all of their dialogue, except that she asked at one point, "How long?" And he replied, in his soft voice, "I don't know. We can't know that. But it shouldn't be too much longer." Afterward he told me more about this foster mother. Kofi was the third child she had taken into her home who would die from AIDS. Though the boy himself did not seem in pain, the suffering of the foster mother was unmistakable. Yet, I reflected, she actually chose this! She had elected to take these terminally ill children, she opened her heart to them, then suffered through their dying.

I found myself wondering what it must have been like for Dr. Bennett to examine this child. Since the boy was obviously dying, it seemed a futile gesture. But when I asked him about this, he replied emphatically that Kofi's physical exam was anything but futile. Yes, Kofi had little time left, but that was all the more reason to continue seeing him in the clinic. I realized that the ritual examination served an important psychological function: Dr. Bennett was telling the boy, through touch and voice, that he continued to care for him. He was also assuring the foster mother that he was still there for her too. He went on to tell me that the patients and parents in his HIV clinic were in some sense the most deeply rewarding of all those he encountered as a doctor. Despite the probability that these children would die of some HIV-related problem, he believed that as a physician he could do much to enhance their lives and, when survival was no longer possible, to help them through the process of dying.

I had known Dr. Bennett for some time. A physician certified both in pediatrics and in infectious diseases, he has had nearly twenty years of experience treating HIV infection in children. He is a superb diagnostician who also runs a clinic for children and adolescents with medical problems that are difficult to diagnose and treat. At sixty, Dr. Bennett is a trimly built man with white hair and a gentle, boxy face. He wears glasses. What is most striking about him, however, is not his appearance but his voice. His accent identifies him as from the Deep South; indeed he was born and grew up in Alabama. He speaks in an unusually soft tone, which children seem to find reassuring. They never have to struggle to hear him, though adults often must listen hard just to pick up what he is saying. Dr. Bennett's direct, no-nonsense style appeals equally to both these young patients and their parents. He is candid, never evasive, and sometimes even blunt, and this style may be one reason why he inspires such trust.

The other most striking thing about Dr. Bennett is his composure. He always remains calm. I have never seen him agitated, never seen him lose his temper. I know when he is troubled because I can see the outline of his jaw moving as he clenches his teeth. But even during those times his facial expression is benign, his body language neutral, his voice low and level.

Dr. Bennett's easygoing demeanor belies the fact that he is not afraid to defy administrative authorities in defending an action he believes is right for a patient. He is indifferent to recent management incentives to economize on time; instead he insists on giving patients the time they need, and in this clinic the needs of these young patients and their caregivers are multiple, varied, and often complicated. Of course, like all of us, Dr. Bennett has his faults. He is incorrigible when it comes to keeping a schedule and is frequently late for the clinic. His office is littered with papers, memos, books, and journals. He does not always call patients back as soon as they would like. He is stubborn and will not "play the game" if he does not want to. Usually the game involves applying for grants for this and that and squeezing more and more patients into smaller and smaller time slots.

Dr. Bennett knows about his reputation for diagnostic skills and attributes this to "whatever it is that allows people to take all their life experiences, and what they've learned from those experiences, and apply them to the present." Besides his work at the hospital, he has a large family that requires his attention and love, and he likes to spend time restoring an old farmhouse he recently purchased, raising chickens, and building furniture. He explains: "I can't deal with the attitude that you're a father, spouse, doctor, and that these are totally separate. The idea that you leave your work when you leave work and you leave your home when you leave home—I've always felt that is just as phony as a three-dollar bill, and not only phony but risky and unnatural. Anytime I confront a problem, I'm hoping that the whole of my life experience will come to bear on it, not just the medical component, but the whole: my spiritual life, my intellectual life, my adventuresome life, my farming life, my life as a father, as a son, whatever I've ever experienced. I'm hoping that wisdom from these experiences will come to bear on understanding the problem."

An example of this approach is Dr. Bennett's attitude toward death, which reflects his religious heritage (his father was a Southern Baptist preacher) as well as a farming background spent growing crops and picking cotton. He believes strongly that children in the last stages of a fatal disease should not have their lives prolonged by mechanical means. He also believes that it is best for a child to die at home, and he is proud that over the past seven years only one child in his practice has died in the hospital. He has helped numerous families through the practical, psychological, and spiritual aspects of a child's death.

Perhaps he is able to do this because his own life has not been without problems. As a person with diabetes who takes insulin and a handful of pills twice a day, he knows that it can be difficult to comply with a strict treatment regimen. Moreover, as someone who underwent quintuple bypass surgery, he understands the meaning of life-threatening illness and values the technological advances that can forestall death. Because of such experiences, he thinks he is more receptive to the suffering of others.

I left the HIV clinic my first day moved, troubled, and shaken. I was ambivalent about going back. On the one hand it had been a powerful and compelling experience. On the other, I felt that if I were to return, it would have to be to help in some way. I did not want just to be there, to watch and witness suffering, unable to do anything. But Angelina and Kofi and his foster mother stayed in my mind and my imagination.

Some nine months later I did return to the clinic. I had an idea — or maybe back then it was only the glimmer of an idea—for a project I might undertake. I would write a book about the children and their caregivers. It would be a book for a general audience rather than one addressed primarily to physicians and scholars, and it would describe through individual case stories the special issues confronting these children and their families. But before such tentative thoughts became actual plans, I wanted to know intuitively that this was the right thing for me to do. And so I started attending the clinic regularly. It did not take long for me to become convinced that this was a book that just had to be written.

The special experience of HIV-infected children and their caregivers is a story that has not been told before. Though a great deal has been written about the experience of adults with HIV/AIDS, there seems to be very little about children and virtually nothing about children with perinatally acquired HIV. There are books by physicians about their adult HIV patients, wonderful books such as Abraham Verghese's *My Own Country*, Abigail Zuger's *Strong Shadows*, Peter Selwyn's *Surviving the Fall*, and Daniel Baxter's *The Least of These My Brethren*. And there are many fine pathographies about adults with AIDS, such as Paul Monette's *Borrowed Time*, Andrea Rudd and Darien Taylor's *Positive Women*, and Catherine Wyatt-Morley's *AIDS Memoir*. But where are the books about children with HIV? There is Elizabeth Glaser's moving *In the Absence of Angels*, which describes how she contracted HIV during a blood transfusion and unknowingly passed on the virus to one child through breast milk and to the next in utero. There is also the celebrated biography of Ryan White, the child with hemophilia who contracted HIV from a blood transfusion. But these children came from middle-class, intact families, and the circumstances surrounding their lives were very different from those that characterize the children in our clinic, all of whom have been born with the disease and most of whom are no longer living with their biological parents.[1]

The incredible foster parents, like Kofi's, whom I met at that clinic during my first visit, impressed me immensely. These were men and women who took such children into their homes and their hearts. I began asking foster parents why they did this. Most of them had difficulty replying to my question, and when they did come up with an answer, it was something brief and matter-of-fact: "It seems the right thing to do" or "These children need care." People who are self-consciously altruistic are generally articulate about the reasons for their charitable acts. These foster parents, however, were anything but articulate. It struck me that they really did not consider what they were doing anything out of the ordinary. To them it seemed only natural to provide a loving home for children whose biological families were unable to care for them.

The stories I proposed to write seemed to shape themselves around two poles, with the children at the middle. On the one hand, there were the social evils of poverty, drug abuse, and unprotected sex as well as the individual problems of many of these children's biological parents, who in most cases had succumbed to such evils. On the other hand, there was "ordinary goodness"—the struggle of an HIV-infected parent to provide for his or her children, the generosity of foster parents, and the energy and patience of people in grass roots community organizations that sought to serve the needy. The book I planned would be hopeful—it would depict unsparingly the troubled (and troubling) background of these children—but it would also show how communities of people came forward to meet their needs.

To describe the special experience of these children means to blend the medical and the personal, interweaving the children's lives with the trajectory of illness and treatment. My experience at

---

[1] Readers interested in books about children with HIV will want to look at Lori Wiener, Aprille Best, and Philip Pizzo's *Be a Friend: Children Who Live with HIV Speak*, a collection of drawings and brief writings by children at the NIH's National Cancer Institute.

the clinic has taught me that it is artificial and even misleading to separate these two. Medical realities are a part of these children's everyday experience. They take medications twice and sometimes three times a day, and they know that for them a cut finger or bloody nose is treated differently from other children. But the full medical context of their stories extends beyond their individual histories of symptoms and medications to the larger history of the disease and its changing treatment and beyond the HIV clinic to the tertiary care center of which it forms a part. Similarly, the other aspect of these stories—the human and personal—cannot focus only on the patients themselves. Because they are still children, often very young children, their lives are inseparable from the lives of their biological parents or of those who actually care for them, whether grandmother, aunt, older brother, foster or adoptive parents. The lives of these parents and caregivers in turn have their own histories and backgrounds shaped by powerful social forces and compelling cultural values that affect the lives of these children for better or for worse. Thus both dimensions of these stories—the medical and the human—come together in concrete, specific, and individual experiences.

Outpatient pediatrics at St. Luke's occupies a suite of sixteen examining rooms in a wing recently added to the main building of the hospital. The children's HIV clinic takes up a quarter of this space, for just one morning every week. Yet in both its medical and human dimensions the importance of what this clinic does belies such narrow measurement. The treatment of HIV forms a crucial phase in recent medical science, and there is little need to dramatize the impact of the disease itself. In the children who attend our clinic, HIV strikes a peculiarly vulnerable and helpless population. Indeed their infection is only one in a host of complex psychological, social, and economic problems.

Medically there are two categories of patients who are treated in this clinic. The first and smaller group are infants whose mothers are infected and who may or may not be infected themselves. The second, larger group are children already known to be infected. Since it is now very rare to contract HIV through blood transfusion, all these young patients have perinatally acquired HIV (sometimes called vertically transmitted HIV). This means that they contracted the virus from their mothers through the placenta, during delivery, or (more rarely) while breast-feeding. The ages of these children range from four weeks to fourteen years. Some have had symptoms or opportunistic infections associated with HIV disease, in which case they are seen by Dr. Bennett monthly. Those who are asymptomatic (only a few) are seen every other month. Many of these children have been coming to this clinic for as long as they can remember.

The cachement area for St. Luke's pediatric HIV clinic covers a fairly large geographical area. A third of our families have a two-hour commute, each way, for medical appointments that occur monthly or every other month. One family drives three hours each way. Patients are drawn, about equally, from cities and small towns. The attrition rate is high for children brought in by young, infected mothers, women who often seem to be children themselves. Sometimes a child does not return because the family moves or the child is sent somewhere else for care, but other times it seems that the mother and child just disappear from sight. Children of Hispanic descent constitute the largest ethnic group in the clinic, Caucasian children make up the next largest group, and African-Americans, the smallest.[2]

Most of these children are on welfare. Many are in foster care either because their parents have died or because their family situations proved so destructive that they had to be removed. Others still live with one or more parents who are themselves on welfare, struggling to comply with their own treatment regimens so they can continue to care for their children, struggling too with the guilt they

---

[2] The racial demographics of St. Luke's clinic differ from those nationwide, where in 1999 children from racial minorities accounted for 75 percent of reported pediatric AIDS cases: of these, 55 percent were black and 20 percent Hispanic.

feel for infecting them. Often there are broken families, long and complex disputes over custody and adoption, frequent changes in foster placement, and extensive family histories of addiction and abuse of all kinds. Clearly the needs these children bring with them to the clinic, and the challenges they present to its staff, are more than medical.

The clinic at St. Luke's has its own history, one that reflects the larger evolution of AIDS and its treatment in America. In retrospect, Dr. Bennett thinks that he saw his first case of HIV infection in 1978. Twelve-month-old Juan was referred to St. Luke's from a community hospital because he had *Pneumocystis carinii* pneumonia. PCP is now recognized as a common opportunistic infection secondary to HIV infection. But back in 1978, three years before AIDS was recognized as a clinical syndrome, PCP in a newborn was very rare and was associated with an inherited immunodeficiency syndrome. As the hospital's specialist in pediatric infectious diseases, Dr. Bennett became Juan's doctor. Juan was treated with Bactrim, his health improved, and he was sent home. But three weeks later his mother, distraught, brought him back with the same problem. This time it was much worse. Juan did not get better, and he died in the hospital.

Dr. Bennett remembers being stymied by Juan's case because it fitted into none of the existing paradigms for congenital immunodeficiency syndromes. It was not until five years later, in 1983, that the first cases of children with AIDS were reported by the Centers for Disease Control. When he read about these, Dr. Bennett remembered the child whose illness had been so difficult to diagnose. He looked back at his records, concluded that Juan must have been infected with HIV, and submitted a report to the CDC, which dispatched a team of physicians and researchers. They tracked down family members, carried out blood work, and easily determined that the child had been infected perinatally with HIV.

By 1984 Dr. Bennett had twenty-five young patients with HIV, most of them Hispanic children. During the 1980s there was little to be done for infected children except to recognize opportunistic infections and then try to treat them. In fact a conscientious physician at this time could do more for these children in the schools than in the clinic. Dr. Bennett was active during these years in designing educational programs and speaking before school boards and at town meetings about AIDS. Our state was no different from others in the way the general public responded with panic to the presence of infected children in the public school system.[3] Much of this fear resulted from a faulty understanding of how the virus is transmitted. To correct such misunderstandings, Dr. Bennett conceived the idea of making films for public school education about AIDS. He realized that it would take a long time to secure a grant subsidy and that these films were needed right away, so he took out a bank loan for $40,000, found a local teacher and a TV producer to help him, and went ahead with the films. Within four months they were completed. They sold well in the area, and after several months the copyright to the films was bought by a distributor of schoolbooks.

The population of children infected with HIV continued to grow at a modest rate through the 1980s. At that time children were much sicker than they are now. Opportunistic infections were much more common, since there were no prophylactic treatments for problems like PCP and MAI (*Mycobacterium avium–intracellulare*). Medical conditions that were a direct effect of the virus, such as HIV encephalopathy, were also much more common since there was no therapy for the virus itself.

Treatment for HIV itself began in 1987 with zidovudine (ZDV; AZT, or Retrovir), which belongs to a class of antiretroviral drugs called nucleoside reverse transcriptase inhibitors (NRTIs).[4] Dr.

---

[3] See Elizabeth Glaser's *In the Absence of Angels* and Ryan White's autobiography for vivid and detailed descriptions of such a response.

[4] A salient factor in therapies for children with HIV is the fact that knowledge about the efficacy and safety of a particular drug is obtainable only through clinical drug trials, and clinical trials for children, until very recently, always followed clinical trials for adults. This meant that if a physician heard about a drug for HIV that had proved successful in adults, he or she either had to wait for FDA approval of the drug for children or go ahead and prescribe it before it was licensed, titrating the amount and timing for a child's or infant's body.

Bennett first acquired the drug by appealing to the manufacturer that it be dispensed for "compassionate need." By the end of 1989 St. Luke's pediatric HIV clinic, like others throughout the nation, was involved in pediatric clinical drug trials sponsored by the National Institutes of Health (NIH). The longest and biggest was PACTG 152, a nationwide trial that introduced didanosine (ddI, Videx) as an alternative or a complement to ZDV.[5] A number of Dr. Bennett's patients were enrolled in this study. He used the NIH funds he received to hire a part-time nurse coordinator to do the paper work for the clinical trial as well as to care for the nonmedical needs of the young patients attending the clinic. Cynthia was not only a fine nurse but also a remarkable human being—"a beautiful person inside and out," as one foster mother remarked. She did far more than her job required: making herself available by phone after hours, providing respite care for some of the foster mothers, and going out on several occasions to help care for a child dying at home.

But in 1993 the government withdrew support for drug trials at pediatric clinics such as St. Luke's, which had only a modest patient population. On the one hand, this decision made sense from a monetary perspective since a drug trial is extraordinarily expensive and since only very large clinics had enough patients to justify hiring someone full-time to gather and process data. On the other hand, it was unfortunate because it meant that a few big clinics received a great deal of money, which could provide nonmedical services for patients and their families, while smaller clinics like St. Luke's received nothing.

When Dr. Bennett's funding for clinical trials ended, hospital officials agreed to continue Cynthia's position for six months so that he could apply for another grant. He did so, but unsuccessfully.

---

[5] The comparisions were between AZT plus placebo, ddI plus placebo, and AZT plus ddI. The results several years later indicated that the best treatment for HIV/AIDS was AZT plus ddI and that the best monotherapy was ddI.

Cynthia was kept on nonetheless for yet another year. When she decided to leave her job to start a family, however, her position was withdrawn. Dr. Bennett's response was not to protest the decision but just to carry on as best he could. For six months the clinic was in disarray. Sometimes parents were called with information about test results, and sometimes they were not. Nonmedical issues posed a major problem, especially since the social worker assigned to the clinic seemed ineffective. Not surprisingly there was a big turnover in clinic nurses during this interval. Administrators soon realized that it was fruitless to prod Dr. Bennett to keep applying for grant money, and though some were annoyed at him, they would not compromise the well-being of so vulnerable a group of patients. Thus a very competent social worker was assigned to the clinic, and eventually the position of clinic coordinator was reinstated.

Though these were dark days for the clinic at St. Luke's, on the national scene research into AIDS and its treatment continued to advance. By 1995 careful analysis of how infected persons reacted to various anti-HIV medications had proved definitively that the use of just one reverse transcriptase drug led to drug resistance and that two reverse transcriptase inhibitors were more effective than any single drug. With this discovery, combination therapy with two nucleoside analog drugs became the approved treatment for HIV.

Soon after, however, a third stage in HIV treatment was introduced when two nucleoside analogs were combined with a new drug called a protease inhibitor, a treatment approved in 1995 for adults, but not until February 1997 for children.[6] Combination therapy with a protease inhibitor has had dramatic results, suppressing the amount of virus in the body, reducing opportunistic infections, and lowering mortality for adults and children alike. At St. Luke's, children on combination therapy with a protease inhibitor not only do better but actually feel better.

[6] One reason approval of protease inhibitors for children was delayed so long was the limited availability of oral preparations. Protease inhibitors differ from earlier HIV medications in that nucleoside analog drugs interfere early in the reproductive cycle of HIV to inhibit replication, whereas protease inhibitors interfere later in the cycle.

When a child's viral load begins to rise despite triple therapy, Dr. Bennett advises changing the child's medications to include a second protease inhibitor. When that combination fails, he substitutes another combination of drugs in the hope of reducing viral load, then another, then another. So far there have always been alternative drug therapies to turn to, and so far, with careful monitoring and judicious changes in medication, children attending our clinic remain relatively healthy.

Perinatal HIV is considered by most physicians to be very different in the clinical manifestations of infection and the overall course of the disease from those in adults since infection occurs while the infant's immune system is still developing. Fewer than 25 percent of children with HIV have the kinds of opportunistic infections that appear in infected adults; Kaposi's sarcoma, for example, though common in adults, is rare in children. In addition, virologic and immunologic markers of infection are different in children and in adults.

Providing state-of-the-art care for children with HIV is difficult not only because of the special nature of perinatally acquired HIV but also because treatment strategies change with the results of pharmacological research and knowledge about the progression of the disease. As Dr. Bennett tells medical students, "HIV treatment is a moving target." Several years ago Dr. Bennett was reluctant to treat asymptomatic infants and children because of the side effects, both known and unknown, of the drugs to which they would be exposed. But since then there have been indications that disease progression is more rapid in infants and children with vertically transmitted HIV than in children and adults who were infected later in life. Knowing this, Dr. Bennett now favors aggressive treatment of all infected infants, whether or not they are symptomatic. If parents elect not to begin treatment, of course he accedes to their wishes. Another example of change in HIV treatment has to do with diagnosing HIV in infants. When I first began attending the clinic, Dr. Bennett could not determine with certainty whether or not an infant born to an infected mother was itself infected until a year or more after birth. These babies were all born with their mothers' antibodies to HIV, and HIV tests before 1996 measured only antibodies. But more recent tests that rely on antigen rather than antibody can usually detect infection at birth or within several weeks, and thus treatment can begin early.[7]

Despite the remarkable advances in knowledge about HIV, its diagnosis, and its treatment, the future remains uncertain. On the one hand, there is a good deal of optimism about treatment of HIV-infected persons, especially children, in the United States. Some believe that HIV is becoming a chronic illness, controllable with the proper medications. It is conceivable that with early treatment of infected infants, begun while their immune systems are still robust, the virus might be so diminished that they will never develop opportunistic infections. On the other hand, because of the capacity of the virus to mutate, any HIV medication has limitations. As I write this introduction in 1999, the production of effective drugs tends more and more to lag behind the pace at which the virus mutates. At St. Luke's, recent viral load testing indicates that for many of our young patients, the virus continues to mutate and multiply. It is now a race between the virus and its treatment, with the lives of these children hanging in the balance.

The possibility of maternal transmission of HIV in the future is also uncertain. Happily, the risk that an infected mother might pass on the virus to her newborn is much lower than it was ten years ago. If pregnant women with HIV undergo antiviral therapy and their viral loads are less than five hundred copies, the risk of transmission is negligible. However, the optimism this lower risk has generated leads some infected women to be less cautious about preventing pregnancies and more ready to accept what seems the small possi-

[7] Regardless of tests results, however, babies born to infected mothers need to be seen by a specialist immediately after birth. If the infant is known to be infected and also symptomatic, pharmacological treatment will begin immediately. For an infant who is infected but asymptomatic, the standard of care varies. Some physicians withhold treatment, monitoring the child's condition every few months. Others, like Dr. Bennett, go ahead and treat an asymptomatic infant as they would a child with symptoms.

bility of perinatal transmission. In addition, the effectiveness of protease inhibitors in reducing opportunistic infections and lowering mortality rates has led to the illusion that there is now a "cure" for AIDS and thus less need for sexual precautions. With infected individuals who receive treatment living longer, and with the increase of the virus in women in their childbearing years, there is statistically a greater probability of infected women bearing children. Some of these children will be born with the virus. Another concern is that perinatally infected children are now living well into adolescence and thus are capable of infecting not only their partners but also their offspring. The history of treatment for HIV thus does not have the happy ending that we all hope for and that some mistakenly assume to be an achieved fact.

In Third World countries the history of pediatric HIV and its treatment is very different. Until recently, few pregnant, infected women received treatment that lowered the risk of maternal transmission. UNAIDS estimated that at the end of 1998, 1,800 infected babies were born every day in underdeveloped countries. The first big breakthrough came in 1999 from studies conducted by a U.S.-Ugandan team, which discovered that treatment with the drug nevirapine was cheaper and more effective than AZT, costing about four dollars per child and reducing the risk of maternal transmission to 13 percent.

The children's HIV clinic at St. Luke's is a busy place. Nevertheless it has a relaxed atmosphere, with children sometimes running up and down the halls and parents often chatting with one another as they wait for the doctor. Many of the children have known Dr. Bennett all their lives. They inevitably become fond of the nurses and can often be found at the nurses' station, asking for juice and crackers, or hoping to be given a lollipop, or just wanting to say hello. Of course the nurses in turn have become very fond of the children, preparing small baskets of candy or small gifts for them around holidays like Christmas and Halloween.

The team approach really works in this clinic. The staff now includes Rachel DeLorca, a registered nurse who is also the clinic co-ordinator, Nicole Jackson, a licensed practical nurse who helps with clinic visits, Ramona Santos, an experienced social worker, and of course Dr. Bennett. In addition, there is often a resident, sometimes a fourth-year medical student, and sometimes a nursing student. Families new to the clinic are often surprised by the number of people in the room with them, but more often than not they quickly grow accustomed to it.

In appearance the two nurses, Rachel and Nicole, complement each other perfectly. Rachel is a petite, dark-haired woman with twenty-eight years of nursing experience. Nicole, on the other hand, is in her late twenties, tall and willowy, with long, curly blond hair. Rachel lives in town, is married, and has a twelve-year-old son. Nicole and her husband, who works in St. Luke's maintenance department, live in the country, where they have chickens and roosters, angora rabbits, donkeys, a goat, a pony, and a potbellied pig named Daisy. To the delight of the children, Nicole's zoo animals frequently attend our annual clinic picnic.

Rachel has the most contact with the children. She is new to the pediatric HIV clinic, though she has worked at St. Luke's in pediatric oncology for ten years. Rachel is a warm, energetic woman with a wonderful throaty laugh. Technically she is superb, possessing an uncanny ability to find the often tiny veins of these children when blood draws are required. She has worked hard to establish links between St. Luke's and local AIDS support services. Rachel is dedicated to her work with these families. This past Christmas, at her suggestion, our clinic "adopted" a family, and she drove out to their home on a Saturday with gifts of food, clothing, and toys. She is aware that there are probably many infected children in neighboring towns who are not receiving treatment, and she has been active in efforts to establish HIV outreach clinics. As a nurse in the oncology and the HIV clinics Rachel has allowed herself to become personally involved with the children and their caregivers, though she knows that a great many of these children will die. When one of her young patients dies, Rachel frequently attends the funeral; it is a gesture appreciated by the bereaved families as well as a way for Rachel to cope with her own feelings of sadness and loss.

Pediatric nurses who choose to work in an HIV clinic are already a special category. As Nicole observes, "Not everyone wants to deal with this population." According to both Rachel and Nicole, their work is rewarding because they get to know the children well and because the families are so varied and interesting. But they also find it hard, largely because of the great disparity between the emotional, social, and economic needs of these children and their families and the extent to which these needs can be actually met by community groups and social structures. Rachel, with her experience in both clinics, can contrast children with cancer and children with HIV: "Both have life-threatening illnesses and heavy medication schedules. But kids with cancer have financial and community support that kids with HIV don't have. People rally around when someone has cancer, but HIV is secretive; it's so much more difficult."

This difficulty is reflected in the frequent turnover of nurses at our pediatric HIV clinic. Dealing with these families involves patient follow-up that extends well beyond clinic hours. The kind of nurse who chooses this clinic finds it hard not to carry out tasks related to the well-being and comfort of the children and their caregivers. But the nurses' schedules often do not include the time needed to do such work, and the result is that they tend to burn out quickly. To prevent this from recurring, and to keep Rachel in particular, administrators have appointed her clinic coordinator and adjusted her schedule to allow for patient follow-up.

However, the position of clinic coordinator itself is threatened by broad institutional policies at St. Luke's aimed at cutting costs and by an increasing shortage of nurses. Of course everyone in the clinic realizes that the cost-saving policies adopted by St. Luke's reflect the way economic pressures are eroding the quality of patient care everywhere. Still, it is frustrating for Rachel when the time allotted for patient follow-up disappears, without notice, for weeks at a time because of a lack of nurses in other specialty clinics. And it is especially frustrating for both nurses when bureaucratic policies interfere with their ability to make quality patient care their first priority.

Ramona, our social worker, is also a recent member of the children's HIV clinic staff, although she has worked at this hospital for fifteen years. When I first came to Dr. Bennett's clinic, I was surprised not to find a social worker who attended the clinic regularly and thus knew the children. There was someone whom Dr. Bennett could call when needed, but when she did appear, she seemed harassed, indifferent, and basically uninterested in the children. As a result, she tended to be ineffective. Ramona is very different. She is an expert in communicating with caseworkers and officials at various child welfare agencies, and she speaks fluent Spanish, which is essential in a clinic with so large a Hispanic population. Since she also works in the adults' HIV clinic, she provides an important link between the two groups of patients.

Ramona is a handsome, large-featured, smartly dressed woman in her early forties who is married to a physician. She relates well to the clinic children, perhaps because she has two youngsters of her own. Her style with adults, both parents and staff, is relaxed yet professional; she is friendly but not effusive. Though some of the problems she is expected to solve are complex, Ramona always maintains her composure. In dealing with parents who need to be reminded to give their children medications or to bring them regularly to their medical appointments, she is patient but insistent.

As with nurses, only a certain kind of social worker chooses to work with HIV patients. Ramona enjoys this clinic because she can actually "do social work," focusing on her clients rather than filling out forms: "I like working with a whole family, the kids and their parents. They let you inside; they're open, honest people. They know why they're here. And I like it that they can be sure that even though we know what they're coming in for, we don't treat them any different from anyone else." She also enjoys problem solving, and there is no lack of problems in this clinic. She knows the geographical area and all its resources, and she finds genuine satisfaction in linking a family's particular needs to community, state, or governmental organizations, agencies, and services.

I continue to be impressed by the number and variety of challenging issues she must deal with. There is Ahsan, a child who comes to the clinic only sporadically and whose mother, also infected, refuses to take HIV medication despite a high viral load. Or there is Carlos, a ten-year-old who is shuttled back and forth between a grandmother and temporary foster placements. Eleven-year-old Michael is in a similar situation. In both cases the children's biological families cannot provide adequate care yet will not permit them to be adopted, in part because they do not want to lose the substantial Social Security benefits that these children bring them. Other problems include the infected mother who continues to get pregnant or who refuses to take HIV medications during pregnancy, thus increasing the risk of perinatal transmission, or the family whose income is just above the poverty line so that they fail to qualify for medical assistance but still cannot afford expensive HIV medications. Ramona believes that she "makes a difference" to these children: "You get a chance to be a part of their lives and maybe make their lives a little bit better."

The book is composed of six extended narratives. Each begins with a vignette of a clinic visit, a reconstruction of conversations and events based on lengthy notes I took during the actual visit. This vignette is followed by a full-length story of a child or pair of children and their caregivers. These stories draw on a variety of sources and include quotations from transcriptions of taped interviews. Each chapter concludes with my commentary on the preceding narrative. Sometimes I focus on a particular aspect of the story that seems to me salient, such as the welfare system or a particular ethical dilemma. Sometimes I link the story to some literary work or works. Since my own training is in literature, it is only natural that this should provide a lens through which I perceive and interpret what I have observed.

As I worked on the book, I read or reread literary works that seemed especially appropriate to what I was learning about these children. Fyodor Dostoevsky's *The Brothers Karamazov*, Albert Camus's *The Plague*, and the novels of Charles Dickens seemed good choices since all of them feature suffering, sick, or dying children. I found that my reading helped tease out and articulate recurrent themes in the real-life stories I was narrating.

In Dostoevsky's *Brothers Karamazov*, for example, though the main plot of the novel concerns parricide, a subplot describes the suffering and death of nine-year-old Ilyusha. As counterparts to the story of Ilyusha, there are images of suffering children throughout the novel: children cruelly tormented by adults, sometimes their own parents; impoverished children afflicted with hunger and cold; children suffering from some mortal illness. For Dostoevsky, the suffering and death of children are terrible realities that cry out for response from all of us. His moral vision is articulated by the dying Markel, a seventeen-year-old who tells his mother, "We are all responsible to all for all." At its most obvious level, Markel's saying points to the moral responsiblity of a society—especially one as affluent as ours—for the welfare of its children. It also implies an almost mystic sense of human community, realized throughout the novel in the way the lives of the characters connect and interpenetrate. It is this sense of an evolving community, responding to and centering on the needs of children, that I have observed in the pediatric HIV clinic at St. Luke's.

Whereas Dostoevsky's fiction explores psychological realities, Dickens's focus is the social world. I found the novels of Dickens less useful for his sentimental depiction of the deaths of Little Nell or Jo, the crossing sweeper, than for his trenchant social criticism, which relates the suffering of individual victims to the larger institutional and economic structures that cause it. Dickens's critique includes both a denunciation of deplorable social conditions and an interrogation of the philanthropic impulse, whether collective or individual. He depicts noble benefactors, but he also portrays countermodels like Mrs. Pardiggle, a formidable lady who enforces charitable actions on her children, and Mrs. Jellyby, a scatter-brained philanthropist who neglects her own offspring while fretting over the natives of Borrioboola-Gha. Dickens's emphasis on philanthropy in all its forms helped focus the theme of service to others that recurs in so many of my stories. Some of the benefactors in Dickens are securely affluent and can afford their generosity; others, like most of my foster parents, are nearly as poor as those they shelter and succor.

The tragedies of Aeschylus, Sophocles, and Euripides remain deeply compelling to me, and I kept coming back to them as I researched this book. "Recognition" and "reversal" are terms from Aristotle's *Poetics* that describe formal plot devices in these plays, and these concepts proved surprisingly helpful in thinking about the possibility of change in human beings. They correspond, as I discovered, to actual moments of crisis and change in the lives of several of the individuals I write about. So too I found that the terms by which the Greeks analyzed human conduct—the paired concepts of *arete* (excellence) and *hamartia* (error or flaw) or the psychology of moral self-definition through choice (*prohairesis*)—illuminated the behavior of those whose stories I tell in this book.

Another theme emerged from Sophocles's *Philoctetes*. Well before my interest in children with HIV, I had been fascinated with this play because of its depiction of the hero's disease and subsequent healing. But after beginning research for this book, what I found compelling was Sophocles' treatment of *philia* in dramatizing the relationships between one character and another. Sophocles led me to Aristotle, who writes at length about *philia*. I came to understand that *philia* is basically an ethical idea. Though rooted in feeling, what we today understand as friendship, it includes a network of obligations, of benefits received and returned. The concept of *philia*, with its intricate bonds of loyalty and mutual obligation, seemed to illumine what I observed at the clinic. Moreover, it proved deeply helpful in my own attempts to form ethically sound relationships with the clinic families. There is no real equivalent in the English language to *philia*. The closest analogue I have found is the concept of moral communities, which provides a model for the way we might ideally relate to one another in our churches and synagogues, hospitals, and workplaces.[8] I think of the pediatric HIV clinic at St. Luke's as just such a moral community, one in which medical caregivers and families mutually give and receive, rather than relate to each other only instrumentally.

Finally, there is the theme of good and evil and the problem of moral judgment. That the books to which I am drawn, from Homer and Sophocles to Dostoevsky and Camus, explore just such moral issues seems to me more than a quirk of personal taste. Such ethical engagement is, I believe, one of the hallmarks of great literature. AIDS is a disease laden with moral meaning. Even more so, in a sense, is perinatally acquired HIV, though the moral judgment is displaced onto the past actions of biological parents and implemented in decisions about guardianship of an infected child.

My exploration of the family histories of our patients has been an education in ranges of behavior and experience that I knew only from newpapers: incest and child abuse as well as prostitution, drug and alcohol addiction, murder, crime and its punishments. But paradoxically, as I learn about these things from people directly involved, my personal sense of evil has become diluted or diffused. Dickens has his villains, monsters of cruelty like Quilp or Sikes, but there are no such villains in the stories in my book. Often the victimizer has him- or herself been victimized. The abusive parent was subjected to abuse in childhood, or the young mother on heroin comes from a family in which drug addiction is a commonplace. Child abuse and drug addiction are surely wrong, but where does one fix blame? How can one not regard the social structure, the cultural forces, and the economic system that permit and even cause such evils as profoundly culpable?

Yet I could not avoid the recognition that the children in our

---

[8] I owe both the term and the idea of moral community to Margaret Mohrmann, who writes about them in *Medicine as Ministry: Reflections on Suffering, Ethics, and Hope*. Mohrmann, a physician who specializes in pediatric medicine, wrote this book after she had gone back to school and earned a Ph.D. in religious studies.

clinic are there because their parents made certain choices—in all cases choices involving either the recreational use of intravenous drugs or unsafe and often promiscuous sexual practices. The disease these children inherited is a consequence of such choices. Though many of the parents have themselves been victimized, they are not therefore blameless, and they remain capable of making choices. In families that seemed plagued by all kinds of social evils, I found individuals who managed to break out and establish new lifestyles, even in some cases arriving at a stability from which they could reach out and help others.

Greek tragedy has been helpful in showing me how human beings can be "fated" in certain ways yet at the same time responsible for their actions through the choices they make. Perhaps the terrible societal conditions into which some people are born, coupled with genetic tendencies and deficiencies, can be considered similar to the Greek idea of Fate. Though in ancient Greek tragedy Fate is expressed through prophets and oracles and intervening deities, these plays can speak of the way forces we might label "heredity" or "environment" impose a fatedness on human life.

The stories in this book concern children with HIV and their caregivers. But whose stories are these? Those of the children and parents whose experience I describe? Or mine, in the sense that I wrote down what I had seen and heard and, in doing this, inevitably altered it? The act of writing or even talking about an experience, whether one's own or another's, changes it: Some aspects may be emphasized more than others, and some may be left out entirely. My telling of these stories is conditioned by how I understand what I have witnessed and what I have been told, and this is an understanding shaped by who I am—my own values, goals, and needs.

In the stories that follow, then, I do not pretend to offer a factual record of the experience of these children and their caregivers, nor do I try to adopt a dispassionate or an objective stance myself. Indeed I do not believe such objectivity possible. My admiration for the doctor I call Dr. Bennett and my pride in the way so many health care providers at St. Luke's try to live up to its idealistic mission will be obvious. I am also deeply involved with the families who attend our HIV clinic. The perspective I bring to their lives is one informed by a strong sense of empathy. Thus my position as I write is that of an involved—sometimes passionately involved—participant.

If it is important to acknowledge the ways in which my book is not factual and objective, it is also important to emphasize that it is not fiction. These stories are based on fact and embody what I believe to be the truth about the lives of these young patients and their families. They are based on notes and observations I made during patients' clinic visits; taped interviews I held with parents or foster parents and later transcribed; conversations with families in person or by phone; formal and informal interviews with caseworkers, friends, and medical personnel who knew the families; and medical charts and records.

I tried to interview parents, grandparents, and foster parents at their own homes. My approach was to begin each interview by reminding them of my aim of presenting, through stories, the experience of infected children and their caregivers (I gave a fuller explanation when asking them to sign consent forms). I told them that I had no particular model for the interview and that I simply wanted to learn from them, in any way they chose to tell me, what it is like to care for a child with HIV. I asked about the child's biological family and about encounters with school, welfare, and medical systems and personnel (Dr. Bennett in particular). Reminding interviewees that names of persons and places would be changed and that I would transcribe the interview myself, I encouraged them to be as frank and open as they thought they could. I explained my wish to record the interview by admitting that otherwise I would have trouble remembering exactly what they said.

I added that I had no training in interviewing techniques and little experience with tape recorders. This inexperience became painfully evident to several of my families. For my very first interview I neglected to bring batteries for my recorder, relying instead on electricity. Unfortunately the electric current in the house went off. The family found me some batteries, which they refused to let me pay for. On another memorable occasion a husband and wife team that directs a community AIDS organization granted me a two-hour interview. Sitting down later at my computer to transcribe my recording, I was mortified to find that there was nothing on the tape. Apparently I had pushed the wrong button. I apologized profusely to my interviewees, and they were gracious enough to find time for another long conversation.

Throughout the writing of this book I have felt a strong tension between fidelity to the text of the taped interviews and the need to edit them to produce a clearer and more coherent narrative. I decided not to make changes for purely aesthetic reasons to achieve a "better story." I did make changes, however, when I thought that otherwise the narrative would have been difficult to follow. Sometimes I shifted the sequence of topics (paragraphs, in my transcription) to present a chronological story. In the interest of confidentiality, I invented substitutions for all names, places, and other identifying information. The older children, at my invitation, chose names for themselves.

The choice of which families to include in the book proved extremely difficult. More volunteered than I had space for. In general, I chose those who, taken all together, would provide a cross section of characteristics typical of the patients we serve: (1) children and caregivers representative of the racial and ethnic groups in our clinic: Hispanic, Caucasian, and African-American; (2) children who have serious and varied medical problems and other children who appear healthy; (3) children cared for by foster parents, by biological parents, by a grandmother or an aunt or some other relative; (4) children of different ages; (5) children harmed by societal problems or helped by community agencies and groups. Of course these categories often overlap.

I asked family caregivers to examine and then sign consent forms. These forms, along with the project, had been approved by the hospital's Institutional Review Board after a lengthy review process. The consent forms outlined the aims and methodology of the project, promised that identifying information would be changed to ensure confidentiality, indicated that I intended to publish my findings as a book, and protected the institution from liability. One consent form was designed for parents and foster parents; another was intended for the child himself or herself. I was instructed to explain the project to all the children and to secure written permission from those seven years and over. Of course obtaining informed consent for research involving patients is important and necessary, but perhaps our hospital's review board overestimated the ability of young children to understand the meaning of their illness or to grasp the purpose of my study. It proved difficult to give an adequate explanation to any but the oldest, the eleven- and twelve-year-olds. I knew that the children and their parents agreed to participate basically because they trusted Dr. Bennett and had transferred that trust to me.

I accepted their trust as both a great honor and a heavy responsibility. The fact that this was a deferred trust made it all the more important that I deserve it. As I got to know these families better, I developed my own research ethic, one that seemed commensurate with this trust. I came to realize that in exploring their lives, I was inevitably forming personal relationships with each of them and that such relationships entailed wider obligations. At the very least I tried to make the relationship itself caring and supportive rather than merely instrumental.

Of course the way in which I related to the children and to their adult caregivers took different forms. I tried to befriend the children by giving out stickers of fish, birds, or stars and sometimes small toys or books when they came for clinic appointments and by remembering to ask about something important to each particular child: cheerleading, or playing basketball, or a pet, or an upcoming trip. With some children I did more, while realizing that such gestures implied a commitment to an ongoing relationship. I had to learn to give of myself while not making promises, especially emotional promises, that I could not keep.

I tried to honor my obligation to the parents by offering various kinds of help and then providing that help when asked. This took very different forms. In one instance a grandmother reluctant to phone Dr. Bennett would call me with medical questions about her granddaughter. Some of her questions I could answer as a mother myself, but most required my calling Dr. Bennett, sometimes after hours and once when he was sick at home. I have taken a child home with me overnight, arranged for a family to receive food from our local food bank, given small amounts of money when money was needed, anonymously paid legal fees, appeared in court in a child custody case, and intervened to make sure a child received the psychiatric treatment he obviously needed. I made it a practice to give out my home phone number. I have attended church services with several families, wishing to show respect for the faith that inspires their actions. Over time, though, I have come to realize that in reality I can do very little for them.

I am grateful to these families. They have given me much more than information; they have allowed me into their lives, sharing with me their ideals and beliefs as well as their struggles and fears, their hopes and joys. They have taught me about kindness, generosity, courage, and faith. I have come to admire those who actually win out over adverse circumstances, especially as I realize the extent of that adversity. I also admire those who simply go on, through poverty and sickness, persevering in their attempts to live good lives. This book is written in honor of them and the children they care for.

TATTOOED HEARTS

Maria and C.J. Montalvo

*Eight-year-old Maria and seven-year-old C.J. (Cesar, Jr.) have peri-
natally acquired HIV. Their mother, who was Caucasian, died of
complications from AIDS when Maria was five and C.J., four. Their
Mexican father, Cesar, now their primary caregiver, is also infected.
Cesar often works out of state as a roofer, and at these times his various girlfriends help care for the children. He has an older child from
a previous marriage who is not infected. All the children attend
school, though the family moves frequently from place to place.*

*Maria was diagnosed when she was sixteen months old. Since in-
fancy she has not done well. She has had growth failure, recurrent diarrhea, and multiple bacterial infections, as well as MAI and CMV
infections. At one point she was thought to be dying, and hospice
care was initiated. For now the progression of the disease seems to
have come to a halt, though Maria is still blind from CMV retinitis.
She copes well with her blindness, navigating through the house by
touch. She enjoys playing with Barbie dolls. C.J., diagnosed at fifteen months, has always been a generally healthy child with normal
growth and development and a minimum of intercurrent infections.
He has a great deal of energy and especially enjoys Rollerblading.
Both children seem stable and happy, despite their HIV status and
problematic futures.*

.　　.　　.

"IF Maria were to die next week, could you pay for the funeral?" It seems a harsh and shocking question. Dr. Bennett is speaking gently and slowly, leaning forward, one elbow resting on the chart splayed out in front of him as he looks at Cesar.

Cesar's response is immediate and visceral. He shudders, and tears well in his eyes as he returns Dr. Bennett's gaze. But he does not resist the implications of the question: that Maria is very sick, that she is likely to die soon, and that there is nothing anyone can do to prevent this. He shifts in his chair and replies softly, "No, I could not."

The Montalvo family arrived fairly early this morning, accompanied by Cesar's latest girlfriend, Bonnie. Cesar is a trim, good-looking Chicano, about thirty years old, with long, curly black hair. He wears several thick silver chains around his neck, mostly medallions of various kinds. He is always dressed carefully and stylishly. Today he's wearing a deep purple shirt, tight-fitting black pants with a large silver belt buckle embossed with the word "Mexico," and black shiny boots that reflect the leather sheen of his motorcycle jacket, which he hasn't taken off though it's very warm in the examining room. Several months ago, when he brought the children in for summer clinic visits, he dressed more lightly in sandals, shorts, and sleeveless shirts that revealed several tattoos on his upper arms. Curious, I noticed that each of the tattoos was a crudely shaped heart with an arrow through it and a name in the center. I had to get closer to read the names. When I did, it was with some surprise—but really no surprise, knowing Cesar—that I realized these were not the names of his girlfriends but of each of his three children, Maria, C.J., and Avricita.

Cesar speaks with a heavy accent. He is articulate and intelligent, and this may obscure the fact that he is illiterate in both English and Spanish. Cesar is clearly embarrassed about not being able to read. At times in the past, he has seemed to the clinic staff cocky, very conscious of his appeal to women, and somewhat defiant. At other times, when not feeling well (Cesar reports that his HIV medications cause stomach upset and severe muscle pains in his legs and face), he is subdued and dejected, his slow, deliberate move-ments reflecting the fact that his whole body hurts. But today Cesar is agitated and voluble.

When Dr. Bennett and I come into the examining room, Cesar is sitting in the chair next to the door. He is leaning back, arms folded across his chest, one leg crossed over the other. Bonnie, the girlfriend, sits in a chair across the room. She seems a pleasant young woman, sweet-looking even, with long and very curly honey-colored hair. Today she is dressed casually in a dark blue warm-up suit. Curled up in her lap is Maria, her fine hair tangled and her face even more pinched than usual, the skin stretched and taut across prominent cheekbones. C.J. is already jumping up and down in excitement: "Do you have a sticker today for me? What kind of stickers do you have today?" (I always bring stickers for the children: neon dinosaurs, glittery stars, iridescent birds or fish.) Cesar shushes C.J., telling him he can go and play on the Nintendo for a while, then begins talking. He is excited because Maria seems better: "I was afraid she would die, and it would be like before, with my wife, in such pain. She [Maria] wouldn't eat nothing, and she wouldn't drink nothing, just like my wife right before she died. It was bad with Maria this time, real bad. On Monday night, I think, 'This is it. She's not going to make it.' But then the next morning, when she wakes up, she's better. She says she wants to go to school, so I take her, and she's doing fine now. She's okay now!" With this last sentence, a big smile spreads across Cesar's face. His face is transformed by that smile: The wrinkles disappear, and his eyes dance.

Maria does seem better—lethargic, but better. Dr. Bennett doesn't really respond to Cesar's description—lengthy, for Cesar—of her im-proved health. He examines Maria, then asks his usual questions about whether she's getting her medications, how well she's eating, whether she has energy, and how many bowel movements she has a day. The answers come easily; this is a ritual with which doctor, pa-tient, and parent are very familiar. In some sense it's a comforting rit-ual. Yes, she's taking her medications, but not always. Her eating is about the same, not very much of anything. No, she doesn't have much energy. She has about three bowel movements a day, more or less. This question, I've noticed, always makes kids of a certain age uncomfortable. They say they don't know; they look away; they giggle and try to elude the question any way they can. Maria, who has just turned eight, is still too young for this, so she just answers simply, directly.

I help Maria down from the examining table. Kids normally hop off the table after their examination, but not Maria. She is totally blind, having contracted CMV retinitis several months ago.[1] I remember only too well the onset of her blindness. She was brought in by her father because she had a fever, she had lost a great deal of weight, she was lethargic, her eyes were red, and she was complaining of not being able to see well. These symptoms, Cesar told us, had been preceded by complaints over several weeks of her eyes hurting and of blurry vision. Dr. Bennett examined her, especially her eyes, and then calmly turned to Cesar and told him she would need to be hospitalized. I knew then that something was very wrong because Dr. Bennett almost never hospitalizes HIV-infected children who have acute illnesses—sometimes to the consternation of the nurses. Instead he usually gives orders for antibiotics to be administered intravenously while the child is at the clinic, writes out a prescription for an oral antibiotic, and sends the family home with a formulaic "Give me a call if anything changes or if she doesn't get better in a day or so."

Understandably Maria was tearful and clingy when she learned she'd have to stay at the hospital. She wanted her father to stay with

[1] CMV—or cytomegalovirus—causes a broad spectrum of diseases in HIV-infected persons, from gastrointestinal problems to infections of the brain, liver, lungs, and eyes. Maria's caregivers, both familial and medical, will not "catch" this virus from her because nearly all adults are infected with CMV anyway. Those of us who are not immunocompromised carry asymptomatic CMV: The virus is there in our bodies, but it remains latent, and if and when CMV-related illness does occur, it is mild and nonspecific. For HIV-infected individuals, however, CMV infections are common and almost always serious. The difference in Maria's case is the locus of the infection; a CMV infection of the retina of the eye is unusual in children.

her, so I took C.J. home with me that day and kept him for the night. Maria's diagnosis upon admission was CMV infection and central nervous system involvement secondary to HIV infection. CMV was confirmed; CNS involvement was not. Unfortunately Maria's eyesight did not improve during her hospitalization. Finally, after six long days and nights, Dr. Bennett signed the release form for Maria to go home, making arrangements for visits from a home health nurse to administer ganciclovir intravenously.

Maria's eyesight has not returned. But she has adapted remarkably well to her loss of vision. At home she gets around by touch and by sound cues. Here in the examining room, once helped off the table, she unerringly makes her way over to where her father is sitting, even though he is not speaking and thus his voice cannot guide her. She climbs onto his lap and snuggles into his arms.

Dr. Bennett sends his nurse to find C.J., who will no doubt resist interrupting his Super Nintendo game for something so trivial as a visit with the doctor. This resistance is always more exaggerated when his sister is really sick. Usually C.J. is seen first, so that he can be released from the examining room as quickly as possible and return to winning car races and zapping bad guys. He is a beautiful child with dark eyes and a head full of thick, black, curly hair, like his father's. He seems always in motion and, like any normal seven-year-old boy, is usually full of himself. The examining room always seems much too small to contain his exuberance.

I've wondered if his eagerness to be out of that room wasn't a response, at some level of childish wisdom, to the confining and encroaching nature of this disease. He knows that both he and his sister are infected with HIV. But the severity and course of the disease have been very different in the two children. He is well. *She* is the one who is sick with it, sometimes unable to eat because of sores in her mouth, sometimes troubled by an itchy rash on her genitals, sometimes up at night with a high fever. It is she who is forced to take ever-increasing numbers of pills and liquids, some of them awful-tasting. He has to take only five pills twice a day while she takes seventeen, some of them three times a day. In addition, just in the last month she has become completely blind. Today, as at the past several visits, C.J. shows no sign that he is upset by this recent development in his sister's deteriorating health. For him Maria's loss of vision seems just the latest in a long series of health problems.

This time C.J. does have something for the doctor to treat. He complains of itching, and there are red splotches scattered all over his body. Dr. Bennett takes a brief look at him and then, his hand resting on C.J.'s shoulder, turns to Cesar and explains what scabies is and how to treat it: "I'm going to prescribe this cream; you'll need to cover him with it when he goes to bed and then wash it off in the morning. You'll also need to wash everything he comes into contact with: his sheets, pillowcase, and all his clothes. If you can, put them out in the sun to dry."

He turns to C.J., who is still sitting on the examining table. "C.J., this itching will go away after you do this."

"Can I go now?" C.J. asks.

"Yes, you can," Dr. Bennett says, and grins at him. He watches, still smiling, as C.J. jumps down from the table, buttons his jeans, puts on his sneakers, and, without tying them, scampers out of the room, back to the video game. Bonnie gets up hastily and crosses the room to go after him. As she opens the door to leave, Cesar asks her to take Maria along. Bonnie picks the little girl up easily. "Bye, Daddy," Maria says, her voice blurry, as she waves to her father.

"Bye, Maria, I'll be there soon," replies Cesar.

The three of us are alone now: Dr. Bennett, Cesar, and I. The room is silent except for the scratching noise of pen on paper, as the doctor writes up his notes for the children's medical records. I imagine Bonnie with the kids out in the waiting room. Maria is sitting on her lap, exhausted, head leaning back, large, sightless eyes gazing out at nothing. C.J., younger by a year but taller and heavier, is playing Stunt Race FX on the Nintendo, the *Super* Nintendo, as he likes to remind me with mock impatience. I wonder what Cesar is thinking.

Dr. Bennett brings us both back to the examining room as he breaks the silence, his voice very soft. "I know it seems she's okay now, Cesar, but she isn't. The fact that she got better this time doesn't change the circumstances. You know that."

Cesar nods.

Dr. Bennett and Cesar both are aware that Maria has sustained serious infections over the years, including numerous episodes of *Pneumocystis carinii* pneumonia (PCP)[2] since she was three months old, intercurrent infections of *Mycobacterium avium–intracellulare* pneumonitis (MAI), and disseminated cytomegalovirus infection that includes not only CMV retinitis but also subcutaneous CMV lesions around her genitalia. Any one of these illnesses could have killed her. When protease inhibitors, the new "miracle" drugs in HIV therapy, became available, Maria's medications were changed, with Cesar's consent, to include indinavir (Crixivan). This was before these drugs were formally licensed for children.[3] Introduction of a protease inhibitor will usually drive even a high viral load down to an undetectable amount. With Maria, though, the change was slight, and this only at the very beginning.

"Cesar, I want you to see these numbers," Dr. Bennett says. Cesar stands up and comes over to Dr. Bennett, looking over his shoulder at Maria's chart. "This one here is Maria's T cell count," Dr. Bennett says as he points to a series of numbers. "You can see how it's

[2] PCP is the most common opportunistic infection in children with HIV. Prophylaxis for PCP was introduced in 1991. Dr. Bennett prescribes Bactrim as a PCP prophylaxis for children whose HIV infection renders them immunosuppressed.

[3] The first protease inhibitor, saquinavir (Invirase), was approved for adults in December 1995. It was not until March 1997 that protease inhibitors (nelfinavir [Viracept] and ritonavir [Norvir]) were licensed for use in children. A major problem in determining the efficacy and safety of HIV medications in children is the lack of phase three clinical trials. Such studies are very expensive and for this reason are almost always subsidized by drug companies. Decisions on performing such studies for certain drugs and certain populations are basically fiscal. A drug company will not run a clinical trial if the market for such a drug is perceived as so small that the company is not likely to be compensated for its expenses. Furthermore, the population of children with HIV/AIDS in the United States is relatively small (about 2 percent of the total number of AIDS cases to date) compared with adults with this disease.

dropped from 1,600, when she was diagnosed years ago, to 170 the last visit. A count of 1,800 to 2,400 would be normal for a child of Maria's age." A T cell count is a measure of the body's immunological defenses and thus predictive of how well Maria can resist infection. Cesar of course knows about T cell counts. Parents who are themselves infected undergo the same tests and receive the same or similar medications, and thus lengthy explanation is unnecessary. He understands that a T cell count of 170 is not good.

"These here"—Dr. Bennett points to another series of numbers— "chart her viral load.[4] You can see that it hasn't gone down as much as I'd like. It's never been lower than 45,000. Even though she's had the newest and the best HIV medications, the virus is still thriving."

Cesar, still listening intently, sits down again. Dr. Bennett continues. "Cesar, it may be that Maria will have a crisis with her breathing and that we won't be able to do anything to bring her back to living a normal life." He goes on to talk about whether it would be appropriate to keep Maria alive, in a hospital bed and on a breathing machine, or to allow her to die. He explains that there is technology now to keep people alive and that there are times when this is appropriate, such as after a car accident or when a child has an illness from which she can recover and return to a wholly or even partially normal life. "But," he observes, "this is not so in Maria's case."

He suggests to Cesar, gently but decisively, that it might be best to allow Maria to die if her health deteriorates to the point where she would require artificial life support systems.

Cesar nods in assent, wiping away tears with the back of his hand.

Dr. Bennett continues. "If she has trouble breathing, don't call an ambulance. Don't call 911. Call my office and they'll page me, and we'll take it from there."

I am impressed by the trust between doctor and parent so evident

---

[4] A newer test that began to be widely used around 1995, viral load indicates the amount of current HIV activity, as opposed to T cell counts, which indicate the degree of immunologic destruction. An individual's viral load rises as the disease advances.

during this painful encounter. Some physicians deal with end-of-life decisions by describing the alternatives and then leaving the patients or families to choose between them. Dr. Bennett is more directive in the way he talks to children and their parents. Critics might perceive this as medical "paternalism" (almost always a pejorative term in medical ethics discourse), overriding Cesar's right to make end-of-life decisions for his own daughter. But to me, Dr. Bennett's paternalism has always seemed not to deprive parents of their right to decide their child's fate but, rather, to relieve some of the burden—and it must be an awful burden—of choosing to allow one's child to die. Parents have powerful protective instincts toward their offspring that become even stronger when the child is in danger, and very few can just set aside those instincts without violating something deep within. It may be a paternalistic gesture for a physician to shoulder such a burden, but it seems to me a generous one as well. It is also true that I have seen parents decline Dr. Bennett's advice to refuse aggressive and invasive treatment for a child with end stage HIV disease, and when this happens, he defers at once to the parents' wishes.

No further words pass between Dr. Bennett and Cesar. There is a knock on the door, and the nurse enters briefly to tell us that the director of social services is on the phone, returning Dr. Bennett's call. Dr. Bennett leaves the room. Cesar and I remain silent while he is gone. He soon returns to report that Medical Assistance does not provide funds for a funeral but that St. Luke's Children's Fund will. He tells Cesar that Maria is now very sick, that it is appropriate for her and the family to receive hospice care, and that he will fill out the forms that authorize this service. He briefly describes hospice, telling Cesar that someone will be calling him at home to explain further and to answer questions. Dr. Bennett remains seated for a few moments, looking intently at Cesar, who returns his gaze. Then he stands, and Cesar stands too. Both men shake hands. Cesar turns, shakes my hand, and gives me a brief hug. "Bring Maria back for an appointment in two weeks," Dr. Bennett says as we all leave the room.

.   .   .

Through many conversations with Cesar (including one lengthy taped session) and through talking with others who know him, I've tried to reconstruct his story, along with that of his children and their mother.

Born in Mexico, Cesar was one of eleven children, two of whom died during infancy. The family was poor. Parents and children alike worked hard in the fields, and even so, they barely had enough to eat. Cesar came to the United States when he was thirteen, sneaking over the border into California. He had older brothers already living in the States, but he didn't want to pick fruit all day as they did to support themselves and their families. He was young and full of confidence, and he wanted a life of his own. Women, especially well-to-do, middle-aged Caucasian women in Southern California, found Cesar attractive. He found it more to his liking (and far more remunerative) to take up with such women than to work long hours in fields and orchards.

Cesar met the woman who became his first wife when he was nineteen. They married, and she soon gave birth to a child, Avricita. Cesar moved his new family to Florida, where his young wife had relatives. But he found it hard to give up other women, and his wife was jealous. After a year and a half they got divorced. Little Avricita was nine months old. Cesar fought hard for her custody, claiming that he could give Avricita a better life than her mother could. He won. He remembers with great bitterness this promise he made to the court, to himself, and to his daughter: "I was so sure I could give her a good life . . . and now, here she's okay, but she has me dying, and her brother and sister will die, and who will take care of her?"

Soon after Cesar separated from his first wife, he began a relationship with Dolores, whom he eventually married and who was Maria's and Cesar Jr.'s mother. Several months after C.J. was born, the family moved from Florida to Liberty, Ohio, a small town about a half hour by car from St. Luke's Hospital and our HIV clinic.

Maria's medical history began when she developed pneumonia at three months of age. She had pneumonia again at twelve months and fourteen months, together with a series of ear infections. All these illnesses responded well to antibiotics. When she was sixteen months old, Maria was admitted to a tertiary care medical center (not St. Luke's) with recurrent aspiration pneumonia, otitis media, and "failure to thrive." By now it was suspected that she might have some underlying illness that caused all these acute infections. At that time chronic lung disease was the primary candidate.

Maria underwent many procedures during this hospitalization, including bronchoscopy, testing for apnea, and several tests for auditory problems. The question of HIV infection came up, but Dolores claimed that Maria had been tested for this during her first pneumonia, when she was three months old, and that the test was negative. More tests were ordered, though not for HIV, since it is illegal to perform an HIV antibody test without written consent, and Dolores refused to acknowledge even the possibility that her daughter was infected. But testing a patient's gamma globulin level is legal, and it was certainly an appropriate step in the attempt to determine what was wrong with Maria. Maria's IgG was found to be high. Since an elevated IgG can be an indirect marker of HIV infection, a culture was sent for HIV testing. It is unclear whether or not permission was obtained from Dolores. The ELISA antibody test (which is predictive of HIV) came back positive, and was confirmed soon after by Western Blot procedure.[5]

Some six months after this last hospitalization Dolores brought Maria to St. Luke's. Again she had pneumonia. Dolores was very angry. She claimed that the other hospital had tested Maria for HIV without her permission; moreover, no one had informed her that the test results were positive. But she accepted the diagnosis of HIV and wanted Maria to receive treatment. At that time our clinic was

[5] The ELISA test, approved in 1985, is used to screen blood for antibodies to HIV. It is quick, it is highly sensitive, and it is inexpensive (about seven dollars from a state-sponsored lab; sixty-five to seventy-five dollars from a private lab). If a person's ELISA test is positive, then the blood sample is automatically sent for a second, confirmatory test, called the Western Blot, a test that is more specific but less sensitive than the ELISA. Combined ELISA and Western Blot HIV testing is 99 percent accurate, except in the case of infants born to infected mothers.

involved in a pediatric AIDS clinical trial research study.[6] Dolores agreed that Maria be enrolled in the study. She was informed that Maria would receive zidovidine (AZT) and a placebo, or ddI (Videx) and a placebo, or AZT plus ddI. Presumably Dolores was also tested around the same time and found to be infected. She went to St. Luke's adult HIV clinic for her treatment, scheduling appointments for herself on the same day that she brought Maria.

Dolores did not want C.J. to be tested. As she pointed out, he was never sick, so why test him? It took nearly a year before she would consent. C.J., by now fifteen months old, tested positive. He was enrolled, like Maria, in the research study. But C.J. continued over the years to be much healthier than his sister. With the exception of fluconazole for an occasional bout of thrush, he was given only the two protocol medications during this entire early period.[7]

By the time Maria was two years old, she was taking Bactrim, Biaxin, and Rifampin as preventatives for PCP and MAI, in addition to the protocol medications. She continued to have a serious cough and recurrent fevers. When she was three and a half years old, her teeth, badly decayed, began to give her pain. She was sedated with general anesthesia, and four primary teeth were removed by an oral surgeon. It was at about this same time that a blood culture revealed CMV (asymptomatic so far). Two years later dual therapy was introduced: AZT (in a lower dose) and ddC (Hivid), both nucleoside reverse transcriptase inhibitors. By then Maria was frequently taking fluconazole, an antifungal medication, for repeated episodes of thrush in her mouth. Six months later, with her T cell count continuing to drop, Dr. Bennett switched to another nucleoside reverse transcriptase inhibitor, subsituting ddI (Videx) for ddC, which she took in conjunction with AZT and Bactrim.

[6] PACTG 152. The results of this study introduced two-drug therapy as the standard of care.

[7] When the study was "unblinded" several years later, it turned out that C.J. had received ddI (Videx) and a placebo for AZT. Maria had been given AZT and a placebo for ddI.

Dolores was the only parent on the scene during the first four years of Maria's medical treatment at St. Luke's. She rarely mentioned Cesar, who she said was always "off somewhere" and was uninterested in the children's medical condition. Dolores was a hefty, boisterous woman, very blond and very loud. When bringing the children for clinic appointments, she would announce her presence to the nurse well before reaching the examining room by hollering: "Hey, Jo! It's Dolores! I'm here!" The children's visits were long, sometimes lasting four or five hours, since the protocol for the clinical trial required intravenous infusions of gamma globulin.[8] The kids were wild, and Dolores had no control over them. She screamed at them constantly, and they paid no attention to her, causing her to scream and yell some more. Once, during a clinic visit, Dr. Bennett said to her in a low voice, "Dolores, you know it's really more effective if you talk softly." She paused, then said, "Do you think so, Dr. Bennett?" Nodding, he replied softly, "Yes, I do." Dolores nodded too. But then, glimpsing C.J. as he clambered up onto the examining table, she turned around and yelled at the top of her voice, "C.J.! You get down from there!"

In some ways Dolores was an attentive mother. She regularly took Maria and C.J. to their medical appointments, and she always made sure there was food in the house. But she indulged the children (her own, not Avricita), giving them whatever they wanted whenever they wanted it, Maria especially. If Maria wanted McDonald's french fries, Dolores took her to get fries, even though it meant driving to the next town. If Maria wanted to stay up late watching TV, she was always permitted to do so. Maria ruled the household. But it was a different story with Avricita. Dolores was

---

[8] Infusions of intravenous immunoglobulin provide antibodies meant to reduce serious infections. In the first year of the study those who received IVIG had remarkably fewer serious infections, as measured by number and length of hospitalizations. In the second year, surprisingly, it made no difference whether or not patients were given IVIG injections. The reason was that in this second year Bactrim was introduced as a prophylactic for PCP. Besides warding off PCP, Bactrim reduced other kinds of bacterial infection as well.

hard on her, telling her that her "real" mother didn't want her and that she should be grateful to Dolores for taking her in.

There was another side to Dolores as well. According to Cesar, she was deceitful about money. He claims that he brought her the wages from his construction work, thinking he was supporting the family. She never told him she was also receiving Social Security benefits for the children and for herself. Much of that money went to drugs, especially cocaine. Moreover, Dolores did not take care of herself. She smoked cigarettes, she did not always keep her own clinic appointments, and she took medications only sporadically, if at all. When her health began to deteriorate rapidly, she continued taking the children for their clinic visits — up until the very end. On several occasions the clinic staff asked her who would care for the children after her death. Dolores indicated repeatedly that she had made arrangements for her parents, who, she said, lived close by, to take legal custody of both children.

Only two weeks after the last time she brought the children for their medical appointments, Dolores died from HIV-related infections.

A week after her death Cesar brought the children for their monthly appointments with Dr. Bennett. None of the clinic staff had ever met Cesar. He was nothing like the "deadbeat dad" Dolores had described. Instead they found him polite, reserved, and closely bonded to his children. He spoke to the children gently, in a soft voice, and they did what he told them to do. Even during this first visit it was apparent that he was more skilled than Dolores in handling them.

But he was also a stricken husband, grieving over the death of his wife and still in shock over the new knowledge — and the new life — into which he had suddenly been plunged. Apparently Dolores never told him that she and the children were infected with HIV. She had explained that she took the children to St. Luke's for chronic lung disease. On occasion he called the clinic to ask about the children, but — in part because Dolores had portrayed him as irresponsible — he was told that such information couldn't be given over the phone and that he needed to come in person to learn about his children's medical status.

During this clinic visit, after Dr. Bennett had examined Maria and C.J. and described their condition to Cesar, he raised the question of Cesar's own HIV status: Was he infected? Had he been tested? Cesar replied that he had made arrangements to be tested that same day. Dr. Bennett asked how he was feeling, and Cesar broke down. "You want to know how I feel? Well, my heart is in pieces. My heart, it's just in pieces." As he described how Dolores had lied to him, his sorrow was punctuated with flashes of anger. It was only three days before Dolores's death that Cesar learned she was dying of AIDS, that his children were infected, and that he probably was too. She had never told her family about any of this, her parents did not live close by, and there had been no discussion with them about who would care for the children after her death.

More than once Cesar told me about the shock of Dolores's deathbed confession. Every time he spoke about it, his eyes welled up with tears, his face tightened, his body contracted. I heard the whole story when I went to visit the family at their new home in Kentucky in May 1998. The children were in school, and Cesar and I were able to talk uninterrupted for several hours. Almost immediately he launched into a description of the time shortly before her death when Dolores told him the truth about herself and the children. I was struck by the intensity of his feeling. At times his voice broke, and when sobbing made it impossible to speak, he was forced to pause. He often rocked back and forth as he talked. It seemed almost as if he were keening, his heavily accented English occasionally lapsing into Spanish. Cesar repeated certain words, such as "pain," over and over during this monologue, and he circled back again and again to lament, "Why didn't she tell me? Why didn't she tell me?" as though it were a refrain.

"This is how it is with my story. The day I found out these problems, it was one of the hardest things. . . . I didn't want to believe it was true. A few days before she passed away is when my wife, she told me she was dying with AIDS. But she didn't want even to tell me about the kids. She said, 'You'll find out when you're at St. Luke's.' But I know now what all those trips with the kids to the clinic were. I turned to her, and I said, 'Why? Why couldn't you ever have been honest with me and told me? Why?' The only thing she said was 'Forgive me, if you can.'

"I was supposed to be moving down with her to Kentucky. All that week I was moving furniture, and the last trip, when I came back for the last things, she was laying in bed. She told me that day she was dying. Her mother was there. She was completely dying. No one could touch her because she was in such pain. I went over to her bed, and she screams and says, 'Don't touch me!' I could just feel the pain in her. She was truly passing away. I couldn't hold her for the pain. I had to take the kids out of the house; that was the night before she died. Even the hospice care worker, she couldn't control the pain. It was so bad, I called an ambulance and they took her to the hospital and hooked her up to IVs. But she wanted to die. This doctor in the emergency room said there was nothing they could do. My wife, she was crying and looking at us and saying, 'Take the tubes out and let me go. Cesar, take me home.'

"So I decided to take her home. After three hours she was still alive. The pain was terrible. I got on the bed next to her and lay down, but I had to be careful not to touch her. I said to her, 'Please, if it's your time, go. I'll take care of the kids until it's the last day I can.' I got up and went to the bathroom, and when I came back, she was gone.

"Right away I had to think, 'How am I gonna explain this to my kids?' The people from the funeral home came and took her away. And I knew my kids had to know. The hospice lady said, 'Do you want us to tell them?' I said, 'No, I have to do this myself.' I stayed in the house for a while. Then I went to my sister-in-law's to pick up the kids and take them back home. When I got there, they saw me with the pain in my face. Avricita said, 'What's happened? Where's Mommy?' And Dolores was not even her real mother, but she loved her. I said, 'I'll explain when we get home.' I was holding Maria when we got there and she said, 'Your heart is beating hard,

Daddy. Where's Mommy? Where's Mommy?' And I just said, 'She died.' C.J. was only three then. He ran into the house and lay on the couch and started crying. All I could think then was: 'She's gone. What are we going to do? How will we manage?' The next few months there were times the kids dreamed that they saw her. I would say, 'It's okay. Your dreams mean that Mommy's still here with us.'

"I think about how it was that she lied to me. Learning this, it was like a lie, that whole time my wife and I were together and had those kids. We were married four years and lived together the year before. Those five years we were together, that was enough time for her to explain things to me. I don't understand why she never told me. When she said the kids had chronic lung disease, I believed her. When she said she was losing her hair because of leukemia, I believed her. By the time I found out it was HIV, it was too late. I was infected by someone I loved and trusted. I never thought I would have a disease like this because I was the cleanest person in the world. When I told my parents about the HIV infection, they didn't want to believe it, because I was so clean all my life. Why did she do this? Why? I don't know.

"I'm alive now because of my kids. What's keeping me going is my kids. I have a lot of pain now. Maria, she worries when she feels me in pain. I think me and Maria feel these things together. I look at C.J., and even though he's healthy, I know he has the same problem. Now I understand: Sometimes you have the pain and sometimes you don't. My kids ask me sometimes about how their mother died. I don't have the guts to explain. I only say, 'It was painful.' I think of my kids with this same disease. . . . I wish someday they'd find a cure and that they'd cure everybody. I deal with this every day, and I try and I try, but I don't have the patience anymore.

"The pain, I try to hide it. I act tough, because I don't want people to see it in my face. And it's not even so much the pain; it's the problems I have to deal with every day. Every day is a different story. It's so complicated. The kids have questions, but I have no answers. They ask, 'Why is Maria so sick? How come they didn't find a cure for Mommy?' I don't have answers for my kids when they ask me about this disease. And that makes me more miserable. And I think, 'What are they going to do after I die? How are they going to go on with this?' It will be even harder for them, especially Maria, with her being blind. And I think about Avricita. She doesn't have the disease. But how is she going to deal with me dying, then the little kids?

"Me, I'm sick of medications. Before I found out we had this disease I would act so strong, and I was so stubborn and I would act so tough. But once I did find out, it brought me down. Now that I've started taking the medications I feel real pain. I can understand why my kids fight me about taking their medications. I'm sick of medicines. They're sick of medicines. Maria will cry and she'll even kick sometimes when I'm forcing her to take them. I promise her the world if she'll take her medications, but I don't have the world to give her. In the end I'm the one that's the liar. Here I promise her the world, and what kind of world am I going to give her?"

Not long after Dolores's death, Cesar began appearing for the children's clinic visits with girlfriends. The first was Tiffany, then came Candy, then Bonnie. It was never certain whether or not he used precautions with these women, though Dr. Bennett more than once warned him about the danger of unprotected sexual relations. When directly asked, Cesar would admit to not using contraceptives, and we would pick up some condoms from the adult clinic and give them to him. Sometimes he told us that his HIV medications made him too sick to enjoy sexual relations. At other times he said that he wasn't interested in sex anymore, that he cared only about his children.

Tiffany, Candy, and Bonnie all were sweet-faced young women, slightly overweight, with long, wavy, honey-colored hair. They were polite but never very talkative. All three in turn seemed devoted to Cesar and to the children as well. At first it seemed that Cesar was womanizing. But before long it became apparent that whatever personal satisfaction he gained from these relationships, he was using his charm with women to attract good caregivers for the children. Cesar's illiteracy was a problem compounded by his unwillingness to admit it. His girlfriends could read prescriptions; they could help deal with the paper work for the children's Medical Assistance; they could read and respond to the notices sent home from school. Sometimes the children were brought in by the girlfriend only, without Cesar. We soon realized that when this happened, he was off working as a roofer for a friend in a nearby state, leaving the children with the girlfriend, sometimes for several weeks. In a way Cesar's lifestyle was that of a traditional husband and father: He worked and brought home money, and his woman —whichever woman it happened to be—took care of the children.

When I first met Cesar and his children, in January 1996, Candy was with them, holding an infant in her arms. Dr. Bennett talked with both Cesar and Candy about the importance of using condoms. Candy nodded, but after she left the room, Cesar confided that she didn't want him to use birth control. In fact, he told us, she wanted to get pregnant by him, and she claimed that the baby she carried in her arms was his!

July 1997

A year and a half after I first met Cesar and Candy, Maria and C.J. are brought in for their medical appointments by a strikingly beautiful woman of about thirty named Lisa Fuentes. Lisa has fine, aquiline features and straight black hair pulled back behind her face, accentuating high cheekbones. She is poised, articulate, and forthright. It is a hot summer day, and Lisa is wearing denim cutoffs and a faded T-shirt. At first I think she is yet another girlfriend, but I soon realize this is not the case. As she puts it, "Cesar and me, we're like brother and sister." Lisa lives in Liberty, as do Cesar and his family—a mostly white, working-class hill town in the Ohio countryside. She was a close friend of Dolores's, and since Dolores's death she has been the one constant figure other than Cesar in the children's lives. At times they stay with her and her own children, especially when Cesar is between girlfriends. She is the person he has asked to take his children when he dies.

When I first meet Lisa, I like her immensely. She seems both caring and intelligent. We talk on several occasions during the times she brings the children in for their medical appointments and later at her home. Lisa gives me a vivid picture of Cesar and his children on the streets of Liberty: "Guys don't dress up there unless they're going to a wedding or a funeral or something like that. But Cesar, for him it was an everyday thing. He'd be walking around in these nice slacks and with dress shoes, and he'd have all these gold chains and shit like that. There was no problem for him to get women, especially in that town. He used to strut his ass up and down the street, and he had his kids with him, and that was just the greatest thing because in Liberty guys don't mess with their kids. So here's Cesar carrying Maria, with C.J. holding his hand, and him walking the dog. Women just loved that!

"He had so many frigging bimbos around. First there was Tiffany. Cesar and his kids were living with me then, and he brought in Tiffany to take care of the kids. Him and Tiffany were playing house, and I was like a maniac: 'You have these three kids now and you're thinking about females? What the hell's wrong with you!' But that's just how he is. Tiffany was good with the kids, though. She was some kind of nurse. She'd make the kids eat dinners and all.

"Then there was this Candy. He was screwing around with Candy while he was with Tiffany. Candy, she was a total idiot. She wanted to have his kid! The first time they were having sex, he didn't tell her about his being HIV. Then the second time he was using a condom and it ripped. He told her, but she didn't care. Then she had this baby, and she said it was his baby. When Tiffany left, Candy showed up right away with this baby of hers. And I was supposed to take care of the baby! In the morning Cesar would be outside cleaning his van, and Candy, she'd be there with him. But this baby, she'd be in the house screaming her head off! So I'd get out of bed—I worked nights, so I slept late in the morning—and get the baby, and then I'd want to kill that Candy. After a few months of this I'd had enough. I told them all to get out.

"Avricita told me later that Candy, she was a real flake. She was stripping and stuff. There was this cop she was messing with. One time—Cesar was off working—she was with this cop in the kitchen, naked, and he had her handcuffed, and she was dancing for him. The kids were right there in the next room watching TV! Avricita says Candy got in a big fight with her and tried to kick her out. Pretty soon after they all left my house, Avricita called me all upset and crying and wanting me to come over. So I drove over there. Cesar was in bed, really sick—he wasn't taking his medicines, and that's what was wrong—and here's this yo-yo Candy out in the kitchen. She had a bunch of people there, and they were drinking. I cleaned them all out and told her, 'You get the hell out and take your fucking kid with you!'

"After about a week Cesar got better, and then there she was, Candy, back again with that baby. He asked me to let her stay until they found out if it was his baby or not. I said okay. But I never thought it was his kid. She's lighter than light, freckles and all. They did blood work on Candy and found out it's not his kid. When I heard that, I told Cesar, 'There's something wrong with this girl. She's trying to get pregnant with your kid, and she's doing this to be with you. And you're going to die, and she knows that. You don't want a yo-yo like that responsible for your kids!' And I told her again to get the fuck out.

"But when Candy went, he left with her and took his kids. They all got an apartment in Moorham. Then one time I see him on the street, and he's with his kids and another girl, not Candy. Avricita was with them, and I asked her, 'Who's that'? She says, 'Well, that's Candy number two.' And I said, 'Oh, my God, here we go again!' This new girlfriend, Bonnie, she was married to somebody else. She had three kids, and she was screwing around with Cesar while she was still married. She tried to be friends with me, but I said, 'No, I don't want no part of you. I don't get involved with Cesar's bimbos no more, sorry. I think you're an idiot. You have your own kids to worry about, and you're going to risk your life for him? He ain't worth it!' After I said that, she stayed away from me."

August 1997

Once more Lisa brings the children in for their appointments. They have been staying with her for the past three weeks while Cesar is out of state doing construction work. As she reminds us, he receives no disability benefits because he never applied for U.S. citizenship. He *has* to work. She adds, "Besides, working is good for him; he feels more of a man." Lisa has four children of her own. All of them, including Cesar's three children, are now living in her trailer, along with several cats and a dog. Lisa tells us she's been temporarily laid off from her work in a nearby factory, where she was assigned to the night shift. She's glad she can be home more, especially while Cesar's children are staying with her and especially since Maria is sick so often and unable to go to school. Dr. Bennett tells Lisa about a nearby school for blind children, suggesting this might be a good thing for Maria and for Lisa too because she'd have more time to herself. But Lisa wants to keep Maria home with her.

Dr. Bennett has already seen C.J. and released him to the Super Nintendo. After examining Maria, he lifts her down off the examining table, positions her in such a way that she faces Lisa, and watches her take the few steps that bring her back to Lisa's lap, where she curls up in her arms, smiling slightly, her eyes drowsy. Maria looks enchanting today, fragile and delicate. I can see that a child like Maria brings out in adults the impulse to nurture and to love. It's as though we feel compelled in some way to try to make up for all the life experiences such a child will never have.

Today Maria's viral load has gone up. This means there is more virus in her system and the disease is likely to be progressing. Lisa explains that she's having trouble—"major trouble," as she says— getting Maria to take her medicines, especially the protease inhibitor Crixivan, which is the most important of all of them but has a terrible taste. Maria resists taking it, and when Lisa can get it down her, Maria not infrequently vomits it back up. Dr. Bennett is concerned. He tells Lisa that Maria's viral load is up to 79,000 and that they need to do whatever they can to try to bring it down. Instead of the dreaded Crixivan he'll substitute liquid Viracept, a different protease inhibitor. Maria loves Ensure, a milklike dietary supplement, and he hopes that if the Viracept powder is mixed in with her Ensure, she'll tolerate it better than she has the Crixivan.

When the children have left the examining room, Dr. Bennett talks to Lisa about plans for guardianship. He suggests that she consult a lawyer so that she and Cesar can be certain of the children's future. He warns her that the issue of guardianship can introduce problems: "Family members will have priority over you if they claim they want guardianship, and their motives may be mixed. It could be that they'll want to take the children because they want their Supplemental Social Security. It would be good if the children don't get involved in that." At this point C.J. bursts into the room, announcing with exasperation that "some other kid" is on the Super Nintendo. He is more than his usual exuberant self. Lisa explains, "School's just about to start, and it's been rainy the last few days and we've all been cooped up together." We realize that it's time to end this clinic visit.

September 1997

Both Cesar and Lisa bring the children in for their clinic appointments today. Cesar has just returned from his out-of-state construction job. He looks good and reports feeling less of the muscle pain that has caused him such misery. He is again wearing his belt with the word "Mexico" etched onto the large silver buckle. Maria traces this with her fingers and says, "Mexico." Cesar corrects her pronunciation. "Me'hi-co," he says, in his fluent Spanish. Maria imitates him: "Mehico." Her Spanish is no better than mine. Indeed both children are more American than Mexican. They can neither understand nor speak Spanish, they don't like Mexican food, and they are unfamiliar with the culture. This has been a problem during visits with their Mexican grandparents, who come to this country from time to time as migrant workers. Though the grandparents are solicitous of the children's welfare, they speak no English and, according to Cesar, have lots of misconceptions about HIV.

The problem today is the same as last time: Maria is not getting her medications. She isn't tolerating the Viracept any better than the Crixivan. She still doesn't want to take it, even when mixed with Ensure. She first resists and protests and, when she's finally been persuaded (or forced) to swallow it, vomits it back up. Dr. Bennett takes all this really seriously. Maria has already exhausted the potential of nucleoside analogs to keep the virus in check. Though protease inhibitors are remarkably successful in inhibiting HIV replication for most patients, if taken inconsistently or sporadically, the virus will continue to replicate, and replication in the presence of antiretroviral agents allows the virus to mutate and become resistant to medications. Because of this, sometimes protease inhibitors are not prescribed for people who admit to being incapable of taking medications on a regular basis.

Dr. Bennett says to Lisa, "If we have any hope of altering the course of this illness, we just have to get her to take this."

He calls Maria to come to him and sits her on his lap, folding his hands around her waist: "The message is this, Maria. You don't have any choice about taking this medication, except for what you take it with. You have to take it. And you have to take it because you want to stay healthy and we want you to stay healthy."

Maria pouts. She asks, "How come I'm sicker than my brother?"

Dr. Bennett says, "Maria, I don't know. Some things are a mystery. C.J. has medications that are right for him, that will keep him healthy, and you have medications that are right for you. He has to take his, and you have to take yours."

C.J. is still there in the examining room. He's more subdued than usual. His eyes have been itching, and Cesar fears that this is the beginning of the cytomegalovirus infection that cost Maria her eyesight. Dr. Bennett examines him and then reassures everyone. "It's okay, don't worry. It's either a viral conjunctivitis or hay fever. This condition is not like Maria's. She was severely immunocompromised, but he's not. He'll be okay." It seems to me that Dr. Bennett directs his comments about C.J.'s eyesight more to Lisa than to Cesar, as though she were the primary caregiver. I know that Dr. Bennett has a full schedule today, with extra patients who have come with serious emergent illnesses. But it bothers me that he doesn't speak with Cesar, doesn't ask him how he is, doesn't ask about the out-of-state job.

October 1997

Lisa is there with the children, once more without Cesar. She doesn't know where he is, and she's annoyed. Cesar apparently is not providing much monetary support for the children, even though he's getting $444 in Supplemental Social Security per month for each child. Lisa is put out about this, especially since school is starting and the children need clothes. Maria was really sick last week with a high fever and chills, so Lisa took her to the emergency room at their local hospital. She describes waiting for what seemed like hours with this child, whose fever seemed to be climbing steadily higher. "I was just sitting there with her," Lisa says, "when suddenly her body stiffened and went into spasms; then she went limp, and her eyes rolled back. I went right through that door, and I told them, 'You got to do something with this kid; she's really sick!' And this doctor guy, he said, 'You've got to wait your turn.' And I yelled, 'I can't wait my turn!' Then I handed Maria to Jill [Lisa's daughter], and I grabbed that guy and took him around the corner and said, 'She has AIDS, and I've never seen her like this. She's got a fever of 104; she's got seizures. Do something for this kid!' Then they jumped right on it." Learning that Maria was a patient at St. Luke's, the attending physician called Dr. Bennett, who suspected the cause might be the ganciclovir she had been receiving for her CMV infection. Dr. Bennett recommended that

Maria be given an injection of Benadryl and that she be sent back home, discontinuing the ganciclovir.

Lisa points out the problems she might have faced during this emergency visit if Maria had required surgery and if Cesar had not been around to authorize such treatments. She knew about Dr. Bennett's and Cesar's decision not to put Maria in intensive care should this be required to keep her alive. But she herself had no legal authority to decide about Maria's health care. Dr. Bennett understood immediately and offered to write a "To Whom It May Concern" letter that would summarize Maria's medical condition as well as his discussion with Cesar regarding end-of-life issues for Maria and that would also indicate that Lisa was frequently the child's caregiver. He wrote this some hours later. Stating that Maria is "profoundly immunocompromised, and at risk for having a fatal opportunistic infection," Dr. Bennett concluded the letter: "In my discussions with Cesar and Lisa, we have agreed that she [Maria] is not a candidate for intensive care. She is not to be intubated or to receive other high-tech medical interventions. We will treat intercurrent infections in an ambulatory setting, and will provide pain medications if such medications become necessary."

November 1997

Cesar comes with the children for the next two clinic visits without Lisa. I ask him about her, and Cesar replies that he has moved back in with Bonnie, taking his kids with him. He explains that he felt Lisa was taking over too much: "She was supposed to help me, not come between me and my kids." He looks exhausted, there are deep circles around his eyes, and his face is lined. I am startled to see, suddenly, a middle-aged man emerging from the face of a twenty-eight-year-old.

Maria has been having high fevers that keep her, and Cesar, up at night. She's been taking liquid morphine for pain. Her mouth is full of thrush, for which Dr. Bennett prescribes fluconazole. Cesar asks him about a rash around "her privates." Dr. Bennett takes a look at it, secures a culture, and tells us that normally this would be presumed to be herpes simplex II, but in this case it's most likely cutaneous CMV. Once the tissue culture has confirmed CMV, he orders a prescription cream for the lesions.

C.J.'s examination is unremarkable, but his viral load has suddenly risen, and Dr. Bennett starts him immediately on a three-drug "cocktail" of two reverse transcriptase inhibitors and a protease inhibitor, the same medications that he has prescribed for Maria.

December 1997

Both children are doing well and are excited about an upcoming trip to Disney World. The whole family will be going, courtesy of the Make-a-Wish Foundation, which arranges such experiences for terminally ill children.

January 1998

C.J. and Maria are late for their appointments, and the clinic schedule is tight because of some "add-ons" with sudden and potentially serious medical problems. There is a long wait before Dr. Bennett can see the children. Since the last clinic visit C.J. has been sick with a fever. In fact the fever was so high that Cesar drove him to the emergency room at St. Luke's, where he was started on antibiotics and sent home (per Dr. Bennett's orders). The trip to Disney World was canceled.

C.J. is defiant today. He refuses at first to interrupt his Super Nintendo game. When he's finally persuaded to come inside the examining room, he starts complaining about his eyes. "They hurt," he says, "and I can't see good." Dr. Bennett examines him carefully but doesn't find anything suggesting CMV retinitis. All the same he sends C.J. to the hospital's pediatric ophthalmologist, just to make sure he hasn't missed something. Afterward I wonder if C.J. could be responding to the recent report of his rise in viral load and the subsequent change in his medication schedule. He has felt safe for so long from the depredations of this illness that have caused his sister such misery, and now, suddenly, he hears that his own viral load is up and finds himself taking the same medications she does.

Maria, on the other hand, looks better today than she has in a long time. Apparently she is also feeling better. She no longer needs Roxanol (morphine) for pain, and she has gained weight. She smiles broadly when we enter the room. Dr. Bennett is surprised, and very pleased. He talks to Cesar and the rest of us about the degree of uncertainty in treating HIV-infected children: "You just don't know how things will turn out!" Before the advent of protease inhibitors it was important to try to prepare parents, and their child, for the death that seemed imminent. Now, however, children with virtually no T cells seem to be thriving, thanks to new medications. Still, there is no way of knowing how long they will stay healthy. Thus the doctor's task is to shape treatment expectations around a radically uncertain prognosis. Many infected adults, after a few years on combination therapy, suffer relapses, sicken, and die of some opportunistic infection. We can only hope that this will not be true for infected children as well.

March 1998

Dr. Bennett's casual remark—"You just don't know how things will turn out"—is true in a way that none of us could have predicted. This turns out to be the final clinic visit for Cesar and the children. Avricita is there as well, along with a nice-looking woman whom I haven't met before. We all think she is another girlfriend, but Cesar introduces her as his new landlady. He goes on to explain that he and the kids are moving to Kentucky and that they're actually on their way there right now! He has left all his belongings in Liberty, where he was living with Bonnie and her two children. Cesar tells us he will be coming back for these things later on. My first thought is to wonder if he's running away from Bonnie, but later conversations suggest that he's running from the father of an earlier (and very young) girlfriend, who has been out to get him for taking up with his daughter. This man has apparently threatened Cesar, telling him, "I'd like to catch you out on a deserted road and shoot you dead!"

Aside from his romantic entanglements, it is understandable that Cesar would want to leave Liberty. It is an all-white run-down mill town that has seen better days. Cesar has been trying to keep his children's HIV status a secret from officials and parents at the school they attend, believing such secrecy is necessary for them to be able to attend at all. He says he has been told that "legally the other parents can do something to you if you put their kids at risk." There are other reasons too why he is uneasy about people discovering his and the children's HIV status. With indignation he tells me about a conversation he had with a "religious person," whose comment on his and his children's condition was only "God gives everybody what they deserve."

Both children are in stable health today. They are excited, and a little scared, about the move. Happily there is a fine tertiary care medical center quite close to the town in Kentucky where they'll be living. Arrangements are made for medical records to be transferred, and Dr. Bennett promises to write a letter summarizing both children's conditions and treatments should there be a delay in sending their records. We say good-bye, and Cesar promises to stay in touch.

Looking back, I realize that Cesar's sudden announcement of the move to Kentucky should not have surprised us. He is a nomad whose life journey has taken him from Mexico to California, then Florida, New Jersey, Pennsylvania, Ohio, California again briefly, then back to Ohio, and now Kentucky. Even during his years in Liberty, he moved from one living arrangement to another, shifting his address as often as he did his sexual partners. What has remained constant in all this restless change is Cesar's commitment to his children; it is after all *their* names, not those of his wives or lovers, that are inscribed in the hearts tattooed on his arms.

THE story of these people—its open-endedness, its touches of humor, and its pervasive sense of life as lived—seems worlds away from the somber, tightly unified grandeur of Greek tragedy. Yet as I think of Cesar, his wife, and his children, I find myself constantly reminded of those ancient plays, whose action turns on some dramatic reversal, often accompanied by an equally dramatic moment of recognition. In the most famous example of such a play, Oedipus discovers his true identity as the man who has—all unknowingly—killed his own father and married his own mother. At this moment of recognition and reversal, his life turns toward tragedy. King of Thebes at the beginning of the play, Oedipus becomes a blind beggar exiled from his country at its conclusion. So too in the drama of Cesar's life there is a recognition and a reversal. Recognition comes suddenly when he learns about the pervasiveness of AIDS in his family: that his wife is dying of the disease, that his children are infected, and that he probably is too. From that recognition comes a reversal, as his whole life is tragically and irrevocably changed.

Like the story of the house of Oedipus, the story of the Montalvo family is dominated by issues of judgment, sexuality, and moral responsibility. The chorus recoil from Oedipus when they learn what he has done, and he himself is so horrified by his incest and parricide that he puts out his own eyes. A similar stigma attaches to HIV: Those infected by it suffer not only from the disease itself but also from the sense of shame and defilement that our society associates with this particular illness. Indeed it was probably this stigma that impelled Dolores to deceive Cesar. For the Montalvo family, a general social prejudice has become directly and tragically destructive.

It is tempting to see Dolores, who introduced HIV into this family and then lied about it, as "bad" and Cesar, the loving father, as "good." But many crucial aspects of Dolores's story—whatever she did that caused her to become infected, her motives in concealing her own and the children's HIV status, her sense of what life would be like for her children and husband after her death—are unknown. Dolores died before I could even meet her, and her side of this story is something we can never know. Finally, she remains an enigmatic figure. There seems a basic ambiguity in Cesar as well. On the one hand, he is a warm and caring father; on the other, he seems an irresponsible womanizer, an HIV-infected man who is promiscuous and who does not always use protection.

Greek tragedy has its own ways of exploring moral ambiguities like those that characterize Cesar and Dolores. Like Cesar, Oedipus is not simply a villain or a hero. He did his best to avoid his crimes of parricide and incest, which were foretold by an oracle. He fled from those he supposed to be his parents, only to encounter his biological father and mother when he slew the one and married the other. What more, the play seems to ask, could Oedipus have done to avoid what seems his destiny? The answer is as inexorable as it is obvious: He must not marry, and he must not kill. The tragic outcome of this play results because Oedipus cannot finally surrender aggression and sexuality, drives that seem fundamental to human nature. It is these basic and instinctive drives that impel Oedipus unwittingly to commit terrible crimes, which in turn infect the whole community of Thebes with plague.

For both Oedipus and Cesar, sickness—plague in the one instance and AIDS in the other—is linked with sexuality. The forms such sexuality takes combine the sanctioned and the transgressive: a legitimate marriage, but marriage tainted in one case by incest or by promiscuity in the other. Similarly, in most parts of the world, HIV is now transmitted through heterosexual relations, often within marriage. There is a good chance that the infants conceived during those relations will be born infected. Paradoxically the sexual drive that is central to love and is the origin of the family can also become the source of disease and death. For ordinary human beings it is extraordinarily difficult to surrender sexual relationships altogether, and "safe sex"—if sex ever is safe—is simply not possible for many people in many parts of the world. Perhaps this inability to surrender the drives of sexuality and aggression is precisely the nexus of fate and character in Sophocles' play: This "paradigm of men" is punished by the gods not for hubris, not for defying or rebelling against the gods, but for acting on those basic drives that make up his, and our, humanity.

AIDS is a disease that uniquely invites judgment. Too often it is seen as the result of some moral failure on the part of the individual who contracts it. But the story of the Montalvo family suggests an ethic that turns not so much on monogamous fidelity or on abstinence or even on observing "safe sex" as on a profound sense of human responsibility. Cesar, despite his faults, takes on responsibility for his children's care. Dolores, despite her virtues, does not act responsibly toward those she claims to love. In concealing her HIV status, she infects and deprives Cesar of treatment, and in harming him, she harms the children, since it is he whose responsibility it will be to care for them after her death. Their story encourages us to consider a moral standard of responsibility that turns not on sexual behavior but on honoring our relationships with and obligations to others. These bonds are often grounded in sexual relations, but the ethic of caring and responsibility that they impose is wider and more imperative than any sexual morality.

It is with this perspective that we can consider what Cesar's children will face if they grow to maturity. Their situation combines a tragic sense of fate with a degree of hopeful uncertainty, thanks to pharmacological and technological advances. In Third World countries infected children almost always die, and die young. But in the United States and other developed countries therapies are constantly evolving, so that there is real hope for infected children to live well into adolescence and perhaps beyond.

Maria and several other children in our clinic have experienced a reversal of fortune, surviving well beyond expectations. But the future for these children—one, or three, or seven years hence—is unpredictable and uncertain. Perhaps in time the virus will develop resistance to these new drugs, with fatal consequences for our young patients. Yet it is also possible that if and when this happens, some new drug that will continue to extend their lives will be available. But even the happiest of endings—the survival of these infected children into adolescence—has its own dangers as they in turn become capable of sexually transmitting HIV infection. Their choices will decide not only their own fate but that of their partners and children. The best hope of breaking what might seem a cycle of predestined tragedy is that they will come to accept, even embrace, an ethic founded on loving responsibility to others.

SQUIRREL PIE AND A PICNIC

Joey and Felicity

Joey was born addicted to cocaine in June 1994. It was not discovered that he and his mother were HIV-infected until he was fourteen months old. His mother continues to have problems with drug addiction. His father is unknown. Joey was nine months old when he went to live with relatives, the Riley family, who adopted him a year later. At six months he had severe pneumococcal meningitis, which left him with a seizure disorder, motor and developmental delay, profound speech and language dysfunction, and subdural fluid collection that resulted in a large cerebral blood clot. Altogether Joey has had eleven hospitalizations for problems related to HIV infection. The Rileys also have a daughter who is now twelve years old and who enjoys taking care of Joey. He's an unusually cheerful toddler, an easy child to love.

Felicity is Joey's half sister. They have the same mother but different fathers. Unlike all the others in this family, who are Caucasian, Felicity's father is African-American. Felicity was born in January 1998 addicted to cocaine and opium. At birth custody was awarded to a twenty-eight-year-old aunt and her husband, the Dawsons, who are in the process of adopting her. It is still uncertain whether Felicity is HIV-infected. Despite a terrible initial period just after birth when she suffered through withdrawal symptoms, Felicity is now a happy, placid baby.

Joey and Felicity's mother is back on the streets and is thought to be pregnant a third time.

.　　　.　　　.

Part I. Joey and the Riley Family

"HEY, Doc, I got a joke for you today. You'll like this one!" Mike Riley announces this confidently, in his heavy Appalachian accent. He speaks quickly and swallows half his words, and it's always a little hard to understand him. Dr. Bennett has just walked into the examination room, trailed by this month's pediatric resident and me. The resident and I move into the corner of the room, leaving Dr. Bennett standing in the center, facing Mike and his wife, Loretta. Mike and Loretta are sitting next to each other, with Joey lying back on Loretta's lap, thumb in mouth. Dr. Bennett smiles at Mike. "Okay," he says, laying the thick chart he's carrying on the table and crossing his arms, "tell me."

"What do you call a girl with just one brain cell?"

Picking up the chart again, Dr. Bennett laughs, somewhat uneasily, and says, "Well, I don't know."

"Gifted!" Mike laughs hard, and Dr. Bennett smiles, then laughs again, a little embarrassed and caught off guard.

Mike is ready with a second joke. "Hey, Doc, here's another one for you. What do you call a girl with two brain cells?" He doesn't pause long before giving us the punch line: "Pregnant!"

Mike roars with laughter, his large belly shaking. Dr. Bennett shakes his head and chuckles, muttering something about how these jokes really aren't too appropriate, then turns around to look at the resident and me. Wanting to reassure him that I'm not really offended by this outrageously sexist humor, I roll my eyes and smile back at him. Mike is still laughing hugely.

Mike Riley is a very large man, sloppily dressed in a T-shirt and a wrinkled, unbuttoned plaid shirt. His blue jeans look clean but worn. He wears heavy work boots that are run-down at both heels. Mike's face is always very red, and he has a gray stubble on his chin, a huge sebaceous nose, and watery blue eyes. Today his iron gray hair is partly covered by a blue baseball cap with words in white lettering announcing: "At my age I've / Seen it all / Heard it all / Done it all" and beneath this, in yellow, "I just don't remember it all!"

Loretta smiles while her husband cracks jokes, but she doesn't say anything. It seems as though she recognizes how important it is to Mike to connect with Dr. Bennett through "guy talk." At the beginning of a clinic visit she is always much less talkative than her loquacious husband. But when they discuss Joey, she joins in; in fact she takes over. Loretta is a large woman with long, thin brown hair and a kind face. She frequently looks somewhat ragged, as though she doesn't have the time or energy to take care of herself. To some extent this is true, since she always puts Joey's needs before her own. But today she's painted her nails with dark purple polish, a color that exactly matches her purple T-shirt. I'm happy to see this because it means that Joey's been doing well recently and that she's had some time for herself. Three-year-old Joey lies back comfortably in her arms. He's probably just woken up and looks out at us vacantly. The most remarkable feature about Joey is his eyes, which are large, very round, and infinitely deep. Their expression is always tranquil and peaceful. Perhaps Wordsworth is somehow right that children carry with them into this life "intimations of immortality."

Dr. Bennett walks over to him. "Hi, Joey. It's good to see you today." Joey smiles back. Dr. Bennett takes him from Loretta, gently, moving slowly as he always does with these children, talking to Joey as he carries him to the examination table. He feels for his spleen, palpates the lymph nodes in neck, armpits, and groin, looks in his mouth, and listens to his lungs with a stethoscope. Joey watches Dr. Bennett during all this, his arms reaching up in a vain attempt to grab the doctor's eyeglasses. Dr. Bennett sits Joey up and uses his otoscope to look into both ears. Joey squirms, but he doesn't seem too bothered. After finishing the exam, Dr. Bennett announces, "Joey looks good. I can feel his spleen, but that's to be expected, and his lymph nodes are not enlarged. His lungs are clear as a bell. Medically speaking, he's doing just fine!"

He turns to the Rileys with specific questions about Joey's health and behavior. "Is he taking his medicines? Is he getting all of it? How many times does he miss?" Loretta answers (as she does every time) that he takes his medicines, that he gets all of it, that he never misses. Dr. Bennett goes over each medication, asking about how much and when Joey takes it. Joey has been on liquid Norvir (a protease inhibitor) for a month. He tells them that he is particularly concerned about this medication since it's vitally important to Joey's staying healthy. Many children have a hard time tolerating Norvir: They just don't like it, or it makes them feel bad, or they vomit it back up. Both the Rileys laugh, and Mike announces, "No, he don't mind it at all. He really likes the taste of that stuff!"

Dr. Bennett asks if they have any questions or concerns. The big issue today for them is the Head Start program[1] in their area. They report that the speech therapist, who has been coming out to the house twice a month to help Joey with communication and feeding problems, has advised them to enroll Joey in the program, suggesting it would be good for him to start interacting with other children. The Rileys have contacted Head Start and made inquiries, citing HIV among Joey's other problems, which include developmental delay, partial deafness, and deficiency in motor and verbal skills. But the people in charge of Head Start seem to be stalling, claiming that Joey might get hurt, that he might pick up illnesses, and so on. The Rileys seem never to push very hard for anything. They say they don't understand Head Start's resistance, and they want to know what Dr. Bennett thinks.

"Well," Dr. Bennett remarks, his forehead furrowed so that it looks as if he's scowling, "I don't think that's the real reason. He won't get hurt any more than any other child."

"Then does it maybe have something to do with his being HIV?" asks Loretta. "They don't seem to know a lot about HIV there. They got no other kids with it. Maybe these people at Head Start think the other kids will catch it from Joey or something?"

---

[1] Early Intervention and Head Start are federally funded child welfare programs.

"Yes, I surely do think it's a possibility they think that."

Mike adds, "They say they have to give preference to four-year-olds, and Joey's still only three. They say they'll send someone out to the house for him—"

Loretta breaks in: "But this here lady that does his therapy, she says he needs to be with other kids right now." Loretta pulls an envelope out of her purse and hands it to Dr. Bennett. "There's this paper that they want filled out by his doctor with all these questions on it. So we brought it to you."

Dr. Bennett glances at the form. "This is none of their business. They don't need this information to provide for his care. But I'll write a letter anyway." He looks up at the Rileys and continues. "As a federally funded organization for children with special needs, they have to take Joey. They don't have a leg to stand on. Just give them a call and tell them you've notified your lawyer, and then they'll be quick to let him in!" He looks at them over his glasses and speaks deliberately, as though he were measuring his words, "You should pursue this. Don't let it go. It's wrong, what they're doing. It's wrong."

The Rileys' response is typically nonconfrontational. "Okay," Loretta says. "We will. We surely will. We'll wait until he turns four and then we'll just *insist* that they let him in!" Mike, his arms crossed over his chest, nods his head vigorously.

This is one of those times when I wonder why a social worker doesn't attend this clinic regularly. Surely a good social worker would pick up on this problem and offer to call Head Start, find out why there should be a delay in admitting Joey, answer questions about safety issues both for Joey and for the other children, and negotiate some kind of arrangement. (As it turns out, some six months later we do get a very competent social worker.)

Dr. Bennett writes the letter to the Head Start administrators. I notice he does not mention Joey's HIV status: "Joey will benefit greatly from the stimulation of the Head Start Program. He is fully immunized and has no health problems which preclude his being in the program." He hands this to Loretta and asks, "Any other problems or concerns?"

"No," she replies. "I expect that's about it for today."

Dr. Bennett stands up, as do Loretta and Mike. He shakes hands with Mike, patting Joey on the back (Loretta is still holding him), and remarks to both parents, "You tell me next time how things with Head Start work out. Joey is doing just fine today. I'm really pleased."

As we start to leave the room, Mike asks Dr. Bennett, "Doc, you doing any squirrels?" Dr. Bennett smiles and shakes his head, "No, not now. I used to, though. My mother would cook up a great pie." Dr. Bennett turns to me and his eyes twinkle: "Do you have any idea what this is about, Anne?" I shake my head. "You Yankees sure miss an awful lot of good things! Mike is talking about going hunting for squirrels, then he cooks them." As he says this, his voice takes on even more of a South Alabama accent. "And they are so good baked in a pie! Squirrel pie, my mother used to make a fine squirrel pie!" Dr. Bennett and Mike both are smiling broadly now. Loretta and I look at each other and laugh, and we all leave the room.

Joey was born eight weeks early, addicted to cocaine. He weighed only five pounds a week and a half later, when he was discharged from the hospital's neonatal intensive care unit into the care of his mother. Ellie was then only sixteen years old. Joey's father could have been any of a number of men, though he must have been Caucasian, since Joey is white (as is his mother). For the first six months of his life Joey lived with Ellie and her boyfriend. A sister of Ellie's helped with his care. Whenever Joey got sick, even if it was only a cold, Ellie left him with her sister, and came back for him when he got well. This sister has since then severed ties with the family, and I was not able to talk with her. Little is known about this early period except that Joey had recurrent pneumonia.

When Joey was six months old, his mother took him to the local hospital's emergency room because he had a fever of 105 and was not responding to Tylenol. He was diagnosed as having pneumonia. Pediazole, a common antibiotic for children, was prescribed, and he was sent home. Angry with hospital personnel because he wasn't getting any better, his mother brought him back that same evening. But she had not given him the Pediazole; in fact she hadn't filled the prescription. This time ER staff were alarmed because besides pneumonia, Joey had a high fever and a stiff neck. He was transported by helicopter to St. Luke's. A lumbar puncture confirmed what they had feared: that Joey had pneumococcal meningitis.

The meningitis left Joey with a seizure disorder, profound speech and language problems, partial deafness, and motor retardation. He could swallow food only with extreme difficulty. He was thought to be blind. In addition, an atrial septal defect (a small hole in his heart) was discovered.

Joey stayed in the hospital for three months. When after several days his mother came to visit him and was told about his medical problems, she left to cash a check and did not come back for a month. When she did return, she explained that Joey's being so sick made her nervous.

Joey's grandmother became involved during Ellie's absence and confirmed what hospital staff by now suspected: that Ellie was not likely to be able to give Joey the care he required. The hospital social worker got in touch with the county's Children and Youth Services, which sent a caseworker to talk with Ellie about placement for Joey. Ellie was angry, demanding how anyone could "dare to judge" her. She began to spend more time at the hospital. The occupational therapists tried to teach her how to feed Joey, who required special techniques to be helped to swallow his food. But typically she became easily frustrated, got angry at them, and walked out of the room. Still, Ellie did not want to relinquish Joey. She was adamant that he not go into foster care, citing her own experience in the child welfare system. She wanted to take Joey home with her and threatened to sneak him out when no one was looking.

At this point Ellie's own mother helped persuade her to let someone else in the family care for Joey. Reluctantly Ellie acquiesced, given the severity of his medical problems, and agreed to his going directly from St. Luke's to the home of her cousin Loretta Riley.

Loretta recalls how this happened: "My grandmother called me and said that Joey was in the hospital and that they weren't going to let his mother take him home because she didn't take care of him right. She said they were looking for a family member to take him in. She told me he was badly retarded, deaf, completely blind, and had no chance of recovery. So I come home and I told Mike about it. He said he didn't want me burdened with something like that. And I thought, 'Well, maybe he's right, but family is family.'

"Then two weeks went by, and my grandmother calls me again. 'It wasn't as bad as they thought,' she said. He could see out of one eye, and he had a chance of recovery. So I go back to Mike and tell him about it again, and he just said, 'Well, I don't know.' Come Sunday he said, 'We're going for a ride.' And I said, 'Where?' We got in the van, and then he said, 'We're going to St. Luke's.' I didn't say nothing then. I was surprised.

"When we got there, we found Joey and visited with him. He wasn't much aware of anyone. He was kinda like a vegetable when we first seen him. I held him, and Mike, he held him, and Mike said, 'Don't get too attached; we may not take him home.' We stayed there about a half hour more, and finally Mike said, 'I think he'll be going home with us.' So we brought him home on June 2, 1995. I'll never forget that date.

"He was home a month, and then he started to have these seizures. That was scary. It was the beginning of July. We rushed him right back to the hospital. They thought it was fluid on the brain, and they wanted to put in a drain. So we said, 'Okay. Do what's best for him.' They put in the drain and a shunt. Then the next day they said it wasn't working and that they'd have to rush him into surgery, his seizures were so bad. When they did the surgery, they found a blood clot formed on his brain. They told us they'd have to cut a hole in his skull to get it out, and they didn't know if he'd make it. We said, 'Just go ahead and do what you have to do.' They did the surgery and got out all they could of that blood clot.

"He did okay, sorta, and after a week we took him home. He was getting better, but then he started getting lumps beside his ears and under his arms. I took him to our family doctor, and he said, 'Take him to St. Luke's.' So we took Joey here, and they did all kinds of blood work; it could have been a lot of dangerous diseases, they said. We brought him home, called them after two weeks, like they said we should, and found out they'd lost everything! So we had to come back and do those tests all over again. But it turned out that all their tests, everything, was normal.

"Then they wanted to have a consent signed for an HIV test. So we did. Later on this doctor (it weren't Dr. Bennett) called us into a room and said Joey was HIV positive. He was fourteen months old. My first reaction was that he wasn't going to make it, that this was the end for him. Then they called down Dr. Bennett, and that was the first time we met him. He told us about the virus, what medications he was going to put Joey on, what to expect. And other stuff. He said he wanted a Living Will–type thing for Joey because he thought that when kids are that bad, it's best to let them go instead of prolonging their life. He said, 'One thing I believe is that they shouldn't be put on a respirator. If they're in that bad shape . . . to keep them on that, to keep them suffering, when there's not going to be any good coming out of it, why do that to them?' Dr. Bennett didn't give him even five months to live. He said to us, 'You think about it, and if you agree to this approach, we'll have it put in the chart.'"

Mike interjects, telling me that he had agreed with Dr. Bennett's advice right away. "What Dr. Bennett does is sit down and talk with you and listen to what you have to say. He doesn't beat around the bush, he just spits it out. 'Course I wish he'd talk a little louder. . ." he says emphatically, and laughs.

It took longer for Loretta to come to a decision about end-of-life care for Joey. "It was kinda hard to accept at first. First it makes you angry, that this could happen to a kid. Then, when you sit down and you listen in your head to Dr. Bennett's side of it, then you realize it's the best thing to do.

"When we got back from the hospital," Loretta continues, "I called my mother and told her I wanted her to come over and to get my grandmom there too, that I had something important to tell them. And I got in touch with Joey's mother to get tested. She went right into denial, said he must've got it at St. Luke's from the blood tests there."

"Ellie was sure she didn't have it because she wasn't sick," adds Mike. "She thought it was some kind of joke. She just laughed it off."

But Ellie consented to testing for HIV at some point during this interval and, not surprisingly, was found to be infected. A treatment program was set up for her at a clinic close to where she was living. Ellie went once or twice to the clinic and was put on HIV medications. But she was never compliant and took her medicine sporadically, if at all. She eventually lost her access card (qualifying her for Medical Assistance) because she moved so much. When it came time to pay the rent, she and her current boyfriend would just move on, never leaving a forwarding address.

"When we first brought him on home," Loretta says to me, "after he was diagnosed with HIV, he was on eight different kinds of medications. He had reflux. He had to be fed with a syringe because he'd choke on everything. It was like his throat wouldn't let anything go down. He was strictly on a liquid diet. My mother and her pastor, they gived us a bunch of support. Without them and the people at St. Luke's, I don't think we'd have made it. I wish *all* my family were this way. My dad, his side of the family, they totally wrote us off. They don't want nothing to do with any of us. They think you can get HIV just by lookin' at someone. After a while we started Joey on baby food; then we would thicken it, a little every week. Finally he was took off his reflux medicine, and he was doing okay. Two months after we had brought him home, he was down to three medicines! And then he stopped the seizure medication too. Now he's only on HIV medications."

The Rileys are proud of Joey's improvement over the past three years. Dr. Bennett remembers seeing Joey in the pediatric ICU, devastated by pneumococcal meningitis: "He could barely see; he was spastic, tight, stayed in one position all the time with his arms turned out. And he couldn't feed. I wouldn't have given a plugged

nickel for him to live. It was around that time that Loretta came on
the scene. The Rileys took him in. I wanted to put in a gastrostomy
tube because I didn't think he could eat at all. The options seemed
limited: put in a gastrostomy tube or send him home to die very
soon. Loretta begged us not to put in a tube. She said she'd feed
him. And she did. I was astounded! It took her hours and hours
every day to do it. This is really one of the most dramatic turn-
arounds I've ever seen in medicine.

"I misjudged the Rileys," remarks Dr. Bennett. "At first I didn't
think they had it in them to take on a profoundly handicapped
child. But I was so wrong! Loretta's been wonderful, just wonderful. And Mike's been very supportive. I learned two lessons from
this: first, that when we make judgments about people, we're commonly wrong, and second, that you just can't make a prognosis with
children. The developing brain has a lot more potential than one
that's developed. You just don't know, you just can't know what will
happen."

Loretta and Mike decided when they took Joey that they wanted
to adopt him, thinking it unlikely that Ellie would ever be in a position to care for a child with such serious problems. But Ellie continued to want him back. The court recognized her legal rights as a
mother, especially since this was her first child, and gave her every
opportunity to try to put her life back together so that Joey could be
returned to her. Loretta, for her part, made it possible for Ellie to
visit with him whenever she wanted. But the visits proved very difficult. Ellie would call and say she wanted to see Joey, plans would be
set, but when the day came, she had changed her mind or had forgotten about it. Later on she would call, angry, accusing the Rileys
of not letting her see her son. Another visit would be planned, and
the cycle would begin all over again. Invariably, during these phone
calls Ellie would tell Loretta that she and her boyfriend were enrolling in a drug detox program, but this never happened.

The Rileys tried their best to accommodate Ellie's wishes, fearing that if they did not "obey her every whim," to use Loretta's
words, Ellie might retaliate by refusing to sign the adoption papers.

They are thankful that Joey was too young to know what was going on during this period.

They adopted Joey when he was two, after he had been with them for nearly a year and a half. They were uneasy throughout the process, thinking that Ellie might change her mind. The day before the adoption Loretta invited Ellie and her boyfriend to come to the Rileys' home, spend the day with Joey, and stay there overnight. But Loretta and Mike, afraid that Ellie would just "take off with him," had Joey sleep in their room. The day of the adoption hearing they all went together to the courthouse. "Just before Ellie signed," Loretta remarks, "the judge told her, 'You do know that by signing this paper you no longer have any rights to the child?' Ellie said okay, and that was it." This final hearing was not really necessary legally since Ellie had signed an earlier form, but Loretta and Mike had been advised to try to have her attend the final hearing and sign again. Their case would be stronger, they were told, if Ellie signed after so firm a statement from the judge.

Now that Joey is legally adopted, Loretta does not feel she needs to placate Ellie. "When I got him adopted, I told her that I've made enough effort now, and if she wants to be Joey's mother and know him, it's her that has got to make an effort to see him. And she hasn't done it. She calls when she has a whim to call. And when Joey's sick, Ellie don't want nothing to do with him."

The Rileys acknowledge that Ellie has had a very difficult life. She was removed from her abusive mother when she was two and, along with her four siblings, put in foster care. She has been on her own since she was twelve. When at the age of sixteen Ellie became pregnant with Joey, one of her sisters took her in so that she could finish school. But with only three months in the school year remaining, she abruptly quit.

Joey has done remarkably well since coming to live with the Rileys, and they have worked hard in caring for him. Since he was a year old, he has been receiving physical therapy and speech therapy, with specialists coming to the house twice a week through the government's Early Intervention program. When he turned three,

Head Start was supposed to take over. After sending out home care therapists for six months, finally, when he was three years and nine months old, Joey was admitted into Head Start's program for developmentally delayed children. He attends four half days a week and seems happy.

The Rileys have an excellent relationship with Dr. Bennett. "He's not just Joey's pediatrician," says Loretta, "he's a friend. I've talked a lot of my problems out with Dr. Bennett. The thing about Dr. Bennett is that he makes you feel comfortable, he's not afraid to be around us, and we can ask questions and we won't get looked at like we're stupid. He loves these kids, and you can tell it. When you give him a picture of your kid, it means a lot to him!"

Mike adds, "Kids can feel it too. . . . They can tell if someone really cares. I just wish there were more doctors like Dr. Bennett that sit down and talk to you and ask you what you want to do when you have to make a decision. That makes you feel that you're a part of it. Dr. Bennett, he's always saying, 'Well that's what I think, and what do you think?'"

Since that first devastating episode of pneumococcal meningitis, Joey has undergone four subsequent hospitalizations for blood infections caused by the same bacteria. "The scariness of the whole thing," remarks Loretta, "is that he can be fine, and then sick the next day. He does real good, and then there's this meningitis-like thing again." Joey's care has always been extremely difficult because he has so many problems in addition to HIV infection and because he is allergic to so many important drugs, including Bactrim (a preventative for PCP), Dilantin (a medication for seizures), and most antibiotics. For more than a year he has been taking the three-drug cocktail that has helped so many children. In his case this consists of the protease inhibitor Viracept and the nucleoside reverse transcriptase inhibitors Epivir and Zerit. Throughout this period his viral load has remained low, though never undetectable.

There is another child in the clinic, almost the same age as Joey and likewise HIV-infected, who also had pneumococcal meningitis during the first year of life. Unlike Joey, this child remains profoundly handicapped physically and mentally: Eric cannot sit or stand, is unable to speak, and has a severe seizure disorder as well as spastic quadriplegia. The child's seizure disorder is controlled with Dilantin and his spasticity with diazepam (Valium). However, his overall condition, unlike Joey's, has not improved.

What accounts for such different developments in two children with similarly devastating diseases, HIV infection compounded by pneumococcal meningitis? To judge from what is known about the biological mother of each child, it would seem that Eric stood a better chance than did Joey of overcoming the sequelae of pneumococcal meningitis. Eric's mother had good prenatal care, whereas Joey's biological mother was an addict who turned to prostitution to support her drug habit. Eric was born several weeks early but otherwise healthy; Joey, on the other hand, was eight weeks premature and born addicted to cocaine. Eric was already diagnosed and receiving treatment for HIV when he was four months old; in Joey's case this did not happen until he was fourteen months of age. Eric remained with his biological family, whereas Joey was removed from his mother's care. It would seem that Eric's situation was in every way more advantageous than Joey's. Why, then, has Joey undergone so remarkable a recovery but Eric none at all? It may be that the pneumococcal meningitis was more severe in Eric's case than in Joey's, but it is also possible that the family's psychological health played a large role. Joey's adoptive family was wonderfully nurturing in all aspects of care. Eric's parents, on the contrary, though they loved their child, had serious problems of their own, including mental illness, mental retardation, and drug and alcohol addiction, that may have compromised their ability to care for him adequately.

Joey is now thriving. Given the possibility that this drastic improvement is due to nurture rather than nature (that is, to the care provided by the Rileys rather than any intrinsic difference in disease process), one wonders what enabled Loretta and Mike to help this child improve so dramatically.

One hot summer day I drive up to Seneca Valley, a rural town in the hill country, to talk with the Rileys about Joey. I turn into a trailer park and pass homes of different sizes and colors as I wind up a long hill. The road ends, and I face a large hayfield that extends down to a grove of trees. I turn off into a short driveway that brings me to the Rileys' faded green trailer. It could be an attractive setting, except that the end of the road, crisscrossed with broken-down barbed wire, is used as a dump for discarded household items. The small yard surrounding the trailer is cluttered with a child's bicycle, toys, various pieces of lumber, and a tractor. There is a shed in which Mike keeps his tools. Attached to the trailer is a very small, half-made wooden deck with a gate, obviously to contain Joey.

I arrive a few minutes early, just before the Rileys drive up in their battered van. I sense that Loretta is uncomfortable about having me come inside, so we sit outside on the deck and talk. But then it begins to rain. Loretta gets up and goes inside to "straighten up," locking the door behind her. I can hear her rushing here and there, plates clinking, furniture being moved around. It's more than sprinkling rain by the time she lets Mike and me go inside. Loretta has covered the kitchen area, both the table and the sink, with bedsheets. She apologizes for the clutter in the living area. I regret that she's so embarrassed by the unwashed dishes and the cluttered living room and try to reassure her that my house often looks the same (which is true).

I spend several hours that afternoon talking with Mike and Loretta and their daughter, Melissa. Joey putters around the room, always busy, always chattering or humming, picking up a toy and carrying it to someone, then choosing another for someone else. He seems a remarkably contented child.

Melissa is a friendly twelve-year-old who strikes me as sensible, mature, and caring, the kind of teenager we all look for as a babysitter for young children. She is large, like her mother. She clearly loves Joey and does not hesitate to tell her friends about his HIV status if she thinks they will understand. "I tell them how he got it and that you can't catch it from hugging or touching or eating the same food. His mother was a drug user. She didn't know how to take care of herself. She just went around with anyone she could find." Melissa tells me that she learned about Joey's medical condition from Dr. Bennett when she was nine or ten. "He asked me first if I knew what HIV was, and I said I'd heard of it. So he explained it. My first thought was that Joey was going to die. I told him that, and he said, 'Probably, but we're going to work on getting him better.' I talk to Dr. Bennett a lot. I go down there when I can, when school is out. He explains things real good."

Melissa is eager to tell me about how she handled the school's AIDS education program. Apparently the school first sent a notice home for parents of sixth graders to sign, indicating whether they did or did not want their child included in an AIDS education class. Of course Melissa's parents signed. Melissa describes what followed: "The nurse passed out this paper about HIV. It said you wouldn't live that long. Some of the information about AIDS was right, but they didn't tell you how you could get it. They said you'd get it through a blood transfusion. So I said to her, 'You can't get it anymore that way; it would be very rare.' Then the nurse said that they don't have a way of testing blood for it. But I know that's not so because Dr. Bennett told me. They also said it could be transmitted through sex, but not very easily. And they said that if you kissed someone with AIDS, you could get it. I told them the only way you can get it from kissing is if you have a draining sore."

Loretta called the school principal after she saw the information that Melissa brought home from school and offered to come in and talk with the children. But the principal, according to Loretta, "felt that these kids were too young for too much information. He said that kind of thing was more appropriate for high school."

At my request Loretta describes her complicated family structure. It is difficult to tease out who is related to whom, and when she is through with her description, I'm still not sure of the facts. It seems that Loretta's cousin married a woman who already had one child, named Sarah. This cousin and his new wife had four children together, the last being Ellie. Loretta then tells me about

Ellie, who is now serving a jail term for a domestic quarrel. "I thought about bailing her out, using the van, but then I thought, 'What if she takes off?' I can't afford that. So in thirty days she'll be out. Anyway, she's on drugs, so she can dry out too while she's there!" Loretta laughs and looks at Mike, who nods vigorously.

"Ellie didn't understand HIV," Mike remarks. "She just didn't get the idea, and there she was pregnant again."

"Ellie likes the idea of being pregnant," adds Loretta. "She likes having babies. She likes all the attention she gets."

I ask Loretta and Mike about their own family backgrounds. Mike begins. He tells me that he is now fifty-one years old. Born into a large family in West Virginia, he "grew up fast." He has had four previous marriages, the first when he was thirteen years old: "I got this girl pregnant, and my mom said, 'Well, then you got to marry her,' and that was that." The young couple were divorced, amicably, several years later. The next marriage ended when his wife, eight months pregnant, died in an automobile accident. His third wife, also pregnant with their first child, was killed in a plane crash. Mike served as a marine in Vietnam, volunteering for the very dangerous job of deactivating bombs. He saw heavy combat; out of 365 men in his division, only 7 returned home. He received an honorable discharge and a medal for bravery but came back to the States with serious psychological problems. A large and powerful man, he could not control his temper, and when he drank, he got into fights. He once killed a man during such a fight, for which he spent five years in the state penitentiary.

Mike and Loretta first got to know each other while he was in prison. She heard about him through her brother's friend, who was incarcerated in the same place as Mike. This friend told her brother, "There's this guy here who's pretty lonely, but he's real nice and would really appreciate getting mail." Loretta agreed to correspond with him. So Mike sent her a letter, she answered it, and they began writing to each other regularly. When they actually met, they were already in love and soon got married. Mike vowed never to touch alcohol again. He has kept this vow, and though he still does get angry—too often, he thinks—the violent behavior that led him to kill a man is a thing of the past. I ask how long they've been married. "Fifteen years," they respond in unison.

When the family moved to Seneca Valley some years ago, Mike found steady employment at a local lumber mill moving railroad ties. His supervisor was very supportive when Joey was in the hospital with meningitis, telling Mike to take off whatever time he needed. "But when we found out Joey was HIV and I told them, then I got canned. They said I took too much time off for Joey and for my own personal injuries." Mike has medical problems of his own that were beginning to interfere with his ability to work at the lumberyard: asthma, emphysema, epilepsy, and severe arthritis in his knees, spine, and wrist. So far, however, these medical problems are not serious enough for him to qualify for disability coverage.

Loretta tells me that her parents, a grandmother, and two brothers all live in Seneca Valley. One brother avoids them entirely because of Joey's HIV status. The other brother lives in the same trailer park, with a wife and child about the same age as Joey. This brother is very understanding, though the wife is uneasy about letting her son play with Joey, fearing he might contract the virus. Loretta remarks that her mother has been supportive, especially at the beginning, before anyone knew Joey had HIV. But she also admits that her mother is uneasy about Joey's playing with his cousin. She is even afraid for herself. Apparently she once refused to kiss Melissa, saying, "Now don't you go and give me AIDS!" Melissa has never forgiven her grandmother.

Loretta suffers from some serious medical problems herself. For years she has been coping with angina and diabetes. Recently she developed cervical cancer. Because of possible complications from her other medical conditions, the doctors at St. Luke's recommended radiation treatments rather than a hysterectomy and chemotherapy. When I talked to her some time ago, she was suspicious of this recommendation, since her regular gynecologist had suggested a hysterectomy. She wondered if her being on Medical Assistance had something to do with the choice of treatment. "Blue

Cross would have paid for a hysterectomy," she observed bitterly, "but Medical Assistance will pay only for radiation treatments."

Loretta underwent five weeks of radiation treatments and then radiation implants. I talked with her several times during this treatment period. I remember that she really disliked the radiologist, who had her sign a consent form while she was being marked for the treatments. "He just handed it to me and said, 'Sign this.' Only afterward I read about the risks." She has not done well since her cancer treatment and is still dealing with nausea, cramps, diarrhea, and a great deal of pain. But now, as she tells me again about her treatment, there is neither suspicion nor bitterness. Loretta seems a basically optimistic person, and negative feelings about other people fade quickly.

Obviously the Rileys have gone through some hard times with family problems on both sides, concerns about money, and serious health issues over and above Joey's complicated medical needs. Even Melissa has a heart murmur. But I'm struck by the extent to which they emphasize the positive. When talking about their lives, they mention first those people who have been supportive and helpful rather than those who have not, and they stress the pleasure they take in Joey rather than the hardships of caring for him. They do not conceal the negative, but when they speak about sad or bad things, it is without rancor or bitterness. It seems as though they *perceive* the good differently, as something that is more important, or more central, than the bad. When asked how others have treated them, Loretta replies, "It's funny how total strangers that you'd think would be sniffy aren't. People that you didn't think would understand do understand, and they really respect you for what you're doing. You do find a few snobs, but that doesn't bother me anymore."

The Rileys live on $864 a month from welfare payments. Mike makes wooden ornaments, shelves, and toys and then tries to sell them. The clinic nurses have been good customers, especially Nicole, whose house must by now be a showcase for Mike's carpentry work. However, recent surgery on his wrist has made this kind of work impossible. Loretta takes in some money from commissions on toys that friends and family order from a catalog. They enjoy being volunteer mentors for Parent-to-Parent, a program sponsored by Early Intervention for parents of disabled children. Their dream is to become even more involved with foster care. Mike explains, "Since we got Joey, we've heard about children who were abandoned, handicapped children. My wife wants children but she can't have no more children. If we could swing it, we want to start a foster home for special needs children. I'd buy a place out in the country, fix it up real good, and we could have these kids with special needs like Joey come and live with us."

Melissa remarks, "People don't understand what can happen to a kid like that; he can turn around and be perfectly fine."

"They don't understand the enjoyment!" Loretta adds.

"You can have so much fun with Joey," says Melissa. "He'll sit there with you and just laugh and laugh. . . ."

Mike summarizes for all three of them: "You have a child like Joey, and you're told he has just so long to live and he'll never do this and never do that, and then you turn around and he's doing all this stuff. It just gives you kind of a feeling of accomplishment that you've fooled the Man Upstairs, that this kid won't be going to Him for a while. I'll take a dozen more like Joey!"

Part II: Felicity and the Dawson Family

It is 8:30 A.M. on a hot Thursday in July. We're all there—myself, the two clinic nurses, and the social worker—all except Dr. Bennett. This is no surprise since he's usually late. Rachel, who serves as both nurse and clinic coordinator, shows us some educational materials that she is preparing as handouts for families. She's working hard to bring order to the clinic, a particularly challenging task since Dr. Bennett is known to be chronically disorganized. We talk about this year's clinic picnic, which will be held as always at a local park. Nicole, the other clinic nurse, will be bringing her various animals, which include rabbits, a goat, a potbellied pig, several

chickens, and a rooster, for a kind of petting zoo. Ramona, the social worker, tells us about the tie-dyed T-shirts she was promised by
a drug company representative: "This box was delivered yesterday
to the Social Work office. It came from that drug company, so I was
expecting the tie-dyed T-shirts. I opened it up to find out how many
she'd sent, and there were these T-shirts advertising some drug,
along with a warning about all these bad side effects! I don't know
what they were thinking of!"

While we are still laughing, Dr. Bennett arrives, and immediately we turn to a discussion of today's patients. When he finds a
newborn named Felicity Benson on the patient list, he remarks,
"So Felicity is here. Felicity is Joey Riley's new sister!" We all look
at him in astonishment, waiting for some explanation.

"You mean, Joey's mother actually got pregnant again?" asks
Rachel. "I thought she was going to get her tubes tied!"

"No," responds Dr. Bennett, "she says she will, but she's said that
before." He explains: "Loretta Riley called me several weeks ago.
She told me that Ellie has had another baby, a little girl. The baby
was still in the hospital. Children and Youth Services weren't about
to release her to Ellie, and they were looking for someone in the
family to take her. Loretta wanted my advice about whether she
and Mike should volunteer. I tried to suggest the pros and cons, and
with the medical problems they already had, it seemed there were
a whole lot of cons. But I told them it was their decision to make.
They said that Ellie has a sister who also might take the baby. So
here's the baby, but I don't know whether it will be the Rileys or
some other relative bringing her in."

Felicity is brought to the clinic not by the Rileys but by a young
couple who introduce themselves as Sarah and Jonathan Dawson.
Sarah tells us she's Ellie's half sister. She is a petite young woman
with sky blue eyes and Shirley Temple–like curly hair. I'm not surprised to learn that she works with children at a day care center.
Jonathan, a slender young man with a constant, if anxious, smile,
tells us he is a security guard at a local shopping mall. Though I
learn later on that both are nearly thirty, they look incredibly youth-

ful, as though they were in their late teens. They also give the impression that they have been untouched by the problems of the world.

Sarah carries Felicity, who is sleeping. Born addicted to cocaine and opium, she is still undergoing withdrawal at five weeks old. Sarah tells us that the hospital's procedure was to "let her go through it natural."

Jonathan adds, "It was a Catholic hospital, and they believe it should be natural. They did give her something, but it didn't work really well. When we brought her home, she cried all the time, she was shaking, and there were even convulsions."

"I just couldn't sit there and see her go through that," remarks Sarah. "It was pitiful just to watch her. It was awful. I thought there just had to be something to take this pain away. So I made an appointment with our pediatrician, and he put her on phenobarbital—that was just a few days ago—to help her off the addiction." Sarah looks down at Felicity, still slumbering peacefully in her arms.

Dr. Bennett asks about Felicity's birth before he examines her, knowing that if he wakes her, she's likely to cry and that Sarah will want to comfort her rather than converse with him. Sarah tells us that Ellie was in the shower at 1:00 in the morning, very stoned. She felt the baby coming, yelled to her boyfriend to call 911, and then passed out. She and the infant were brought by ambulance to a nearby hospital. Ellie was released in a day or so, but the baby was kept for a week because of the addiction problem. Ellie claims that the father is her current boyfriend, Julio, but Julio is Puerto Rican whereas this baby is black. Moreover, Julio was in prison when this baby was conceived.

Sarah tells us that Ellie wanted to take the baby home with her. She told the hospital staff that all her brother and sisters were dead, her mother was missing, and she had no relatives in the area. At Ellie's insistence, a caseworker came out to the place where she and her boyfriend were living but found it to be "a drug house." The apartment had no heat, no refrigerator, no furniture but a mattress, and a leaking gas stove. "When the caseworker smelled the gas for herself," says Sarah, "that was it!" Ellie's medical chart and police record soon revealed that she did have relatives living close by. The authorities contacted Ellie's mother, and she told them how to get in touch with both Loretta and Ellie's half sister, Sarah.

Dr. Bennett asks Sarah about HIV testing for Felicity, observing that the medical records forwarded to St. Luke's include no information about this. Sarah thinks she was tested and the results were positive. Dr. Bennett then asks whether this was an ELISA or a PCR test, a question that neither Jonathan nor Sarah can answer. Jonathan thinks it was an ELISA test but admits he is not sure.

"If it was," explains Dr. Bennett, "a positive result won't tell us whether she's infected, because a newborn carries its mother's antibodies to the virus for a year, sometimes longer. So we don't know whether ELISA testing measures the mother's antibodies or the infant's. PCR is a new test that's more helpful because it measures antigen, not antibodies. If Felicity had a positive PCR test, there's a strong chance she's infected. I know you must be anxious to find out," he goes on, his voice slowing. "We'll try to locate those records, but she needs another PCR test today anyway, so let's go ahead with that."[2]

Turning again to Felicity's chart, Dr. Bennett observes, "It looks like she's been on AZT since she was born."

"Yes," replies Sarah, "since birth."

"Do you know whether Ellie took AZT during her pregnancy?" he asks.

"No, but I think it's highly unlikely," Sarah responds.

"And of course, since the baby was born at home," comments Dr. Bennett, "she didn't receive AZT during delivery."

---

[2] PCR testing is performed on infants born to infected mothers in the first twenty-four hours of life, again at one to two months of age, and once more at three to six months. If the results are positive on two separate blood samples done at least a month apart, the baby is infected and pharmacological treatment can begin. If the test is negative, the baby is probably not infected. But certainty that a child does not have HIV cannot be arrived at until the child is fifteen to eighteen months of age, with a negative ELISA (antibody) test.

Dr. Bennett asks Sarah to lay Felicity down on the examining table. Felicity wakes up, but she doesn't cry; instead she looks up at her mother, then at Dr. Bennett. We all notice right away that Felicity has the same round, gentle, liquid brown eyes as Joey. Dr. Bennett examines her carefully. He says to Sarah, "She looks good. There are no enlarged lymph nodes, no signs of HIV infection at this time. But this doesn't mean she's not infected. The probability that she didn't get AZT during pregnancy and the fact that she didn't get it during delivery does raise her chances of being infected.[3] Keep her on the AZT until she's six weeks old. We'll do a PCR test on her today and call you with the results in about a week. If this test is negative, and if she has no symptoms by the end of next week, you can stop giving her the AZT. If the test is positive—and of course we all really hope it isn't—I'll advise that she start HIV medications."

At this point Rachel, who has gone to track down the earlier test results, comes back to report that she can't get through to anyone at Shopes Community Hospital able to locate them. "I'll keep trying," she tells Jonathan and Sarah, "and I'll call you as soon as I find out."

Sarah and Jonathan have many questions for Dr. Bennett: about immunizations, about risks of infection, about kinds of formula. After answering these, he remarks, "I know the biggest question for you is whether or not Felicity's infected. We should be able to give you information about that real soon. Now you take this," he says, handing Sarah a standard test request form, "and go on over to the lab and she'll get a PCR test."

"I'll show you how to get there," Rachel says. As we all leave the room, Rachel adds, "I hate to leave you hanging like this. I'll get back to you just as soon as I can about all these test results."

---

[3] The use of zidovudine (AZT) dramatically reduces the risk that an infected mother will give birth to an infected infant. Studies conducted in 1994 and 1995 (PACTG 076) demonstrated that if the mother takes AZT beginning in her second trimester, if AZT is administered intravenously during delivery, and if it is given to the child for six weeks after delivery, the chances of transmission decrease from 25 to 8 percent. Felicity's chance of being infected is greater than this since she received AZT only after delivery.

Over the next four months there are several important events in the Dawsons' life. The first is the good news that on the basis of two PCR tests, it seems Felicity is not infected. Sarah and Jonathan are immensely relieved.

The second is that Sarah is now pregnant. "We've been trying for a baby for years," she says, "and now we'll have two!"

Soon after reporting her own pregnancy, at Felicity's next clinic visit, Sarah tells us that she hears that Ellie too is pregnant. She is angry not only with her sister but with those she perceives as being in a position to prevent this. "Why don't those doctors do something!" she exclaims. "Why do they let her go on having babies? Why don't they make her have her tubes tied!"

I'm eager to find out what Dr. Bennett thinks about Sarah's declaration that doctors should forcibly persuade women like her sister to undergo sterilization. After the clinic, over lunch, I ask him.

"I understand Sarah's point of view," he says. "I do think these women should limit their pregnancies, and I also believe that they should tell their sexual partners that they're infected. I've been treating children with HIV infection for more than fifteen years now. I've routinely encouraged most of the infected mothers we see in the clinic to have tubal ligations. My view has changed somewhat, though, over the past two years, and this has to do with the greater probability now that perinatal transmission can be avoided, thanks to 076.[4] I don't feel as strongly about encouraging infected women to have tubal ligations because there's been a change in the facts. But this is still a very important issue—the rights of mothers versus the rights of the child—and it's much broader than HIV transmission. This is a very complicated issue, and I certainly don't have the answer. My hope is there might be widespread, serious, heartfelt debates that would cause people to think about these things, talk about them, and understand them better. So far that isn't happening."

Two months after this clinic visit and my conversation with Dr.

[4] Dr. Bennett is referring to PACTG 076 (see note 3).

Bennett, Sarah brings Felicity in for a checkup and for repeat HIV testing. The results are sent to her pediatrician, a resident at the hospital's general pediatric clinic. Felicity's PCR test is positive. Despite Dr. Bennett's earlier prediction, there now seems a strong likelihood that she is in fact infected with HIV. The general pediatrician has the unhappy task of telling the Dawsons about this change in her HIV status. Unfortunately she does not do a very good job. She reports Felicity's test results not as "positive" but as "problematic," while assuring Sarah that "we'll still take care of her." Sarah and Jonathan are understandably confused and upset.

The Dawsons bring Felicity in to see Dr. Bennett soon afterward. The first thing he does when he walks into the room is to address the issue of the new test results. "I've heard about the positive PCR test," remarks Dr. Bennett, "and I know it's really hard for you to think that she might be infected. You should remember that Felicity has absolutely no sign of HIV disease. That's good. And frankly, I'm surprised by this positive test result. I really did believe that she was not infected."

Sarah asks, "Does this mean Felicity will need to go back on medication?"

"Yes. But I want you to know that if you go to different clinics or hospitals, places with fine doctors, you'll get different advice about treatment for children with HIV. There are three strategies. The first is no treatment at all until her viral load reaches four or five thousand. The second is to use AZT and ddI, the standard treatment for HIV, and then introduce a protease inhibitor, which is a new drug, when these fail. The third strategy, and this is the one I'm recommending, is to treat it the way we do cancer, as rigorously as we can from the very beginning. The object is to give her aggressive treatment in the hopes that the virus will be suppressed and she'll remain asymptomatic as long as possible. If you decide to go with my recommendation, I'll be giving her three different kinds of medication: AZT, Epivir, and Viracept. We don't have a track record for treating newly diagnosed infants with this combination of drugs because it didn't exist until recently. We'll monitor her blood at regular intervals—every two weeks at first. Then we'll see her monthly, mostly to monitor for drug toxicity."

Jonathan nods and looks at Sarah. Sarah asks about risks to other children, "especially the new baby."

The longer we've been working with kids with HIV," replies Dr. Bennett, "the more confident we have become that there is minimal risk of the virus being transmitted by ordinary family contact. There is a risk for health care professionals. If I get stuck by a needle that's been used on a person who is known to be infected with HIV, the risk is 1 in 300. That's not very much, but it's still a risk. But there are no reports of HIV transmission in households, playgrounds, or schools. The longer the epidemic goes and the more data we collect, the more confident we become that the risk is nil of passing on the virus in this way."

"We've been wondering what the difference is between HIV and AIDS . . ." asks Jonathan tentatively.

"Well, there's not a real difference," Dr. Bennett answers. "'AIDS' is an obsolete term. It was used in the early eighties, when the cause of the disease was not known. Once the virus was identified and we knew something about it, then the term 'AIDS' was no longer appropriate. Let me give you an example. Do either of you know what infantile paralysis is?"

They look at each other; then both shake their heads.

"Do you, Anne?"

I breathe a sigh of relief. For once I know the answer to the medical questions he likes to ask me. "Polio," I reply.

"Yes, that's right. Because the virus hadn't been identified, it was called infantile paralysis. Then, when the polio virus was identified, the disease was named polio. It's the same with HIV. They called it AIDS when it was a disease of no known cause. In pediatrics we never used 'AIDS'; instead the terms were 'asymptomatic HIV' and 'symptomatic HIV.'"

Dr. Bennett goes on to tell the Dawsons about Viracept—that it comes in a powder and has to be mixed with milk, when they need to give it to her, and so forth—probably giving them more information than they require at this point. I can tell that he's shaken by the new test results. He talks more than he has to, and he overstays the clinic visit. Though his expression remains composed, as always, I know he is upset because I can see his jaw working as he grinds his teeth.

To me, Jonathan and Sarah appear less upset during this clinic visit than does Dr. Bennett, perhaps because they've had more time to absorb and process the bad news. They seem resigned, telling us that they knew when they first took Felicity that she might have HIV. "We love her already," remarks Sarah, "and we love her whether she has HIV or not."

Dr. Bennett suggests they get in touch with the Rileys, indicating that they've been through all this with Joey and could be very helpful. Sarah and Jonathan look at each other. There is a moment of silence. Sarah takes a deep breath and says simply, "I don't want any contact with any of them. I was sexually abused as a child by Ellie's father; that's Loretta's cousin. I avoid that whole side of the family."

I learn more about this complicated family history when I drive out to the Dawsons' home and talk with Sarah and Jonathan. I also learn a good deal more about Ellie. The Dawsons live in a small "starter" house in a suburb of Harperville. Mounted on the wall of their living room are several wedding pictures of the couple. There is also a large, familiar picture of a haloed Jesus gazing off to the side. The living room is neat. They have a big dog locked up in the kitchen during my visit and a very small black-and-white cat that darts past me from time to time. Felicity, now plump, sits on a pink baby blanket on the floor, surrounded by toys. She looks at me intently, and when I smile at her, she smiles back. Soon after I arrive, Sarah carries Felicity off and puts her to bed.

Sarah and Jonathan tell me that they themselves are the product of foster care. Jonathan was given away when he was two days old to an aunt, who adopted and raised him. When he turned eleven, he was asked to choose whom he wanted to live with. He elected to be formally adopted by his mother but to stay with his aunt (who is now dead). Though such a choice was very difficult, he was glad to have been permitted to make it. He sees each parent from time to time, and his relationship with both is good. His father has been supportive about Felicity; his mother, less so.

Sarah was in foster care between the ages of four and sixteen. Sarah and Ellie's biological mother was abusive to her children. When they did something wrong, she would beat them around the head, and when they said something wrong, she would put hot pepper on their tongues. Sarah and Ellie, along with the three other children, were placed in foster care—some permanently, some semipermanently. Sarah was one of the children who were sent back and forth between their mother's home and various foster homes and institutions. Sarah's mother at one point told her about her biological father, giving her his name and telling her that he was a married man with whom she had a brief affair. Four years ago, with Jonathan's help, Sarah found where he was living, tracked him down, and talked with him. While admitting that he had a "one-night stand" with her mother, he denies paternity of Sarah.

Sarah is the oldest child. After she was born, her mother married and gave birth to four more children, two girls and two boys. Ellie, born eight years after Sarah, is the youngest child.

"I was the first one to go into foster care," Sarah observes. "Ma was abusive. I was taken out somewhere between three and five. From then on I was in and out of foster care. Some of that time I lived with Ma. I went back and forth. This place where she lived, it was a nightmare. I didn't think I'd ever grow up. I thought I'd die. I saw a guy getting scalped; I was in first grade. One time I was in the pool, and there was a lady there beside me, treading water. I dived under, and when I came back up, she was lying facedown with a pool of blood around her. I never knew if she was knifed or shot."

Sarah continues, in a flat, matter-of-fact tone. "I was sexually molested by my stepfather. This started when I was three. He was a sick man, a very sick man. Denied it till his dying day. But he did it, and he did it to Maureen [her other half sister] too. He was sentenced to four years in jail for molesting his children and other children, but he served only a year."

I ask Sarah if her mother knew what was going on. "Yes, she did. The first time that she caught my stepfather sexually molesting me, I was five or six. She walked in. She pulled him off of me because he was drunk and passed out on me, and I was underneath and stuck there. I was taken out of the home for a while, but they sent me back, with him still living there. And she would leave me there with him, unattended. He died a couple of years ago, and she wanted me to go to the funeral. I said, 'No way, I'm not going!' She couldn't understand why I wouldn't want to go. 'But he was your father!' she said. And I answered her, 'What kind of father does the things that he did to his children?'

"When I was being molested . . . I think the state didn't have a definite law on that yet. I wasn't allowed to speak in court. Because I was underage, I had no say. I remember asking not to be adopted by him. But they wouldn't listen. I remember him saying, 'I'm going to adopt you.' And I said, 'I don't want that. I don't want you to be my father.' I was six then."

After this court hearing Sarah lived with her mother and stepfather off and on for four years. "When I was ten," she remarks, "I was taken out permanently. He had sexually molested some other kid, and then they found out about the sexual abuse that went on at home. That's when Ellie and the other kids were taken out too. Ellie was about two years old.

"I asked to be emancipated when I was sixteen. Ma was there at the hearing trying to get custody of me, saying I should be placed in church custody and that she'd set it up through her church. But I said, 'No, I want to be on my own.' And the court respected that."

To grant her request to be legally declared an emancipated minor, the state required that Sarah have a place to live that was approved by Children and Youth Services. She remembered a woman whom she liked, a hall monitor at one of the schools she attended, and asked to be placed with that person and her family. Sarah stayed with them for nine months. She credits these foster parents and their daughters with turning her life around. "Through them I learned what a family was like, and I learned that was the lifestyle I wanted. They showed me what love really was; they showed me what it means to be a family. Even now they call me their daughter. When I talk to people about 'my parents,' I mean them. They really are my parents. That's where my heart is."

Sarah and Jonathan married young, when she was eighteen and he, nineteen. "For a long time I couldn't get pregnant," Sarah says. "Because of the sexual abuse, I had endometriosis. There was so much scar tissue." Jonathan adds that several years ago, thinking they couldn't have a child of their own, they decided to open their home to foster children. They went through most of the steps required for certification.

"Around that time we were called about taking Joey," confides Sarah. "Even though we were certified by then, I knew we couldn't do it. He had too many problems, and we both had jobs; there was no way we could give him the care he needed. But several years later, when they called and asked if we would take Felicity, something clicked inside me, and I said, 'We've got to do this.' I want Felicity not to be abused by the system and to have the opportunities I didn't have."

I ask Sarah about what happened to her brothers and sisters. She tells me that the oldest brother was "adopted out" as a young child and "wants nothing to do with the family." The sister who befriended Ellie during her first pregnancy avoids her now and recently severed ties with the rest of the family. Sarah's younger brother, Larry, now twenty-four years old, is severely dysfunctional: "He was born with water on the brain. He has an eighth-grade education. I think he needs to be institutionalized, but he's out on the streets. He's capable of killing somebody. He doesn't know his own strength, and when he gets angry, he can't control it. He's supposed to be on medication for ADD and something else. He's not the safest person to be around. He can be together one minute, but the next minute he doesn't know what he's doing. We were close earlier on, but I don't see him now. It's scary to be around him, and I'm

afraid for my life. . . . Larry fathered a child with a mentally retarded girl. The child—she was born around the same time as Felicity—is being cared for by the girlfriend's mother."

Sarah recites all this in a surprisingly even voice. When she talks
about Ellie, however, her tone becomes more inflected and emotional. Sometimes Sarah disparages her sister, and sometimes,
when she talks about Felicity, her voice turns downright bitter.
"Ellie was taken out as an infant and put in foster care. She stayed
there until she was twelve. Then Ma decided she wanted her to
come home. Ma thought she could handle her, so she pulled her
out of foster care. I think that's where all the problems started for
Ellie. They were living in a terrible place; it was a drug house with
prostitution, murders, everything. Ellie started staying out late and
mouthing back at Ma, and Ma couldn't handle it. She's an abusive
mother, always was and still is. When Ellie was thirteen, she was
caught having sex with a guy older than her. She accused him of
raping her, so Ma took her to the hospital. But it came out that
Ellie wanted sex with him; it wasn't rape. I warned Ellie about
AIDS then. I told her, 'You're going to end up with AIDS or die on
the street!' And now look what's happened. She wouldn't listen.
She won't listen to anyone.

"Jonathan and I—we were married then—we told Ma, 'You have
to put her back in foster care. You just have to!' Ma did this through
her church's foster care program, but none of those homes lasted
long. Ellie started accusing all the men in her foster families of molesting her. I know this had something to do with me. Ellie always
believed her father was totally innocent. She blamed me for breaking up the family and sending him to jail and for him and Ma getting a divorce. Of course it wasn't me who first told on him.

"When Ellie was fifteen, Ma tried a tough love approach through
her church, locking Ellie out of the house when she wouldn't keep
to a curfew. But this was the wrong time for tough love. Ellie could
have used her mother's love during that time, and it wasn't there."

Sarah jumps from Ellie at fifteen, just before she got pregnant
with Joey, to Ellie at twenty-one, having given birth to Felicity.

"She only calls when she wants to visit the baby. She leaves no number or anything. Half the time nobody knows where she is. She's back now with her boyfriend. He says he wants Felicity, but he's never seen her. He says they're saving money, they want her back, but he's done nothing.

"We didn't have the baby a week, and Ellie was calling here and wanting Felicity's birth certificate and Social Security number. She was going to go down to the Medical Assistance office and get her card and stuff. I said, 'Ellie, we don't have any of that information. That's all been taken care of by Children and Youth.' But she kept asking for Felicity's access card, and I kept saying, 'We don't have it because they're taking care of all that now.'" The Dawsons believed that Ellie wanted this information so that she could get at the money allotted for Felicity's care. As the biological mother she had the legal right to do this. But Felicity's caseworker at Children and Youth Services, anticipating the problem, had already made arrangements for Felicity's care. The Dawsons could tell Ellie in all honesty that Felicity already had an access card and that everything was being taken care of by her caseworker.

The adoption process has been easy for the Dawsons. It is being handled through SWAN (State Wide Adoption Network), an agency that arranges for everything and costs the adoptive family nothing. Since Jonathan and Sarah had already been certified as foster parents through a private agency, procedures for temporary placement as well as for adoption were much simpler than they would have been otherwise.

In general, the process of assigning a child to foster care or arranging for adoption is intricate, as the court tries hard to balance parental rights against the welfare of the child. When Felicity was born, there was a court hearing for emergency placement. It was decided that she would remain with the Dawsons for six months, during which time Ellie would be allowed monthly visitation rights. Ellie was told that if she wanted Felicity back, she had to comply with a number of court-ordered provisions within those six months: enrolling in a drug rehabilitation program, finding a place to live, entering into family counseling, taking parenting classes, and staying on birth control. Moreover she was told that it was *her* responsibility to keep in touch with Children and Youth Services. Ellie fulfilled none of these conditions.

"She went wacko," Sarah reports, "when she found out what she had to do to regain custody of Felicity. I told her, 'You need to start doing these things if you want Felicity back. Don't get angry at me; talk to Children and Youth. All this happened because of what you chose. These are the consequences of your choices.'"

Ellie visited Felicity only twice during those six months. Sarah describes one of those visits: "It was like a social call. She held her like she was a doll. There was no emotion. Jonathan told her we thought Felicity was HIV positive. And Ellie said, 'Oh, that's okay, they'll just give her medicine.' She didn't care."

When Felicity was six months old, there was a dependency hearing. Ellie didn't show up. The Dawsons petitioned the court to terminate parental rights and permit them to adopt Felicity. The court, always mindful of the rights of parents, notified Ellie that she had another thirty days to begin to comply with the set of provisions she had been given. But she did not do so, and she failed again to show up for the court hearing. Parental rights were legally terminated at that time. The Dawsons are now moving ahead in the process of adopting Felicity.

I ask Sarah how she would explain the contrast between Ellie and herself and how she had found her way into a different and more constructive life. It is obvious that she has thought a good deal about this. She gives me several reasons for her change, each belonging to a successive period in her life. From earliest childhood Sarah felt a strong wish to find "a way out" of what she saw going on all around her: "I remember when I was a little girl, growing up, even before I was taken out, I knew I wanted something different for my life. I didn't want that lifestyle. I didn't like what was happening to me, I didn't want to live it." Sarah speaks with emphasis, punching out her words. "I didn't know what I *did* want; I only knew that I didn't want what I had."

When she became a teenager, this childhood attitude of negative determination took the form of a strong sense of self: "I had an attitude when I was growing up. I cared for me and only me. I wanted what I wanted. I was after a better life for myself, and I didn't take crap from anybody. If teachers made me upset, I'd tell them off. Whenever somebody got in my face, I'd blow up."

Sarah's voice hardens as she says these things, as though she were reverting to the pugnacious teenager she once was. Listening to this tough street talk, I hear Ellie speaking, and I comment on this to Sarah. "No," she says decisively. "It's different. My type of blowing up, I'd yell and scream and then be done. Ellie can't do that. She holds grudges, gets violent. I never did that. I was never violent. Ellie does things out of spite and revenge and jealousy. That's the difference." The hardness in her voice turns to bitterness. "You know, she thinks everything was handed to me on a silver platter. That I got everything I wanted. She's jealous of the life I have now. But to tell you the truth, I've worked for the life I have!"

When Sarah turned sixteen, this determination fueled her insistence that the court grant her the status of emancipated minor, which would allow her to choose where to live. At the same time, a strong sense of her own self and worth, coupled with the negative determination of her childhood, seems to have directed her to an adoptive family that was not only loving but could provide her with a model lifestyle. As she remarks, "Once I moved in with that family as an emancipated minor, I knew that was the kind of life I wanted."

I ask Sarah if there wasn't anyone earlier in her life who helped her in some way, and she tells me about her relationship as a ten-year-old with a Big Sister. When Sarah mentions this young woman, her voice softens. "She was my saving grace. She even wrote a poem about me in a book she published!"

Today the Mormon Church provides Sarah and Jonathan with a supportive community as well as a set of values that reinforce those Sarah learned from the family she stayed with. She exclaims, "It was the first church where I actually felt the Savior's love. We've gone to many churches, but there was just nothing there. For the Mormons the highest value is the family. That's their main thing. Family first." Sarah describes the active support she received from church members when she first brought Felicity home: "I told them about her, and the same night there were bags and boxes on the front steps—baby stuff. It was unbelievable!" Even later, when the Dawsons learned that Felicity was probably infected with HIV, the church community remained staunchly supportive.

We are interrupted by a phone call. While Sarah goes to answer it, Jonathan and I talk. He tells me that he was raised as a Methodist and she as a Baptist, but clearly he is as happy with the Mormon Church as she is. He explains that they don't accept everything the Mormons stand for. For example, they chose not to pursue adoption through their church because mothers have to agree not to work outside the home. Sarah enjoyed her part-time job teaching nursery school and was unwilling to give it up.

Sarah returns and changes the topic back to Ellie and Ellie's new pregnancy. I observe that some people might consider Ellie just as victimized as the children she brings into the world. Sarah responds heatedly: "No. She had a choice. I grew up in that same environment, and I knew my choices. I knew right from wrong. She's a smart girl, a bright girl. She got all As in school when she was with her first foster family. She knew right from wrong. Everyone has a choice whether to sleep around or not. She's the one who decided to have these children; she's the one who keeps bringing them into the world."

As she talks about her sister, Sarah's face is flushed; she becomes excited and tends to repeat herself frequently. Ellie, she declares, will continue to get pregnant until she dies and is unlikely ever to be able to care for the children she brings into the world. "Things should be changed," Sarah exclaims, and repeats an opinion she has shared with Dr. Bennett and me before, this time at greater length and more vehemently. "I think if a person has a first child and makes a mistake, you take the child out of the home and help the mother get her life back together. But if she's not going to try, and she's going to keep having babies, like Ellie's doing, and just walk away, then somebody needs to say, 'Okay, that's enough, you went and had a second child. That's it, you're unfit. You get your tubes tied.' I know that's taking away their reproductive rights. But what right does an HIV positive woman have to bear children? Think of these poor children who are coming into the world and being raised in these situations, stuck in foster care or stuck with unfit parents! Someone needs to say, 'Okay, that's enough! It stops here!' They need to make tougher laws on that, for the children's sake. Because if they don't, the cycle is just going to keep going."

Sarah is more heated now than at any other time during the interview. She pauses, then continues, her voice breaking. "I love Felicity dearly. I look at her face, and I think, 'How can this go on? How can the state allow this to happen to innocent children?' Somebody has to step in and do something. For men who molest children, it's three strikes, you're out. Why isn't it the same for women who bring children into the world like this?"

Jonathan adds, "If you robbed a bank, they're not going to leave you out there to rob more banks. You go to jail—"

Sarah breaks in. "So why not with this? It might be taking a constitutional right away, but what about the child's rights? If Felicity is HIV positive, where's her right to have children, to have a normal marriage, a normal life? These innocent children that come into this world, their lives are being taken, they're being robbed of their lives. If you can stop child molestation and child abuse, you should be able to stop this. Children are our future. If we don't take care of our children, what kind of future is there?"

As I leave the Dawsons' home, I realize how surprised I am by Sarah's vehemence and anger toward Ellie and other women like her. She seems very different tonight from the gentle, worried young woman who brought Felicity in for her clinic visits. I want very much to understand the reasons behind that animosity and not to judge Sarah, as Sarah has judged Ellie. At times I felt as though I had tossed a match into dry leaves. Sarah repeated the same beliefs and ideas over and over as if she were trying to rid herself of her negative feelings toward Ellie, while really only intensifying them. Perhaps for Sarah, Ellie represents the lifestyle she managed to turn away from, and her judgmental attitude toward her sister reflects the energetic repudiation she needed in order to break away. Perhaps securing a better life for herself has deprived Sarah of some compassion for those unable to make such a change. Her harshness may be the cost of the success that has saved but to some degree hardened her.

Reflecting on their shared biological family, I am not only struck by the differences between Ellie and Sarah, differences that grow more marked the more I learn, but also curious about the relationship between them. They seem to exhibit ordinary sibling jealousy, but the family life of each has been so distorted that the stakes in their rivalry are now exceptionally high. According to Sarah, Ellie resents her for sending her father to jail and dissolving the family, though most of the children were already in foster care by the time "Pa" went to prison. Sarah senses that her sister is envious of the attention Sarah received when it became apparent that her stepfather had been sexually abusing her. Ellie's accusations of molestation by foster fathers began soon after her father's conviction. No one I have talked with who knows Ellie credits these accusations. But Ellie believes them, and whether or not she was actually molested, her belief that this happened suggests complicated feelings about her father as well as a cry for attention.

Another factor complicating the relationship is their different experiences of childbearing. For a long time Sarah seemed unable to conceive a child, while Ellie can do so easily and often. Apparently Ellie promised their mother that she'd be the first in the family to give her a grandchild. With Joey's birth, she kept her promise. It is ironic that just recently both sisters may have become pregnant at almost the same time. When Ellie found out that Sarah was also to have a child, she was angry and resentful. "Now that you're pregnant," she announced to Sarah, "you don't need my baby, so I'm going to work real hard to get her back!" Ellie may not be able to regain Felicity, but she can always produce another baby, and another, and another.

Of course the most striking difference between them is that Ellie is floundering and Sarah is not. Ellie carries on the lifestyle into which she was born: poverty, drugs, violence, and babies who must be removed from her care. But Sarah has successfully broken this cycle, moving out of the destructive conditions of their childhood and into a happy, constructive life. It is true that Ellie, at twenty-one, is much younger than Sarah, who is nearly thirty. Perhaps she too in time will break the cycle. Mike Riley, as we have seen, turned his life around at a much later age. But so far the record is not promising. Ellie does not take her medications, she cannot hold a job, and she continues to have drug problems. She has already had to give up two infants, and if she is indeed pregnant with a third, it too will almost certainly be taken from her and placed elsewhere.

Inevitably I find myself wondering how Ellie would understand the contrast between herself and her sister. I wish it were possible to talk openly and trustingly with Ellie, eliciting her views of what her childhood was like and of what her life is like now. I did try to do this, but Ellie quickly became defensive and antagonistic. So I cannot relate her story in her own voice, or the reasons she would give for her choices, or her reflections on deprivations she suffered as a child and problems she faces as an adult.

Reflecting on Sarah's description of Ellie's childhood and adolescence, I wonder to what extent it was shaped by her antipathy toward her sister. I think about Ellie, at the sensitive age of twelve, suddenly taken by her mother from what seems to have been a successful foster placement—her home for ten years—and brought to her "real home" to live in a slum. Perhaps Ellie's quick decline into sexual promiscuity reflects her anger over this sudden, and senseless, displacement. Then there is her insistence that she was sexually molested. The first time she made this claim she was thirteen, and it was "proven" that the act was consensual. Soon after this event Ellie was put into foster care, where she proceeded to accuse one foster father after another of sexually molesting her. Perhaps indeed these things didn't actually happen. But until she was two years old, Ellie lived at home with a father who was convicted of sexually molesting his three-and-one-half-year-old stepdaughter. It seems not impossible that this father molested Ellie as well and that she may have displaced whatever memory she retains of this event onto later relationships with older men.

Ellie certainly seems to lack two things important in Sarah's experience: a strong sense of self and the presence of positive role models. Sustaining any sense of self-worth must be hard for a child who is abused by her mother and lives surrounded by poverty, drugs, and crime. Moreover, though programs like Big Brothers and Big Sisters seem feasible and effective even in the inner city, it may be that Ellie did not have the opportunity to participate in them.

I think about Ellie's strong wish to become pregnant, and this brings to mind Sarah's fierce comments on reproductive rights and their conflict with the rights of children yet unborn, particularly in the case of women who are infected with HIV or who are addicts. Current social and legal policies in this country tend to favor the mother rather than the child and the biological family rather than a foster or adoptive family. In some sense this imbalance reflects the confluence of two very different positions: the older belief that children were possessions who belonged to their biological parents to do with as they wished and contemporary views that women have a constitutional right to decide about their own bodies. Sarah's views about the reproductive rights of women like Ellie may carry a kind of authority in that she not only is Ellie's sister but is voluntarily taking on the task of raising Ellie's child. The conflict between maternal rights and those of children is a complicated problem. But we need at least to recognize the importance and urgency of the issue as well as its complexity. One can only echo Dr. Bennett's wish for "widespread, serious, heartfelt debates" that will weigh the arguments on either side and lead to some shared understanding.

Coda: The Picnic

The picnic this year turned out wonderfully. It didn't rain, the "petting zoo" was a great success (especially Daisy, the potbellied pig); the T-shirts were not missed since only the staff knew about them; and the ever-present bees were kept at a distance by moving soda and pop bottles away from the area where we were eating. Dr. Bennett played softball, as he always does with the older children. He even clambered up onto the jungle gym and went down the slide, to the delight of the youngsters who had congregated below to watch him. When the games stopped so that we could eat, he went from group to group, sitting down and talking with parents and relatives.

About seventy-five people came this year—clinic children, staff, and the families of both. The Dawsons brought with them not only Felicity but also Sarah's elderly foster parents, the couple she refers to as "my real mom and pop." The Rileys came with Joey and Melissa—and Ellie too. To my knowledge, the two families never actually mixed. But I knew about Sarah's aversion to "that side of the family," and I was impressed that she had agreed to come at all, knowing that Loretta and Ellie would be there. At times during the picnic, when Ellie felt self-conscious, she was bad-tempered and either uncommunicative or defensive. But there were other times that she seemed to be enjoying herself. She would relax, and her face would soften as she sat and gazed at the children playing. We were glad for Ellie's presence.

Our annual picnic serves a symbolic as well as a practical function. Practically it brings together parents and foster parents so that they can share with one another the experience of caring for a child with HIV, makes it possible for infected children as well as siblings to spend time among other children with this disease, and allows children and their parents to interact with clinic staff (especially Dr. Bennett) as people rather than as medical personnel. Symbolically the picnic is an expression of the way the clinic functions as a moral community, enabling the staff to nurture these individuals

whose medical needs we serve and to celebrate the spirit of hope
that binds us all together. For a few hours the tragedy that threatens
these young lives seems suspended; for a few hours we live in a
world of celebration and good cheer.

THE communal festivity of the picnic seems almost Dickensian.
Indeed much in the stories of Joey and Felicity reminds me of the
novels of Charles Dickens. Yet even Dickens, despite his fondness
for melodrama, might have hesitated to depict a family as dysfunctional as Ellie and Sarah's: a mother who is abusive; a father/step-
father who molests his children; a brother who, brain-damaged and
potentially violent, fathers a child. Perhaps not incidentally Sarah
and Ellie's mother, raised in an institution, is herself the product of
the child welfare system. What is so terrible about all this is its
cyclical nature; the misery of this family reproduces and perpetu-
ates itself. Mother and father abuse or neglect their children, and
these children, when they become adolescents, often give birth to
children whom they are unable to care for.

It is to be hoped that such children can be placed where they will
be loved and protected. However, we have a child welfare system
already strained to its capacity. In a single year Children and Youth
Services in just one county of this state were more than a million
dollars in the red. Furthermore, not all foster parents can make up
for damage already done by the child's biological family. In the case
of children with perinatally acquired HIV infection, the harm in-
flicted by the disease itself is pervasive and permanent. Not only are
these children born with a fatal disease, but they are likely to require medical treatment on a monthly basis throughout their lives;
they are subject to serious opportunistic infections that often require hospitalization; they will not be able to have children of their
own (if they live that long) without the risk of passing on the virus;
and they have a disease surrounded with a penumbra of shame, a
disease they acquired, as they eventually learn, through a parent's
careless promiscuity or illegal use of intravenous drugs.

Yet in life as in Dickens, people somehow survive dysfunctional families and remain capable of happiness and even generosity, despite their own backgrounds of adversity. The Rileys are a case in point. They have, quite literally, saved Joey's life. Yet Loretta belongs to the same biological family as the father who sexually abused his children, and Mike's history includes childhood poverty, four marriages, traumatic military experience, excessive drinking, violent behavior culminating in manslaughter, and five years in prison. The Rileys have a solid marriage and a happy family life and even dream of setting up a home for handicapped children, though their health and financial problems would seem to preclude this. In their case the welfare system is working, not only providing for their needs but also enabling them to provide for others.

Many of the real-life people I have described tend toward moral extremes, seemingly akin to the idealized good characters and villainous bad ones that populate Dickens's fiction. Some, like Sarah and the Rileys, seem exemplary in their willingness and ability to care for those in need; others, like Ellie and Sarah's abusive parents, seem reprehensible in the way they harm others. Then there is the extraordinary difference between Sarah and Ellie, children of the same mother, who grew up in similiar conditions of material squalor and moral depravity. It is not hard to understand why Ellie has the problems she now has. It may be more difficult to comprehend how Sarah was able, in her own words, to "break the cycle." The child welfare system seems to have failed both these women, but especially Sarah, in returning her to a stepfather known to have molested her. Yet not only has she survived, but she is flourishing; furthermore, she is willing and able to be a mother to Ellie's child, with all the pain that this will inevitably entail.

The living conditions that Sarah vividly sketches when recounting her childhood are as terrible as any Dickensian portrayal of a nineteenth-century London slum. She not only is abused by her mother and molested by her father but witnesses murders, brutality, and violence of all kinds. In twentieth-century America we have one of the most advanced welfare systems in the world, whereas in Dickens's time such programs were nonexistent or in their infancy. Still, reflecting on the conditions under which Sarah and Ellie grew up and that still entrap Ellie, one must conclude that even today our ability to protect children from terribly abusive situations is tragically limited, resulting in situations not unlike the appalling mistreatment of children that Dickens describes graphically in novels like *Nicholas Nickleby* and *Oliver Twist.*

Dickens's "moral fiction," with its underlying optimism, suggests one way to interpret what I have described in this chapter. Much of his work, especially his early novels, seems based on the premise that people are for the most part innately good and that the lot of humankind, especially the welfare of children, can be bettered through social reform. This view suggests that if we provide better laws to protect children (both the living and those not yet born), if we work harder to secure loving homes for them, if we provide them with education and take care of their medical needs, then it is possible that the cycle of familial dysfunction can be broken.

Besides social reform, there is the virtue of personal generosity. Nearly all of Dickens's novels include benevolent individuals whose kindness affects in some deep way the lives of individuals victimized by circumstance. Dickens knew that no child—or adult, for that matter—can thrive without love. His novels are peopled with generous and kind surrogate parents such as Jarndyce in *Bleak House* or Brownlow in *Oliver Twist*, characters who open not only their purses but also their hearts to orphans they take in. Complementing this rescue motif, there is the recurring pattern of young heroes like David Copperfield and Little Dorrit (and Dickens himself) who make their way from poverty and oppression to a successful maturity. Dickens recognized that there is a hidden force of life in children enabling some of them not merely to survive but to achieve a better life—and then reach out to help others.

SOME VERY LARGE ANGELS

Angelina Morales

Angelina is eleven years old. Her parents are from Puerto Rico. Both are dead from HIV-related infections (her father during her infancy, her mother when she was eight). Other family members have abandoned her. Angelina was diagnosed with HIV when she was four years old. She began treatment at our clinic when she had just turned six. At that time her T cell count was 268 (two years later it dropped to single digits). Angelina has been in foster care since she was nine. She has serious psychological and behavioral problems that have caused numerous changes in placement; in fact she has been with six different foster families over the past two and a half years.

Her medical history is remarkable for frequent pneumonias, thrush, impetigo, molluscum contagiosum, severe anemia, disseminated MAI, and recurrent psychotic episodes. Two years ago her health deteriorated so badly that she was believed to have end stage HIV infection, and she was placed in hospice care. To the astonishment and delight of everyone involved in her care, she recovered remarkably. Her viral load, while never undetectable, has remained at a reasonably low level for the past two years.

Right now Angelina seems to be thriving. She is in sixth grade, has a "best friend," sings in the church choir, and is fascinated by R&B.

.   .   .

ANGELINA looks down, fidgets for a few seconds, and looks back up at Dr. Bennett. "Tell me about the disease I have," she says, almost in a whisper. A shy little girl, worried-looking, with a sweet, round face and round eyes, she's standing in front of him, and he's sitting in the chair adjacent to a small white plastic table, writing up his notes. He stops writing and looks up at her, pencil in hand, then puts his left arm around her waist and draws her next to him. I wonder how he'll explain this complicated disease and its equally complicated treatment to an eleven-year-old. He speaks slowly, his voice low. "Well, Angelina, it's like this. You catch HIV from your mother's blood. It gets in your blood cells; then it gets in your spleen and lymph nodes. It lives a very long time and kills off the cells that prevent infection. This virus doesn't go away like other viruses do. With other viruses, like a cold, your body fights them off. But with HIV that's harder to do. You get infections because your body can't fight back as well as it should. The medications help your body fight back; they help get the disease out of your body. One of the tests that we do measures how well your body can fight back. We do this test every so often, and it helps us know what medications to give you." Dr. Bennett smiles at her, pauses, then asks, "Does that help you understand?"

"Yes," she replies softly as she turns her head slightly to the side, dropping her eyes. She focuses on a pretty beaded bracelet on her left arm, which she turns around and around with her right hand. Dr. Bennett's arm is still around her waist. She shifts her weight to her left leg, still looking down at her bracelet.

Dr. Bennett continues. "Angelina, we're really happy that you're so healthy now. A few years ago you weren't doing so well. You were one sick little girl back then. And now you're so much better! It's really important that you keep taking these medications, and take them just like you're supposed to. They're helping you not get sick."

"About those medications . . ." asks Angelina's foster mother, a large, genial, comfortable-looking woman who has been sitting in the chair beside Dr. Bennett. "The county caseworker wants to know what she's taking and what it's for. I know what she's taking, but I sure can't remember what it's all for!" She laughs and shakes her head.

Dr. Bennett turns to face Mrs. Carver as she speaks. Angelina walks over to where I'm standing, looks up at me, smiles, and asks, "Do you have any stickers today?" I reach in the pocket of my jacket, peel a shiny neon-colored fish off its paper, and put it on the back of her hand. She holds it up for me to see and beams.

Mrs. Carver has brought all of Angelina's medications in a plastic bag to the clinic visit, as Dr. Bennett suggested last time. There are twelve bottles of pills on the table. He picks up three of them. "These three, the Norvir, Epivir, and Zerit, these are for the HIV infection. The Norvir is a protease inhibitor. Epivir and Zerit, these are called reverse transcriptase inhibitors. What these three drugs do, in combination, is reduce the amount of virus in her body."

He turns back to Angelina, who is still standing next to me. "Angelina, are you listening to this? I want you to be hearing this too. Are you taking your medications?"

She nods.

"All of them, all the time?"

She nods again.

"Well, I'm glad to hear that," he says.

Mrs. Carver is making notes as Dr. Bennett recites which drug is for this and which one is for that. He goes on, picking up another bottle. "This is Bactrim; it's to prevent her from getting *Pneumocystis carinii* pneumonia—PCP. The folate, it's to remedy a folic acid deficiency. We're hoping it will prevent her from becoming anemic and then she won't need injections of Epogen in the future. Rifampin, Biaxin, and Myambutol are all for her MAI infection—that's short for *Mycobacterium avium–intracellulare*. MAI can lead to serious problems, so we want to fight that aggressively. Fluconazole is for her thrush; it looks pretty good this time, so you can stop that after two more weeks. And the Prednisone, remember that you're not going to give this to her anymore, now that those mouth ulcers have cleared up. You can keep it because she might need it again. But don't give her any more now.

"These"—he holds up the two last bottles—"clonidine and Risperdal, they're to help Angelina with her psychological problems. They've been prescribed by Dr. Hartman, the psychiatrist she sees at the Centerville hospital. You'll have to ask him if you want to know more about them. Does that answer your questions?"

"Yes," she says, laughing, "but I have a feeling I'm not going to remember all this!"

"Oh, that's okay," he replies. "We can always go over it again." He turns back to Angelina. "Anyway, soon Angelina is going to know what all these medications are for and then she can tell you. Right, Angelina?" he asks as he looks over at her, smiling. She smiles in response and looks down again.

"Any more questions for me today?" he asks Angelina.

At first she doesn't answer. Then Mrs. Carver says to her, "Angelina, remember what you were going to tell Dr. Bennett? About going out for recess?"

She shakes her head.

"Do you want me to tell him, or do you want to tell him?" asks Mrs. Carver.

"You tell him," says Angelina slowly, her voice soft and her head still down.

"Well," says Mrs. Carver with a big sigh, "there are problems with recess. Angelina doesn't want to go out, and she's telling her teachers that she's too sick to go and play outside."

"I know about that," says Dr. Bennett. "Last week I got a call from Laura Freedman, the counselor from Dr. Hartman's office. I told her that it's just fine for Angelina to go outside for recess." He looks over at Angelina. "And I'm telling you too, Angelina. You can go outside for recess. In fact that's good for you. You need exercise. Do you like to jump rope?" She nods, smiling. "Well that's good. You go outside for recess and play jump rope. Angelina, you're not sick now. You have an underlying infection, but you're not sick. You should go out for recess. And I'm telling that to Laura, your counselor." Dr. Bennett knows that Angelina, like many children with HIV (or any chronic illness), can be extremely manipulative, using their illness to get special privileges or to secure release from tasks they don't want to do. When such issues come up, he always adopts the position that a child with HIV, when not sick, should be treated just like any other healthy child.

"Angelina," says Dr. Bennett, "it's good to see you. Next time I want to hear what you can do with that jump rope."

She looks up at him, a big grin on her face this time.

"Okay," he says. "You go get your blood work done, and I'll see you again in a month."

She leaves the room, and Dr. Bennett asks Mrs. Carver, "How are things at home?"

"Better," she says. "The counseling has been great. It helps me deal with the problems she's causing for my other children. I wish the counselor, Laura, would stay longer, though. I know Angelina still has a lot going on inside her head. She doesn't talk much about her thoughts, and I worry that she's keeping things bottled up inside. . . . I really love Angelina, and I want to keep her, but I don't know if I can take another episode like what happened before."

Mrs. Carver is recalling how three months ago Angelina was hospitalized for an acute psychotic episode. She had problems sleeping, she was frightened by voices and faces "from dead people," and she told Mrs. Carver on several occasions that she wanted to kill herself. When she threatened her ten-year-old foster sister with a big kitchen knife, Mrs. Carver took her to the emergency room at the local hospital, where she was admitted to the psychiatric ward. She stayed two weeks. Angelina was very penitent about what she had done and begged Mrs. Carver to let her come back to what she now called home. She was released to the Carvers on a regimen of antipsychotic drugs and weekly counseling.

Also living in the Carver home are three biological children: a seven-year-old boy, a girl of ten who is in the same grade at school as Angelina, and an older girl of thirteen. Mrs. Carver told us last month that Angelina very much wants to be like everyone else; she avoids thinking about the psychological problems that led to her being hospitalized and does not like being reminded of her HIV status at all. She does not want to be singled out as different from the Carver children. This is one reason why the weekly counseling sessions with Laura Freedman involve the whole family and are more oriented toward family therapy than individual help for Angelina.

Dr. Bennett asks, "Is she still seeing Dr. Hartman, that psychiatrist at Centerville?"

"No," responds Mrs. Carver. "Not anymore. Not really. He just monitors her medications. He sends out the counselor from his office, and I guess she reports back to him."

I ask Mrs. Carver whether an arrangement might be made so that the counselor could spend some time with Angelina, one-on-one, in addition to the family counseling. She tells me that she thinks this would be possible, that the county caseworker told her more visits could be authorized if Angelina needed them. Intervention right now seems important, I observe, so that Angelina gets the help she needs to be able to stay with their family.

Mrs. Carver adds, "The problem now is with my older daughter, Karen, the thirteen-year-old. She says she doesn't want to get to know Angelina because she thinks Angelina's going to die."

"Well," replies Dr. Bennett, "we don't know that she's going to die. I thought so a year ago, but Angelina's doing fine now. About a year and a half ago she was deteriorating rapidly. Sometime around the middle of December we got hospice involved in her care, expecting her to die in a few months. We were still continuing to treat the MAI aggressively, and as a result of this her hemoglobin began to come up. But she still had that molluscum, which was really disfiguring. You saw her then, Anne. I remember your being here." I nod, remembering what she looked like, with hundreds of warts covering her arms and face, even her lips and eyelids. "Well" — he goes on — "in March she had surgery for the molluscum, and their removal had a major effect on her sense of herself. She felt so much better about herself. Then she was put on a protease inhibitor last August, and that's helped too."

"You know," observes Mrs. Carver, "I think the molluscum seems to be coming back."

"I've noticed that too," says Dr. Bennett. "But the warts are still very small. We can have them removed again like we did before. It won't be such a big operation this time; she can do it as an outpatient. But let's wait a little for that until things calm down for her. Now about Karen—maybe she needs some time with her mom. Time that you can be together, just the two of you. Can you try to spend some more individual time with her, things like errands?"

"Okay, I'll try that," she says.

Dr. Bennett stands, handing her paper work from the clinic visit. "Keep up the good work, Mrs. Carver. I know it can be hard. Raising children is hard, even without introducing foster children into your home. Angelina looks really good, she's gaining weight, and her viral load is down. I'll see her in a month. You can call my office if anything comes up before then."

The story that follows is one that I have struggled over, trying to avoid oversimplification and distortion but also trying to present a coherent and sequential narrative. My first problem was that Angelina was not able to provide much information. She is a shy, somewhat withdrawn, and not very communicative child. She deals with her past by claiming to have forgotten whatever happened and with her present HIV status by asserting that she doesn't know anything about it. Those responsible for her care believe this to be a successful coping mechanism for now. She is thriving, and she seems happy. I have never pressed Angelina to talk with me about anything related to her disease. From the very beginning my relationship with her has been a simple friendship. Of course I'm there at the clinic when she comes in for her monthly appointments with Dr. Bennett, and in this capacity I've followed Angelina's story through four of her six foster placements. I've become extremely fond of her and think that our relationship right now is more important than initiating discussions about a past that seems too painful for her to talk about or even remember. As one of Angelina's caseworkers observes, "She's pent up this stuff for so long that it's hard to get to it. She doesn't want to talk about it. She extends herself only to a certain point into her past, and that's all she's capable of doing."

Another difficulty I confronted was the sheer number of people in Angelina's life. Besides her foster families and her medical providers (Dr. Bennett, her psychiatrists, and her counselors), there are at least four persons appointed by the court who share responsibility for her in different ways. I spoke with ten different people about Angelina: six foster parents (from five foster families); a visiting nurse who cared for Angelina's mother when she was dying; a young Hispanic caseworker, Teresa, who knew the family and befriended Angelina before she was placed in foster care; a caseworker from Children and Youth Services; and, lastly, Dr. Bennett and the nurse who served as his clinic coordinator when Angelina first came for treatment.

At times this multiplicity of sources and perspectives inevitably led to confused or conflicting versions of events. When there is consensus among my sources, I present what is reported as "fact."[1] But when there is no consensus, I try to preserve inconsistencies and contradictions, quoting individual informants (while disguising their actual identities) without trying to reconcile or smooth over their differences.

Angelina Morales was born in Puerto Rico in 1986, just before Christmas. She remembers virtually nothing of the first four years of her life. Her mother, who contracted HIV from Angelina's father, did not know she was infected when Angelina was conceived. There were four older children, all healthy. The father abandoned the family not long after Angelina was born and died in Puerto Rico when she was still an infant. Angelina was diagnosed with HIV when she was four, her mother having taken her to the hospital in San Juan for treatment of pneumonia.

When she was five years old, Angelina, her mother, and her four

---

[1] I put the word "fact" in quotes to signal my awareness that none of this material, gleaned through the memories and perspectives of others, can truly be called factual.

siblings moved to Pittsford, a small city some thirty miles south-
west of St. Luke's Hospital. In January 1993 Angelina, then six
years old, was brought by her mother for her first appointment
with Dr. Bennett. At that time she had a CD4 count of 268 (several years later it dropped all the way down to 2). Dr. Bennett and
his nurse both remember Angelina's shyness. They have little
memory of her mother, except that she always looked haggard and
ill. She spoke little English and was usually accompanied by another family member. Angelina soon developed facial warts that
were diagnosed as molluscum contagiosum. The warts spread
rapidly, and within a year covered her face and arms. The molluscum was very disfiguring.

At first Mrs. Morales did a good deal of "doctor-hopping," taking
Angelina alternately to a doctor in Pittsford and to Dr. Bennett for
repeated episodes of pneumonia. Somewhat later it was discovered
that she was not telling either doctor about the other, to the consternation of both physicians. Mrs. Morales did not seem to be giving Angelina her medications regularly. Though Dr. Bennett had
prescribed Bactrim, Mrs. Morales told the doctor in Pittsford that
she never gave it to Angelina. Nor did she give her the antibiotics
prescribed when she came down with pneumonia.

The Morales family tried to conceal from others the fact that
Mrs. Morales and Angelina were infected. Perhaps too they denied
it among themselves. A Latina nurse involved with the family believes that the sense of shame generally associated with AIDS is especially prevalent among Hispanics. "AIDS is a stigmatizing illness
for Latinos. They feel it reflects negatively on them as a culture.
They are poor, they have so many problems, and now there is
AIDS. So AIDS is something Hispanic families don't want to acknowledge and try to keep secret. This family just didn't want Angelina. They were afraid of the illness, afraid it was contagious. And
it brought them shame."

Near the end of 1994, when Angelina was almost eight years old,
Mrs. Morales became very sick from an AIDS-related infection.
There was a local AIDS hospice in the area, and the care provided

was exemplary, but Mrs. Morales did not become involved with this program. The hospice director, though well intentioned, was known to be indiscreet. To alert the community to the needs of individuals with AIDS and to help raise money for the hospice, she solicited media coverage and allowed the names of her clients and even their photographs to be printed in local newspapers. Because of this, people who could have benefited from her program were often unwilling to expose themselves and their families to the shame of a disease with so powerful a stigma.

Visiting nurses came out to provide care for Mrs. Morales at home, and in this way others in the community became aware of the family's situation. The four older children ranged in age from ten to twenty-one, and there was also a grandmother. Angelina barely remembers this grandmother, who refused to have anything to do with her after Mrs. Morales died.

Angelina and her brother, ten-year-old Roberto, were expected to care for their dying mother. Angelina knew that she had the same disease, and she confessed to the visiting nurses her fear that she would die a similarly painful death. Descriptions of just how she experienced her mother's death are not entirely consistent, but that experience seems to have been traumatic. According to Teresa, the caseworker who befriended the young Morales children afterward, "Angelina watched her mother die. That's a really painful, scary memory for her. Her mother was in a lot of pain at the end, and she cried and moaned and kicked and screamed, and there were times she was too weak to do anything but open her mouth and moan. Angelina would bring cold cloths to put on her forehead." According to a nurse involved with the Morales family, Angelina regularly slept in the same bed with her mother but was not allowed to do so the night of her death. That morning, at 2:00 A.M., Angelina was awakened and told, in a blunt and matter-of-fact way, that her mother had died. But Roberto was actually in the room when his mother died, and her very last words were addressed to him. She asked him to promise to take care of Angelina. Roberto still remembers that promise, and he is still trying, in his own way, to carry it out.

January 1995–December 1996: The Morales Brothers (Angelina Is Eight Years Old)

After Mrs. Morales's death, legal guardianship of Angelina and Roberto passed to their eldest brother, then twenty-two years old. They moved in with him and his girlfriend, who had five children of her own. The apartment building in which they were living was ridden with drugs, prostitution, and violence. The girlfriend resented having to care for two more children and took an active dislike to Angelina, a child with AIDS who was disfigured by facial warts. It goes without saying that Angelina was unhappy. Once she tried to run away. Her brother found her a mile or so from the house, walking toward the center of Pittsford. Reports were made to the county Children and Youth Services that the children were being abused—that the girlfriend hit Angelina over the head repeatedly with a hairbrush and that the brother beat her with his belt—but these reports could never be verified.

Teresa remembers the Morales family as "in every way extremely dysfunctional. They were ignorant and poor. They were always shouting at each other. The older brothers were troubled kids. They drank, they did drugs, they were in trouble with the law." Several agencies in Pittsford came together and found Angelina's brother and his young charges a subsidized apartment, then furnished it and delivered food regularly. They also organized a crew of volunteers who came in the morning to make sure the younger children got breakfast and went to school. These same volunteers were to pick them up when school was out and take them home, then stay around and help with homework until an adult showed up. But the plan didn't work. When a volunteer arrived in the morning to get them ready for school, the children didn't answer the door, and sometimes they weren't even there. It soon became apparent that they were left alone in the apartment whenever the older brother stayed at his girlfriend's place. The children rarely went to school. They ate what they could find. Angelina describes how she and Roberto cooked for themselves: "You fill a pan of water and you put an egg in it and you put a hot dog in it and you cook them at the same time. Then you eat. Hot dogs and eggs are good together!" Not surprisingly, Angelina was not given her medications regularly, and she frequently missed medical appointments.

Angelina began to spend more and more time with her other brother, who was nineteen, and his girlfriend. This young woman seems to have been the only member of the family to care about Angelina, and Angelina remembers her with fondness. But the nineteen-year-old brother suddenly abandoned his girlfriend and returned to Puerto Rico. He told her and Angelina that he was going only for a visit. But he informed everyone else, including Dr. Bennett, that he was leaving permanently. After he left, Angelina and Roberto spent more and more time by themselves in the subsidized apartment.

Sometime during the year after their mother's death Angelina and Roberto were befriended by a young Hispanic caseworker, Teresa Diaz. Teresa was concerned because the children were so frequently left alone. She often brought Angelina in for her clinic appointments and then took her to lunch—sometimes at the hospital cafeteria, sometimes at McDonald's. Angelina recalls with pleasure that people who saw them together assumed that Teresa was her mother. Teresa took her on trips and brought her home to play with her own children, two boys around the same age. "I remember one Christmas," Teresa remarks, "she and I went out and bought her gifts, and she was so happy. We came back, and she lay down on my bed, and we just talked and talked. Girl talk. Then there were also times she was really sad. She seemed far away, so far away, and then I felt that I couldn't reach her." There were limits to what Teresa could do for the Morales children. She was a single mom with three young children of her own, an infant she had recently adopted, an elderly parent, and a full-time job. Often phone calls had to substitute for visits.

Angelina's health deteriorated remarkably over the year that followed her mother's death. The molluscum on her face and arms
continued to spread. She began to avoid going out in public. Opportunistic infections increased in frequency and severity. Near the
end of that same year she was hospitalized on four separate occasions for severe anemia and pneumonia. All this was surely a consequence of the neglect by her older brothers.

On several occasions Teresa and others involved with the family
notified Children and Youth that Angelina and Roberto were not
properly cared for. Each time they were told that the agency could
not intervene since there was no evidence of actual abuse. However, sometime in November Angelina was brought, presumably by
her brother, to the emergency room of their local hospital with a
temperature of 104.9, cough, lethargy, and bone ache. She was
transferred to St. Luke's by ambulance and arrived alone. At St.
Luke's she was treated for anemia and found to have disseminated
MAI. Children and Youth was informed of all this. They contacted
the brother who still retained custody of the two younger children
and recommended placing Angelina and Roberto in foster care.
But he was reluctant to do so. Dr. Bennett recalls conversations
during which this brother vigorously maintained his wish and his
right to retain guardianship of Angelina, but he believes that the
brother may have been primarily interested in the generous Social
Security benefits Angelina was receiving.

The situation finally resolved a month later, during the Christmas holidays. On Christmas morning Teresa called the children
and discovered that they had been alone for several days. When she
heard Angelina coughing as they talked over the phone, she became alarmed, drove over to the apartment, and brought both children to her own home. Realizing that Angelina had a fever as well
as a cough, Teresa took her to the local emergency room in Pittsford. She was diagnosed with *Pneumocystis carinii* pneumonia and
once more sent by ambulance to St. Luke's Hospital. This time authorities intervened, and arrangements were made for Angelina
and Roberto to be placed in foster care.

December 29, 1995–January 6, 1996: Mrs. Alloway
(Angelina Is Nine Years Old)

After her second St. Luke's hospitalization, Angelina went directly to her new foster home, and soon after, Roberto was placed in a different foster home. But Angelina's first placement didn't work out, partly because of the foster mother's expectations and partly because of Angelina's behavior. For Mrs. Alloway,[2] a Caucasian woman who had heard about the family's problems, Angelina was a kind of pet, in every sense of the word. Mrs. Alloway wanted to care for her as a helpless little creature, and she wanted to be admired for taking a child with AIDS into her home. But Angelina, devastated by the abrupt separation from her family, began having severe and violent temper tantrums. After only a week Mrs. Alloway called the agency responsible for Angelina's placement and demanded that she be removed immediately, despite the fact that the town was paralyzed by a severe blizzard. The agency contacted community volunteers from a local service organization called FIA (Faith-in-Action).[3] These people found a four-wheel-drive vehicle

[2] To avoid confusion, the pseudonyms for each foster family begin with a successive letter of the alphabet, from Alloway to Blosser, and so forth.

[3] FIA was started in 1993 by four people from Pittsford who felt a commitment to caring for people with AIDS. Several of the founding members of FIA were involved with home health care through the Visiting Nurse Association. Their work brought them in contact with young men with AIDS who had come home to die, young people who were abandoned by their churches (and sometimes by their families as well) because of their sexual orientation. In speaking with several of the group's founding members, I was struck by the fact that while FIA was started by churchgoing people motivated by a desire to put their faith into action, it was initially the community rather than the churches that responded to the group's efforts. Though it is a faith-based ministry, the primary goal of FIA is to provide services like housing and transportation. "We don't have the goal of making people Christian," Mrs. Zurko (a founding member of FIA) told me. "Our work is an expression of our faith, not a demand of theirs." The group began as a volunteer organization. In its second year it was awarded a $25,000 grant from the Robert Wood Johnson Foundation, and now, with a budget of $200,000 a year, it is supported by state and federal money, the community hospital, the local board of realtors, area churches, businesses, and individual donors.

and with great effort drove to the house, shoveled out the driveway, and took Angelina to the home of an elderly Caucasian couple, the Blossers, who were also volunteers with FIA. Mrs. Blosser knew about Angelina and Roberto from her work with the Visiting Nurse Association, through which she had become interested in and involved with the needs of AIDS patients and their families.

It was unfortunate that this displacement from her first foster home coincided with the anniversary of her mother's death a year before, an extremely difficult "anniversary" for Angelina. She had watched her mother die, knowing that she had the same illness. Then came the sudden separation from her family, followed by another sudden expulsion from Mrs. Alloway's home after only a week, events that must have intensified the issues of abandonment with which Angelina was already struggling.

January–April 1996: The Blossers
(Angelina Is Nine Years Old)

Because of their age—he was near seventy and she in her midsixties—the Blossers had agreed from the beginning to take Anglina only temporarily, until permanent placement could be found. As it turned out, she stayed with them for eleven weeks. Angelina thrived under their care. She thought of them then, and thinks of them now, as her foster grandparents. They have tried to stay in touch with her whenever possible over her subsequent placements through letters, birthday presents, and visits.

When I first met the Blossers, the couple struck me as quintessential grandparents—kind, generous, and interested. Lucinda Blosser is a tiny woman of boundless energy who laughs and talks a lot. Elvin Blosser, a lean, angular man who is a retired machinist, is much less voluble, though he always has a smile on his tan, creased face. The Blossers are eager to talk about Angelina. They show me snapshots and letters she has written to them. My favorite photograph is of Angelina holding a "stuffy," a little brown and white stuffed rabbit with floppy ears that they gave her on Easter.

The picture was taken several months after she had come to stay with them, during one of the annual Easter egg hunts that the Blossers hold for neighborhood children. The grass is very green, and the yard seems very big. Angelina is wearing glasses with pink frames and smiling. At that time the Blossers had a real rabbit named Whiskers, the kind of rabbit that has long, floppy ears, with whom Angelina had fallen in love.

When Angelina first came to live with the Blossers, she was very thin, her teeth were brown and spotted, and she was still recovering from her last bout of pneumonia. "She was such a sorry little thing," Mrs. Blosser recalls. "She had this infection around her nose and in her nose, and she had scabs down her face, oozing scabs, and she had that molluscum; the visiting nurses told us it was cancer. She was one sad-looking little girl. She was coughing up this terrible stuff, she had rales, and she was so weak I had to help her bathe. She had I forget how many cavities, and severe gingivitis too. And she just ate all the time. She couldn't get enough, she practically inhaled her food!"

For the first time Angelina was keeping her clinic appointments on a regular basis. The Blossers got to know Dr. Bennett. Mr. Blosser remembers that when they were thinking about keeping Angelina permanently, Dr. Bennett sat down with them and talked at length about the emotional toll of taking on such a child. "That Dr. Bennett," remarks Mr. Blosser, "he was just wonderful to us and to Angelina. One time when we went to court about getting rights to make decisions about her medical care, the judge called Dr. Bennett from the courtroom to get his input, and he gave it over the phone, and the judge said, 'This is the first time we've had that much cooperation from a doctor!'" The respect this judge felt for Dr. Bennett was evident when, during Angelina's placement with the Blossers, he gave Dr. Bennett legal responsibility for end-of-life decisions.

The Blossers made it possible for Angelina to spend as much time as she wanted with Teresa, the young caseworker she had become so fond of during the difficult months she was living with her older brother. Mr. Blosser took Angelina regularly to see her brother Roberto, then twelve years old, who was staying with a foster family in a nearby town, and Roberto in turn came to visit them. He too began to call them Grandma and Grandpa. Roberto has always felt responsible for Angelina, perhaps ever since his mother on her deathbed asked him to take care of her. "He was always very protective of Angelina," says Mrs. Blosser. "But he was so harsh on her. He'd put her down. He'd always find something wrong with her. She was always seeking his approval, and he wasn't generous about giving it."

Socially Angelina was having a hard time. Though her health gradually improved over the first few months at the Blossers, the disfiguring molluscum remained. People stared at her in the supermarket or the drugstore. Mrs. Blosser remembers the extraordinary insensitivity of some people who asked, "What's that? What does she have?" Angelina increasingly avoided going places. For several months she had been too sick to go to school, and now she didn't want to go to school for fear of being teased.

In late February, a month and a half after she had come to stay with the Blossers, Angelina was referred to a plastic surgeon to determine whether the molluscum warts that covered her face and arms could be safely removed. Roberto, whom Angelina still saw regularly, was strongly opposed to the surgery. According to the Blossers, he thought that the warts "were a part of who she was." Nonetheless in March the warts were removed by a long and difficult surgical procedure. When the scars healed, the result was transforming, and Angelina became much more willing to go out in public.

Plans were already in the works for her to attend public school. To help her catch up, the principal of the elementary school that she was to attend came to the house three times a week for several hours of tutoring. "It was so wonderful to see this child using her mind, feeling more like a child her age should feel," remarks Mr. Blosser. "Mrs. X wasn't just a principal; she was also a great teacher.

She was only reviewing things, but Angelina loved it. She was really happy doing that."

Angelina also began attending services at a Methodist church with the Blossers. She loved singing in the choir. Mrs. Blosser observes: "On Sunday mornings we didn't have to leave until about eight-thirty or nine, but she'd get up at six and come and knock on our door. I'd say, 'Yes, Angelina, we're here,' and she'd say, 'Lucinda?' or 'Grandma?'—she called me either one, depending on what mood she was in. Then she'd say, 'What time is it?' I'd tell her the time, and I'd say, 'Honey, you have two hours before you need to get up.' She'd say, 'But I'm hungry!' Of course we weren't going to let her stand there at our door, hungry, and so we had early breakfast here every Sunday. If something came along so that we couldn't go to church, that would throw her, and she'd be moody all day. And, oh dear, could she be moody!"

Indeed after a month or so Angelina began having tantrums again. "At least one thing we know caused her rages," says Mrs. Blosser, "was Hispanics. We went for pizza one time, and we sat next to this Hispanic family. In the car on the way home she started one of her episodes. She said, 'I can't breathe! I can't breathe!' and then, when she got home, she went into one of her rages. This happened again when we went to the grocery store and she saw a woman with her children who looked like she might be Hispanic; you could just tell that it broke Angelina's heart. It was like she became a different child. I've often said that there are two Angelinas. And I've been saying that for a long time. I do think that there's a split there somewhere. At first I looked at it as an anxiety thing— separation—but now I think, yes, there really are two Angelinas because she's like two different children."

At least twice the Blossers sought psychiatric treatment for Angelina. In March they took her to a psychologist at St. Luke's. For the most part he directed his intervention to Mr. and Mrs. Blosser, telling them how to handle her behavior, which he referred to as mood swings. Mr. Blosser was convinced that something more than just mood swings was going on. "I really didn't think he understood the situation. Angelina's a clever little girl. I don't know if that psychologist at St. Luke's knew he was being fooled, but he sure was!"

Angelina's rages became more frequent and more violent. During one episode, after screaming and crying and kicking, she tore down the curtains in the dining room, bending the curtain rods, then threw the dining room chairs, breaking one and chipping the table. During another episode she became really violent, and when Mrs. Blosser tried to restrain her, Angelina bit her finger quite deeply. The Blossers sought psychiatric help once more, this time bringing her to the emergency room at the local hospital. But Angelina quieted down while in the waiting room and seemed fairly calm when seen by the staff psychiatrist, who made no recommendation for further treatment.

The Blossers began to think that they were too old to deal with Angelina. "I wish we had been younger," Mr. Blosser observes. "Physically it was so demanding, we just couldn't do it. But we're still here, and we're always here for her." The situation was complicated by the absence of children in the Blossers' home and by Angelina's desire to be with her brother. Roberto was living with a family, the Carvers, who had children about the same age. The prospect of moving in with Roberto's foster family seemed very attractive to her. Since Angelina had not only a serious illness but also severe behavioral problems, the judge responsible for her placement this time went through a private agency.[4] It was agreed by all that the Carvers would take Angelina to live with them, thus providing her with a permanent home as well as reuniting her with her brother.

---

[4] When a child requires foster placement, the county's Children and Youth Services first turns to a list of foster families kept on file. But for a child with special needs, or when prior foster placements have not worked out, Children and Youth often uses a private agency for placement. Though it costs the county more, this agency finds (and trains) parents willing to care for special needs children and often provides other services as well, such as psychiatric counseling in Angelina's case.

April 1996–October 1997: *The Carvers* (*Angelina Is Nine and a Half*)

In April 1996 Angelina moved in with the Carvers, her third foster home in four months. A solidly middle-class Caucasian family with three children of their own, the Carvers lived in a nice house in Meadville, a suburb of Pittsford. Mr. Carver had a well-paying job at an insurance company, and Mrs. Carver was a friendly woman who clearly loved children, especially babies.

At first Angelina seemed happy. She was frequently able to visit the Blossers, often accompanied by Roberto or one of the Carvers' three children. She was now with her brother, and she also had a foster sister her own age. Furthermore, she appeared to have a very close relationship with her foster mother. Indeed she was always to be found sitting on Mrs. Carver's lap. They even had their own song—"I can see that look in your eyes, I'll never leave you, I'll take care of you forever"—that Mrs. Carver would sing to her. Mrs. Carver put Angelina's wishes and needs before those of Roberto and even before those of her other children. But this attachment may have unwittingly harmed Angelina, both by inciting jealousy in the other children and by promising Angelina more than she could ever give her.

Perhaps the Carvers miscalculated the severity of Angelina's medical problems and underestimated the extent of her psychological and behavioral problems. They may well have believed they were providing care for a dying child and could thus lavish time, energy, and affection on her because they expected her not to live very long. This is Mrs. Blosser's point of view. "When we met the Carvers," she says, "I was a little surprised to find out that in preparing for Angelina to come there, they had told their two older children that she had AIDS and she would probably die. Of course her CD4 count was terrible, but it was always terrible. We tried to tell them that we really didn't feel there was any impending doom at this point. But they had already told their older children this." In Angelina's medical records there is no evidence that she was perceived at this time as dying. Indeed she had been in more danger some months before, while living with her brothers, than when she first came to the Carvers.

Mrs. Carver claims that the agency told her that "the only problem Angelina had was AIDS," concealing the fact that she was prone to violent outbursts of temper. "I was prepared to deal with a child with AIDS," she says, "but not with a child who had tantrums like that." The Blossers, on the other hand, maintain that they met with the Carvers well before the Carvers consented to take her. "Early on," remarks Mrs. Blosser, "we told them that Angelina had problems. We all sat in this room [in the Blossers' house], the children were out in the yard playing, and we told the Carvers about her behavior. But somehow, that didn't connect with them. We said, 'You need to know that Angelina has problems.' We described exactly what she did, the fact that I had been bitten, the fact that she would get totally out of control."

Roberto, though still protective of his sister, became jealous of the attention she was receiving and started to act out. Fights among the older children increased. Once Roberto threatened thirteen-year-old Karen with a knife, though he claimed he was only trying to scare her. He was even rougher with the younger daughter, Julie, putting her in a headlock and then pummeling her on the head. Roberto's increasingly violent behavior finally led the Carvers to ask that he be placed elsewhere.

At first, declares Mrs. Carver, "Angelina was nothing like him. She was good." But after about three months the relationship between Angelina and her foster family deteriorated. Her rages began again. The agency that placed Angelina had promised that she would receive weekly counseling. But counseling was inconsistent; the therapists frequently failed to show up, and when they did, their intervention did not prove very helpful. Angelina's tantrums became more frequent and more violent. Mrs. Carver describes these episodes: "She scratches; she bites; she'll try to stab you with pencils; she's like a wild, crazy person. Not like a regular child. She'll kick and scream, destroy everything. Like one time she went into the bathroom, pulled the shower curtain down, poured shampoo all over the rugs, and when I went in, she had that shower curtain pole there waiting for me."

Medically Angelina's condition worsened. She was not responding to HIV therapy, and her T cell count continued to drop. In July she came down with pneumonia. In August she had large, raw, painful-looking ulcers in the back of her throat. These were treated with Prednisone, which caused her face to swell. At the beginning of October, Dr. Bennett began giving her Norvir, a protease inhibitor. Though Norvir had not been licensed for children, it had proved very successful with adults and Angelina had not responded to other HIV medications. By the end of October she seemed no better, continuing to have frequent fevers and now complaining of stomach pains. By December not only was her physical health poor, but the molluscum lesions were returning, she had frequent tantrums, and she suffered from insomnia. When she saw Dr. Bennett in mid-December, he had our hospital social worker initiate plans for Angelina to receive hospice care.

Near the end of December, Angelina became psychotic. "Just before Christmas," says Mrs. Carver, "she got suicidal and said she was hearing voices. It started with her telling us how she was going to kill the family, especially my daughter Julie, and then telling me the details of what the voices were telling her, how to stab Julie in the heart and then kill herself with the same knife." The Carvers were terrified and once more had Angelina brought by ambulance to their local hospital's emergency room, the same place to which the Blossers had brought her. She was admitted to the psychiatric ward, where she reported that she had indeed been having thoughts about stabbing her foster sister in the heart, but that *her* heart told her not to do this. She was discharged after a week's stay. Only a few days later she was admitted again when, after more talk of suicide, she actually ran into the kitchen, claiming she was going to find a knife and stab herself.

Reports vary on what happened during these hospitalizations. Personnel at the hospital claim that Angelina talked about her illness and her impending death and sought reassurance about the idea of heaven. But Mrs. Carver blames the hospital psychiatrist for telling Angelina that she was going to die soon. Angelina herself, during a later clinic visit, confided, "The doctor there told me I would die while I was young," adding that she was "very scared." The second of these two hospitalizations lasted only three days. Angelina was pathetically eager to return to the Carvers. They agreed to take her back, understanding that the goal was for her to "die at home" and that her death could be imminent, an understanding that psychiatric personnel apparently encouraged. She was sent home, her HIV medications supplemented with Risperdal (an antipsychotic drug) and Prozac and with a plan for psychiatric counseling on a weekly basis.

We will never know what actually transpired in those conversations between Angelina and the hospital psychiatrist. Her medical records do show, however, that the formal request for hospice care was entered on December 18, shortly before her psychosis began. Perhaps there is a link between her understanding of hospice care and her violent threats and actions. Were her condition and the nature of this care explained to her? Were communications between Dr. Bennett and Angelina's psychiatrist adequate? It seems possible that Angelina's Christmas psychosis was a combination of several factors, including confusion about hospice, her fear that she would die, jealousy of her healthy foster sister, and the memory of her mother's terrible death two years earlier. Somehow, somewhere, communication among the many individuals involved in this child's life seems to have failed.

I asked Dr. Bennett whether he remembered any conversations with Angelina about hospice or about the likelihood that she would die. He does not remember talking with her in this way and thinks it unlikely that he would have initiated such a discussion for the simple reason that even though he arranged for hospice care, he did not believe she was dying. He talks about dying with children who are very near death, even, as he remarked, "helping them put their affairs in order." But Angelina was not dying. Her diagnosis at the time was "advanced HIV disease": The virus was not responding to HIV medications; she had had several major infections secondary to HIV; her T cell count was near zero. For most children in such a condition, death is likely, perhaps within six months. But Dr. Bennett never "predicts" death, in the sense that a patient might be given six weeks or six months to live, because, he claims, "we just don't know."

It soon became clear to her foster family that Angelina was not in any imminent danger of dying. Indeed, with the exception of painful mouth ulcers and despite her having a T cell count of two, her health began to improve. Nevertheless, Dr. Bennett does not think his decision in December to initiate hospice care was wrong. Given her condition at the time, death seemed probable. Angelina's condition had continued to deteriorate, and Dr. Bennett believed her chances of remaining at home during her last days, something he considers very important, would be much greater if hospice were involved. He also thinks Angelina's recovery might have had something to do with her response to the drug Norvir, which she began taking in November. Without protease inhibitors, at this time the new "wonder drug" in HIV therapy, many children like Angelina who are alive and thriving today would be dead from AIDS-related infections.

Angelina's health over the next few months continued to improve. Her viral load decreased, and in April she had the recent molluscum lesions removed. She wrote to Mrs. Blosser about her upcoming surgery: "Dear Grandma. I'm getting the bumps off my face. I'm happy about it, but not happy. I'm happy because I don't have to be teased all the time. I'm not happy because they are on my face. And I think I'm not so happy about it because I'm afraid it's going to hurt bad. But I am brave and I can do it." The surgery was again successful and not overly painful.

The court permitted monthly supervised visits with her older brothers while Angelina was staying with the Carvers; these were to take place at the office of Children and Youth Services. Only twice did any such visits materialize. Instead various members of the Morales family would, without notice, show up at the Carvers' front door wanting to see Angelina. The Carvers refused to allow these unplanned visits. In April, to Angelina's delight, her older sister returned from Puerto Rico. She was permitted to visit Angelina at the Carvers'. But the relationship between the two girls had its sinister side. According to Mrs. Carver, the sister when visiting "would bring a pocket knife and they'd play with it. They'd pretend they were jabbing each other."

Angelina's relationship with her foster family continued to sour. Though Mrs. Carver reported that they never received the respite care that had been promised, they chose to decrease and then terminate Angelina's visits with the Blossers and with Teresa. Perhaps they thought this might help her feel more a part of their own family. After Angelina's last hospitalization they had been promised counseling sessions at the house twice a week. But this was family counseling, and though helpful for the family, it does not seem to have been directed toward enabling Angelina to confront and deal with her psychological problems.

Angelina's misbehavior became more pronounced, and her tantrums continued. Mrs. Carver tried to discipline her in the way the counselor suggested—by sending her to her room for a specified length of time—but this never worked for very long. Angelina at the time had severe insomnia. She prowled the hallways at night. She saw menacing shadows. She claimed that on several occasions she saw and spoke with her mother. When Angelina was able to sleep, she would wake up screaming from nightmares about people coming back from the dead. These experiences may have had something to do with beliefs and practices in her biological family—"a mix of Christianity and Voodoo," according to Mrs. Carver, "animal sacrifice and all that stuff. The family is Catholic, but they believe that the dead will hurt you and come back and get you. . . . Angelina would be afraid to go to bed at night. She told me once that in Puerto Rico there's this lady who can tell you when you're going to die and how you're going to die . . . and when she tells you you're going to die, you die!"

When we saw Angelina at the clinic, she rarely volunteered information about her feelings. One time Mrs. Carver encouraged Angelina to talk to Dr. Bennett about her nightmares. She did, reporting that on several occasions, when she was in her bedroom alone, her mother appeared to her. Dr. Bennett asked her how she felt about this. When she confessed to being scared, he told her to remember that her mother loved her and that in essence what she was seeing wasn't real: "Angelina, sometimes we can see things that aren't really there. You're seeing her through your memory, like a picture in your brain. You may be seeing your mom, but she's not really there. I know that sounds strange, but it's true. You need to tell Dr. Hartman [the psychiatrist] about this the next time you see him."

It may be, on the one hand, that the Carvers' relationship with Angelina deteriorated because they had expected her to die soon, only to find, on the contrary, that her health improved. On the other hand, it may be that they kept her as long as they could, until in the end her rages were too much for them. When I spoke with Mrs. Carver about Angelina, she conveyed a marked (and understandable) ambivalence about her. She clearly loved the child, and Angelina could indeed be lovable, but was frightened by her violent temper, frustrated by her misbehavior, and baffled by the alternation between her wish to stay with them and her wanting a different placement. It was particularly hurtful when Angelina, in an angry mood, told her caseworker that the Carvers were physically abusing her.

At the beginning of October, nineteen months after Angelina's arrival at their home, the Carvers gave notice to the agency that they could no longer keep her. Shortly thereafter, in the middle of the night, Mrs. Carver discovered Angelina in her eight-year-old son's bedroom, standing over him as he slept. The next day, while changing Angelina's bedsheets, she found a knife. Frightened, she called the placement agency, then Angelina's CASA,[5] asking that the child be removed immediately. At first it seemed that no family could be found to take her and that Angelina would have to be institutionalized. But authorities persevered in their search, and Mrs. Dettweiler, a wonderful foster mother known to all of us at the clinic, agreed to take her in.

October 1997–April 1998: Mrs. Dettweiler (Angelina Is Eleven Years Old)

In October 1997 Angelina arrived at her fourth foster home. Mrs. Dettweiler, who is Caucasian and has been a widow for some eight years, lived in a modest house in Springtown, a small city about the same size as Pittsford. A charismatic Christian and a nurse, she was an experienced foster mother who had cared for a number of HIV-infected children, several of whom died of the disease in her home. At this time only one foster child was living with her: Jamal, an eleven-year-old African-American child with HIV infection. Jamal had been living with Mrs. Dettweiler since he was two.

There are different stories about how Angelina came to stay with Mrs. Dettweiler. Mrs. Carver claims that she persuaded Angelina's CASA to call Mrs. Dettweiler and ask her to take the child. Mrs. Dettweiler maintains that she had agreed to provide respite care for Angelina only over the weekend. On Sunday night, instead of picking her up, the Carvers called to say that they wouldn't be able to take her back at all, that they were sorry but that they had no recourse, and that they knew Angelina would be well cared for. Soon after, the Carvers changed their phone number to an unlisted one.

---

[5] CASA stands for "court-appointed special advocate," a volunteer assigned by the judge to a particular child and given the responsibility of representing the child's needs and wishes in court. Some counties have adopted the CASA system to make sure that there is one individual with legal standing who knows the child over time. Given the frequent turnover of caseworkers in child welfare agencies—52 percent in just one year in Jackson County—CASAs serve an important function.

Mrs. Dettweiler cheerfully told us this story when she brought Angelina and Jamal in for their clinic appointments. When we asked how long Angelina would be staying with her, she replied, again cheerfully, that this placement was either "permanently temporary" or "temporarily permanent." In other words, she would be keeping Angelina indefinitely.

But Angelina was not happy during her six-month stay with Mrs. Dettweiler and Jamal. She claimed that her foster mother was "old" and "mean." She never bonded with her, as she had so easily from the very beginning with her last two foster mothers. Jamal, her new foster brother, had psychological problems of his own and was clearly jealous of Angelina. They fought frequently. One bond between them was the fact that in their own biological families both children had been exposed to Santeria and Voodoo, blends of Catholic Christianity and African animist religions that are popular in Puerto Rico, especially among the very poor and disenfranchised. Santeria and Voodoo can for some people involve witchcraft, curses, and the return of the spirits of the dead. Jamal had for some time been reporting that he heard voices telling him to kill his foster mother. He would leave objects lying around the house that he believed had magical powers to cause harm. He claimed to have placed curses on Mrs. Dettweiler as well as on others. Now that Angelina was spending so much time with Jamal, she began to talk more about visits from her mother and spoke of fears about people coming back from the dead.

There were major problems at school, and the rages had begun again. Mrs. Dettweiler, when she brought Angelina in for her clinic visit, seemed somewhat frazzled but optimistic: She claimed that she had been prepared for these tantrums and believed she could handle them. "I just showed her she wasn't in charge!" she exclaimed. Despite these problems, Angelina was doing well medically. She was gaining weight, and her viral load was low.

In April, after six months, this living arrangement broke down completely. Angelina threw one of her fits: She screamed and kicked, then ran to a window, opened it, and tried to throw herself out. Mrs. Dettweiler feared that she wouldn't be able to prevent Angelina from hurting herself and called Children and Youth Services. The agency arranged for an ambulance to take Angelina to the same psychiatric ward where she had been before. While there, she told hospital personnel that she was being abused by Mrs. Dettweiler. But Angelina had said the same thing about the Carvers the last time she was hospitalized, an accusation she had later withdrawn. Though Children and Youth realized she might not be telling the truth, they could not return her to Mrs. Dettweiler without a full-scale investigation. Mrs. Dettweiler was not willing to submit to this. "I've heard that even if you are found not guilty," she explains, "it's a very unpleasant and humiliating experience. I'm willing to take Angelina back, but only if she withdraws those accusations."

Mid-April–June 1998: *The Evanses* (*Angelina Is Eleven and a Half*)

After two weeks in the psychiatric hospital Angelina was released to her fifth foster family. This time the court explored different foster care agencies, even going out of the county in the attempt to find a family appropriate for her. The agency they chose offers more services than others: Foster parents receive more training than is required by law, the agency provides individual counseling on a weekly basis, and a caseworker sees the child for an hour two times a month (once a week at the beginning) and shares with the foster mother the task of bringing her to St. Luke's for medical appointments.

The Evanses live in Patterson Creek, a small town in eastern Ohio some two hours' distance from the clinic at St. Luke's. Mr. and Mrs. Evans are an African-American couple who are devoutly Christian. Angelina's new foster mother is a lovely woman, young-looking and somewhat shy, with a serene expression. The Evanses have a twelve-year-old daughter, and there are two older sons in their twenties who have families and homes of their own. The

Evanses have been serving as foster parents for three years. I ask Mrs. Evans why she chooses to do this, and she responds: "I'm a religious person, and these kids need care. God has blessed me so, and when he blesses us, he does this so that we can give to others. He gives us love and joy and happiness, and we are to pass these on."

When Angelina comes in for a clinic appointment in May, she tells me that she saw her family (her biological family) when she was in the hospital. It turns out that her older sister, whom she had not seen for years, was actually in the same psychiatric ward. Angelina was reunited not only with her sister but also with her two older brothers and their girlfriends and children when they came to visit. Angelina discovered there was a new baby in the family, making her an aunt. She tells me, confidently, that the Morales family will be going back to Puerto Rico and that she'll be going with them. They have bought her a plane ticket and promised to contact her when the time comes. I ask Mrs. Evans about all this, but she knows nothing. I call Angelina's caseworker and discover that the family has disappointed her, as they've done so often before. They have already returned to Puerto Rico, making no attempt to take her with them. They never tried to contact her, and they didn't even call to say good-bye.

When Mrs. Evans brings Angelina for her clinic appointment in June, all of us are struck by the change in attitude: She's resistant, recalcitrant, and even defiant. Dr. Bennett tells her in a matter-of-fact way that her dosage of Viracept needs to be increased. She responds by announcing that she DOES NOT WANT to take Viracept at all. Clearly surprised, he tells her that we all have to do things we don't always want to do and reminds her of the importance of this medication if she is to stay well. She responds by letting us know that she also DOES NOT WANT to be in a special school. We learn afterward from Mrs. Evans that it is a Christian school for adolescent girls with behavior problems. Angelina is the youngest. This school placement seems to me far from ideal. However, Mrs. Evans is affiliated with the school, and this arrangement is a compromise between a foster home and placement in a residential institution. The court is trying to avoid institutional care for Angelina.

Given Angelina's expectations of reunion with her biological family at the time she was placed with the Evanses and her disappointment when this failed to materialize, I am not surprised that this placement doesn't work out. Angelina does not want to take her medications, she does not like baths, she refuses to do as she is told, and she is rude. As Mrs. Evans puts it, "She really has an attitude!" Mrs. Evans realizes the crucial importance of Angelina's taking her medicine, and she has adopted a strategy that, while draconian, seems to work. She measures everything that Angelina needs to take and, when she resists, just tells her: "If you want to die, that's okay. Because that's what you're doing when you don't take these." Then she walks away. Eventually Angelina takes her medications.

The turning point for Mrs. Evans comes when her twelve-year-old daughter, who has been disturbed by Angelina's attitude toward her mother, announces that she has her clothes packed and wants to go live with her grandmother. She tells Mrs. Evans, "I just can't stay around Angelina anymore, with the way she disrespects you." When Mrs. Evans tells me this, I ask her whether she was warned of Angelina's problems before taking her into her home. She responds with a sigh and a smile. "Yes, I was told about her former problems, and I had read her record, but I thought, 'Maybe this time it'll be different!' "

June 1998–Ongoing: The Fanthorpes
(Angelina Is Eleven and a Half)

After a little more than a month Angelina moved during the summer to her sixth foster family. She was happy to learn that she would be attending the local public school in the fall. The Fanthorpes are African-Americans and Pentecostal Christians. Mrs. Fanthorpe is a large woman with a big smile. Mr. Fanthorpe drives a delivery truck and is very involved with the Promise Keepers, a fundamentalist Christian movement for men that endorses traditional family values. There are other children in their home: a niece the same age as Angelina, two children from Mr. Fanthorpe's first marriage, and another foster child, a girl fifteen years old. Mrs. Fanthorpe's biological children are grown and have children of their own.

When Angelina comes in for a clinic appointment with Letitia Fanthorpe (whom she calls Tisha), she seems remarkably different. There is no attitude, no contentiousness She is calm, her eyes are bright, and she seems happy and fond of both her foster parents. Of course this is still the honeymoon period for Angelina and her new family.

The Fanthorpes live simply, believing that "God will provide." They reside in one side of a two-family house in a seedy area of Webster, a city in eastern Ohio. There is litter of all kinds in the streets and graffiti written wherever graffiti can be written. Across the street is a playground, mostly asphalt. Next door to the playground is a derelict factory with broken windows. What makes the Fanthorpes' dwelling distinctive is the large sign on the glass front door, obviously made by children. At the top WARNING is inscribed, in big red letters. Beneath that, in different colors: "This house is being protected by very large angels. Welcome to the Evans, Morales, and Coates Resident [*sic*]." Underneath the sign there is a drawing of a cross surrounded by pink flowers, also obviously drawn by children.

When I visit the Fanthorpes' home, rather than talk with the foster parents, I take Angelina out to lunch. She likes Chinese food, so we drive to China Wok, a restaurant tucked into the corner of a big mall. Angelina, who has a very good sense of direction, helps me get there. We talk about how her best friend at school has the same name; about how she is learning to play the clarinet; about the Spice Girls. We do not talk about HIV. When we return to the house, I make arrangements to talk with Mrs. Fanthorpe during Angelina's next clinic visit, scheduled for October.

Angelina comes in for her medical appointment, and Dr. Bennett is delighted to find that she is healthy and seems happy. When he has completed his examination, she takes off for the Super Nintendo, and he sets off to examine another patient. Mrs. Fanthorpe tells me her story.

"Well, first of all," she says in her deep, sonorous voice, "I've had a lot of stuff that I went through in my life. I used drugs intravenously, I shared needles with people, and I had all the risk factors for HIV. I lived like this for years, and then God saved me. I had an experience with the Holy Spirit. Then I spent a lot of time praying and reading my Bible and getting to know God. I said to God, 'Whatever you want me to do, Lord, I'll do it.' And this is what he told my heart to do: to care for children. I didn't know I would get children that were HIV positive. All I knew was that my husband and I, we prayed about it, and we said, 'Okay, God, we're trusting you. Whoever you send to our house, we will take that child, we will love that child, we will nurture that child.' And that's what we've done. The first child that God sent to our house was Angelina. . . . I just believe that anything that happens is God-ordained, and I believe that everybody that comes into my life God has sent to me."

The Fanthorpes attend church every Sunday morning and Wednesday evening, and they get up every morning by five for prayers and devotions. The children participate in the last ten minutes of these morning devotions, just before they go to school. Mrs. Fanthorpe tells me: "I spend a lot of time praying and reading my Bible and getting to know God. God has done so much for me. I hear his voice—some people prefer to call it conscience, but I prefer to believe that God speaks to me directly—so I follow that voice, as long as it's not telling me to do something that is contrary to what God's word says in the Bible. . . . I have peace and joy that's so deep it's really hard to shake that, no matter what. I don't worry where money is coming from. Lots of time we don't have money to pay our bills. We do what we can, and I just tell people, 'Honey, when the Lord gives it to me, I'll give it to you. Now you have a nice day!'"

There is a knock on the door of the examining room. It's Angelina, with Dr. Bennett standing right behind her, one hand resting on her shoulder and the other holding some papers. "I can give you the results of Angelina's blood work, Mrs. Fanthorpe," he says, coming into the room. He reports that Angelina's health is excellent. Angelina lounges against the door, curious about my conversation with Letitia. I tell her that we've been talking about her, about how well she's doing, and also about religion. Angelina beams and tells all of us that she got an A on a social studies test. Mrs. Fanthorpe nods in assent. "Yes, she surely did!" she announces, emphasizing every word. Angelina looks wonderful. Her eyes are shining, as is always the case when she is happy. Her skin seems to glow. Her hair has been elaborately done up in cornbraids, a ritual that she and her foster sister perform together every week. Dr. Bennett looks at her with real affection and tells her, "Angelina, you encourage us by your staying so well. It's really good to see you today!"

THE maxim "It takes a village to raise a child" is surely true in Angelina's case. When Angelina's biological family failed her, as they did through their fear of contagion, their neglect, their broken promises, and their abandonment of her, members of the community came forward to make up for their failure. When Mrs. Morales died and Angelina and Roberto were remanded to the care of their eldest brother, it was a local organization of volunteers that found housing for the family and tried to look after the children. When this arrangement broke down and emergency placement was needed for Angelina, it was a volunteer couple from this group, the Blossers, who took her in.

If one pictures the communal "village" as a widening series of rings centering upon Angelina, the closest and most intimate circle of caregivers are foster families like the Blossers. No doubt, in retrospect, one might question the suitability of Angelina's placements or the motives of some of her foster parents. But my

overwhelming impression is that these are compassionate and dedicated individuals who have cared for Angelina in every sense.
They have offered her affection, striven to cope with her violent
outbursts, and let her go, in some instances, only when their other
children were threatened or harmed. To this day Angelina returns
periodically to visit the Blossers.

The next circle of support, less intimate than the foster family
but directly and personally involved with Angelina, consists of her
medical and psychiatric caregivers. Angelina has received expert
care at St. Luke's for her HIV disease and intercurrent infections,
and her relationship with Dr. Bennett seems exemplary. Indeed he
and the clinic remain almost the only constants in her life. On the
other hand, Angelina's psychiatric treatment leaves much to be de-
sired. She receives pharmacological therapy as well as counseling,
but these two therapeutic interventions are performed by different
people. Moreover, there is no continuity even within each type of
therapy, since her psychiatrists and her counselors change with
each new agency brought in to oversee her care. Perhaps, if her psychiatric care had been better coordinated and there had been more
communication between Dr. Bennett and psychiatric personnel,
things might have gone better for Angelina. But competent psychiatric treatment is notoriously expensive, and the financial support
Angelina receives from the state is already high. How does one balance the extraordinary cost of psychiatric treatment against a limited state budget for child welfare?

A still wider circle is the social welfare system, in which the
closeness and intimacy of Angelina's families and doctors give way
to the larger, more complex, and more impersonal array of lower
courts and government agencies. It may be hard to think of such institutions as parts of a communal village, but of course even Angelina's foster parents are agents and representatives of this social
system, which trains, accredits, compensates, and supervises them.
Moreover, the support Angelina receives from this larger system
has not been faceless or remote: Teresa Diaz, Angelina's caseworker, has also become her friend. The welfare system may have

faltered in allowing six different foster placements in two and a half years, but this same system has persevered in trying to find ways to meet her needs.

As a ward of the state, Angelina's welfare is overseen by Judge Marks, who represents the Jackson County Family Court. This same judge sits on the bench each time Angelina comes in for a hearing, which happens twice a year. Others with legal responsibility for her are an attorney, her CASA (court-appointed special advocate), a caseworker from Children and Youth Services, and another caseworker from the placement agency. The agency caseworker is directly responsible for setting up and monitoring other services as needed. In Angelina's case these services include regular visits to the HIV clinic at St. Luke's, medications, weekly psychiatric counseling, and participation in a local program for HIV-infected children.

The financial support required to meet the needs of a child like Angelina is substantial. In her case the cost to the state has risen as her needs have become greater and as it has become more difficult to place her. Angelina's foster parents now receive around eighteen hundred dollars a month for her care. The agency placing her receives an additional fee for the services it provides, which in her case are extensive. But it is economically prudent as well as in Angelina's best interest to pay whatever is necessary to keep her in foster care. The next step up is institutionalization, and should this become necessary, the cost triples.

The process of placement involves difficult decisions. When the plight of a child like Angelina is brought to the attention of Children and Youth Services, the first recourse is to arrange for supportive services that will enable the child to stay with the parents. If placement seems necessary, the court will look first for another family member. A foster home is very much a third choice, and even when a child is placed in foster care, the court tries to maintain visits between the child and family members. For Angelina, these interactions seem to have been devastating. Nevertheless, contact with her brother Roberto has recently been resumed, though he is now institutionalized for uncontrollable and violent behavior.

The reasons that the system prefers the biological family turn on financial, legal, and philosophical considerations. Financially it costs much less to provide services that enable a family to keep a child than to place that child in foster care. Legally the court is extremely reluctant to override parental rights if the parents want to keep the child. Philosophically the state favors keeping a child with his or her biological family unless removal is absolutely necessary. I have asked attorneys, judges, and caseworkers involved with the welfare system about the reasoning behind this policy. Judge Marks believes that "there is a bond, usually of some level, in the family. If you start taking actions whereby you're severing that bond, it takes a toll on the family, on the child, and on all other people involved. I think the family is a viable unit that should be preserved if at all possible." The alternative, she concludes ominously, is "casting [the child] into the foster care stream, and God knows where that's going to lead."

But several caseworkers have told me that they think the welfare system goes too far in preserving the biological family and in protecting parents' visitation rights, often to the extent of irrevocably harming the child. One caseworker says, "I guess the biggest frustration in the work I do surrounds issues of termination of parental rights. There are a lot of people in this world who do not deserve children, who have abused them horribly, but then we go on and send these kids back to them. These parents may have rights, but they have no right to abuse a child. These decisions about whether or not to send kids back to their parents can be really hard, I know, but I see what happens when they're sent back and they shouldn't have been. Sometimes the laws are more restrictive for animals than for children." The emotional toll on child welfare caseworkers is considerable, as is reflected by a turnover rate of 52 percent in Jackson County in a single year.

At the center of this sizable array of foster parents, doctors, psychiatrists, counselors, caseworkers, and judges who have sought to help her is Angelina, who remains an enigmatic figure, troubled and troubling. On the one hand, we have the whole intricate medical, legal, and social system designed to care for children like Angelina. On the other hand, there is the child herself, who repeatedly baffles the system's best-intended efforts. While there may have been flaws and lapses in coordinating those efforts, it would be hard to fault either the professionalism or the concern of the individuals and agencies involved. This is not a story of gross mistakes or shocking omissions.

The deepest problem in Angelina's case history may not be the changes in her medical condition but the alternating cycles of her behavior. The pattern of iteration in Angelina's placement is reflected in compulsive acting out. To quote Mrs. Blosser, there seem to be two Angelinas. One is a shy, winsome, almost angelic child, and the other is a child who seems almost demonically possessed by her ungovernable fury, who wreaks havoc on everything and everyone around her, whose fantasies are violent and suicidal. And there may be a third Angelina between these two extremes: the unsleeping child who cries out in the night, haunted by voices from the dead and the visitations of her mother.

The causes of this turbulence and division remain hidden and inscrutable. Are they rooted in nurture or in nature? Is Angelina's compulsive misbehavior a response to early and continued trauma: her mother's painful death, her dysfunctional biological family and their repeated abandonment of her, the cruel stigma of her disease, and the constant shifting from one foster family to the next? These external factors may explain a greal deal. But Angelina's older sister was also fascinated by knives and confined in the same psychiatric ward, and her brother Roberto has exhibited similar outbursts and threats of violence. Perhaps there is a genetic factor too, something internal and inherited of which Angelina is as much the victim as she is of her disease. I do not pretend to know the answer to these questions, but the fascination, and the importance, of Angelina's story are that it compels us to ask them.

It is difficult to predict what the future will hold for Angelina. Besides having an illness that is not only terminal but socially stigma-tizing, she has serious psychological and behavioral problems and a track record with foster placements that is far from encouraging. From another perspective, she is doing well medically, she is cur-rently placed with what seems a superb foster family, and the sys-tem is fully engaged in trying to help her.

Whatever her problems, Angelina is capable of eliciting love from those involved with her. I have felt this myself, and others with whom I've talked have repeatedly testified to their affection for her. All along the way she has encountered people like Teresa Diaz or the Blossers who really care for her, taking her into their homes or going out of their way to spend time with her and show her kind-ness. Angelina also has always demonstrated the capacity to give as well as to receive love. It is this, I believe, that has caused her such pain, but it has also kept her emotionally alive. She is a remarkably resilient little girl, both physically and emotionally. Her heart re-mains open. Though intensely vulnerable to being hurt by others, she remains capable of welcoming and responding to their love.

SIMPLE GIFTS

Carlos And His Caregivers

Carlos Mendez is an eleven-year-old Hispanic boy who has been coming to the clinic at St. Luke's since he was five years old, when he moved with two older brothers to Springtown to live with his grandmother and uncle. The man presumed to be his father, who is not infected, lives in Chicago. His mother died when he was six from AIDS-related pneumonia. Soon after, Carlos became quite ill with chronic pneumonia, persistent ear infections, and severe gastroenteritis. His grandmother seemed unable to give him medications regularly or take him to the doctor. Increasingly, a community HIV service group called Loaves and Fishes began providing his care.

Carlos's health continued to decline over the next year and a half. When seven and a half, he spent two weeks in the hospital on ventilator support. His T cell count was ten. A few months before Carlos's eighth birthday Dr. Bennett put him on morphine and called in hospice support. But Carlos rallied. He gained weight. When protease inhibitors became available, he responded beautifully. By the time he was nine, his main problems were morphine addiction, returning to school (he had missed nearly two years), and his family's inability to regulate either his morphine or his HIV medications.

Carlos is an engaging child who is very responsive to affection and affectionate in return. He likes the things most eleven-year-old boys like—Nintendo and PlayStation games and action figures—and *makes friends easily. He is back in school and off morphine, though problems regulating his HIV medications continue.*

.   .   .

Clinic Visit, May 1997

"HELLO, Carlos. How are you today?" asks Dr. Bennett as he enters the room.

Carlos doesn't answer. He is sitting on the examination table, bent way over, his head down. This is not the first time he has been unresponsive during a clinic visit. But there are also times, when he's feeling good, that Carlos is quite talkative, even garrulous.

Isabel, a young woman from an AIDS service group called Loaves and Fishes (L&F), has brought him to his appointment today. She's sitting in the chair next to the examining table. "He's feeling pretty bad," she says. "He hasn't been getting his morphine. When I picked him up this morning, and his grandmother and I put together all his medications to bring in, we couldn't find the morphine. It's supposed to be refrigerated, isn't it?"

"Yes, but it's disappeared before. What happened to those fentanyl patches[1] I prescribed?" Dr. Bennett asks her. "I did that to avoid situations like this."

"Well, he's got one on now," Isabel replies as she gets up and walks over to where Carlos is sitting. "But it looks to me like it hasn't been changed for a while.

"Hey, Carlos," she tells him, "sit up just a little. I want to show Dr. Bennett your patch." Carlos straightens up as Isabel lifts his shirt to reveal a badly crumpled and dirty patch, about two square inches, attached to his chest on the left side.

"That's not going to do him much good," observes Dr. Bennett, shaking his head. He then turns to Carlos, speaking slowly. "Carlos,

---

[1] Fentanyl is a morphine-like drug available in a transdermal patch. It is used for the treatment of chronic pain over time.

you've got to change these every two or three days for them to work. The reason you're feeling bad now is that you're not getting the medication that comes from this patch. And if you don't get that, you're going to start hurting."

Carlos looks up briefly, then looks back down. He is a round-faced little boy with a big dimple on his cheek and sad eyes. Today his eyes seem glazed.

"Isabel, I'm really frustrated. I don't know what more to do to get his grandmother to give him his medications. Is there any way you or Bill can help with this?" Bill Henderson is Isabel's father. He and his wife started L&F some years ago. The staff is still composed of the Henderson family, though the number of their clients has grown considerably over the years. I've known Bill and Isabel ever since I started attending Dr. Bennett's HIV clinic, because they often provide transportation from Springtown to St. Luke's for our young patients. But they do much more than that. Their mission is to serve the needs of these families, whatever those needs may be.

This time, however, Isabel seems stymied. "I don't know what more we can do either," she replies. "They always wait to call me until a medication he needs is completely gone. Then they call and tell me I have to do something about it right away. 'Pronto! Pronto!' I wish they'd call when they still have two or three doses left, and I've told them this, but it just doesn't get through."

"Who changes his morphine patch?" I ask.

"Well," answers Isabel, "it's supposed to be either his grandmother or else his uncle, that's Ramon. But usually Carlos does it himself."

"It's the same with all his medications," observes Dr. Bennett, turning toward me. "We've tried everything. We made charts, we made boxes, we did things in Spanish, we made trays; we just did everything we could think of. But basically he's self-medicating." He pauses, then speaks to Isabel. "What I'm going to do right now is to ask Rachel if she can find some morphine to make him feel better. And I'll write another prescription for fentanyl patches. Isabel, can you get these filled on your way home?"

"Sure," she says. "No problem."

"Carlos, let's go through your medications," says Dr. Bennett as Isabel hands him a large paper bag. "How about this one?" he asks, holding up one of the bottles. "This is Zerit. When do you take it?"

"I take one of those at breakfast and one at dinner," says Carlos.

"Okay. Now how about this one," he asks, holding up another pill bottle. "Do you know what this one is called?"

Carlos shakes his head.

"This is Bactrim. How often do you take it?"

Carlos shrugs.

"You take Bactrim once in the morning and once in the evening, but only three times a week. All the others you take every day. This medication, though, you take three times a week—like, say, Monday, Wednesday, and Friday. Then there's Rifampin and Biaxin." He holds up two more bottles. "You should be taking one of each of these in the morning and another in the evening. Is that what you're doing?"

"I think so," says Carlos.

Dr. Bennett picks up another bottle. "Fluconazole," he announces. "He was supposed to stop this last month. Carlos, are you still taking these pills?"

Carlos nods.

"You don't have to take them anymore. They were for the thrush you had in your mouth—those white patches, remember? But you don't have thrush anymore, so you don't need to take these."

The bag is now empty, and there is a row of bottles lined up on the table. Dr. Bennett pauses, then asks Isabel, "Where's the Norvir?"

She looks through the bottles of pills and shakes her head: "I took all these off the shelf where they keep his meds. I did look in the refrigerator for his Roxanol [morphine], but I didn't think to look there for the Norvir. Was it supposed to be refrigerated?"

"No. It should have been with the rest of his medications. Carlos, do you remember taking any other drug besides these?" Dr. Bennett points to the bottles of pills on the table.

Carlos shakes his head.

"Last time you were here I prescribed a new drug for you. You were supposed to take it three times a day. Do you remember doing that?"

Carlos looks up at him. "I don't think so," he says hesitantly.

"Hmm," says Dr. Bennett, turning back to Isabel. "Well, I don't know what's happened. Maybe they forgot it. They shouldn't have run out; maybe they didn't even fill the prescription. Norvir is a protease inhibitor, and it's really, really important that he take it and that he take it regularly. Isabel," he says, "we need to get Mrs. Alejandrez in here. Do you think you could persuade her to come next time?" Mrs. Alejandrez is Carlos's grandmother. She comes only rarely to his clinic appointments. "I think she's more reliable than his uncle. We'll get a translator, and I'll explain to her again how important it is that he get his medications."

"I'll try, anyway," says Isabel.

Carlos is still sitting in the same position on the table. Dr. Bennett leans over, his elbows resting on the table, so he can be closer to him. He speaks very softly. "Carlos, I'm sorry you're feeling so bad. You've just got to get your medications. It's so important. It will make a difference to how you feel. I can promise you that."

Dr. Bennett then reaches for the otoscope. I know he'll want to examine Carlos's ears because he came in last time with a bad middle ear infection. I know he'll also want to look in his mouth. Carlos has some badly decayed teeth and needs to be seen by a dentist, but there have been difficulties finding someone in Springdale who will treat children on Medical Assistance. I leave the room to find Rachel and deliver Dr. Bennett's message about getting morphine for Carlos. The same problem has come up before, so Rachel will not be surprised at this request.

Carlos and His Grandmother

Carlos is the youngest of four children born to the same mother, Elena, each by a different father. Mrs. Alejandrez, his grandmother

and legal guardian, believes that Elena acquired HIV from her husband, but she also admits that Elena used drugs. Understandably
Mrs. Alejandrez does not want to see her daughter as directly responsible for her HIV infection. "It was her friends that ruined
her," she says.

Elena did not tell her family that she and Carlos were infected
with HIV until she became very sick. When she could no longer
care for her children, she sent three of them, including four-year-
old Carlos, to Springtown to live with their aunt. This aunt also had
HIV, as did one of her own three children. Mrs. Alejandrez often
found herself caring for all six grandchildren.

Carlos was first taken to the HIV clinic at St. Luke's when he had
just turned five. Though diagnosed at birth, he had never received
HIV medications. Dr. Bennett prescribed AZT and Bactrim. For
several months Carlos was brought to his medical appointments
regularly. But then for a long time, nearly a year, either his appointments were canceled or he did not show up. When he finally
did return, Pastor Bill Henderson, who drove him to the clinic, told
us that there had been several deaths in the family from complications related to AIDS: an uncle, an aunt, and Carlos's own mother.

At that point L&F was already very involved in caring for the
needs of the Alejandrez family, and Bill drove to Cleveland to visit
Elena close to the time of her death. "What a story!" he remarked
when he told me what happened. He found Elena in a shabby,
overheated hospital room. She was emaciated, in pain, suffering
uncontrollable diarrhea, and having difficulty breathing because of
pneumonia. Shocked by the deplorable conditions of the hospital—the indifference of the nursing staff, the absence of pain medications, urine-soaked bed linen, bloodstains on the floor, and
cockroaches everywhere—he arranged for her to be transferred to
another institution that would provide hospice care. Perhaps more
important than this promise of better care was the comfort of his as-
surance that her sons were well cared for. The very next day, before
the transfer could take place, Elena died.

Carlos and his brother Alonzo moved in with their grandmother and an uncle after their mother died. This was a hard time for Mrs. Alejandrez, who was devastated by the deaths of so many in her family. She placed, one by one, the cardboard boxes holding the cremated remains of her daughters and her son on the top shelf of her china closet. Maybe she just wanted to keep her children with her a little longer. Or maybe she was waiting for the others who had HIV to die, so she could bury all of them together. There were now only two members of the family with HIV still alive: Carlos and a younger cousin named Tony. Of these two grandchildren, Tony was hospitalized with end stage AIDS, hooked up to tubes and in a great deal of pain. It seemed to her only a matter of time before Carlos too would sicken and then die. Indeed, when he returned to the clinic, Dr. Bennett found that his health had deteriorated remarkably since his last appointment, ten months ago. Perhaps this was the result of his not receiving HIV medications, or perhaps it had something to do with the trauma of so many deaths. His T cell count had dropped from 312 to 42. He seemed plagued with chronic ear infections, stomach pains, and a cough that was soon to develop into pneumonia.

Dr. Bennett had told me that Mrs. Alejandrez was "emotionally unable to participate in Carlos's care." I discovered this to be true. She found it extremely difficult to come to his clinic appointments because it reminded her that Carlos has the same disease that killed her children. For the same reason, she could not seem to remember to give him his medications. So it was his uncle who frequently accompanied Carlos on clinic visits, but the staff soon learned that he was no better than the grandmother at making sure Carlos took his medications. Though Ramon was pleasant, cooperative, and well-meaning, he had a severe learning disability that made it hard for him to oversee Carlos's demanding medical regimen.

Carlos came regularly to see Dr. Bennett thanks to Bill and Isabel, who drove him to clinic appointments. But getting him to take his HIV medications proved a nearly insurmountable problem for everyone. Dr. Bennett and his nurse pleaded, threatened, flattered, and cajoled Mrs. Alejandrez—usually through Bill or Isabel.

She was given special pill dispensers with pockets for appropriate pills at the appropriate times. A chart of Carlos's medication schedule was made up in Spanish. Several times Dr. Bennett warned that he would report her to Children and Youth Services. Once he refused to sign disability papers until Mrs. Alejandrez herself came in with Carlos, so that he could talk with her about the problem. Whenever she did appear at the clinic, Dr. Bennett emphasized with the help of an interpreter how important it was that Carlos take his medications. She would smile and nod. But nothing changed.

About a year and a half after the death of Carlos's mother, a memorial service was held at an Episcopal church near Mrs. Alejandrez's home for her three adult children, including Carlos's mother, and a grandchild. Carlos's younger cousin Tony had recently died of medical problems secondary to AIDS. Though Mrs. Alejandrez herself attended a Spanish-speaking evangelical church, this particular Episcopal parish had been very involved with the AIDS community. The whole extended Alejandrez family—some twenty-five of them—were there. It was mid-November, and it was cold. First there was a service in the church, then the burial of the ashes outside in the church's memorial garden. A square hole had been dug in the ground, and one by one each person came up, took some of the ashes in their hands, and placed them in the grave. Carlos and his two brothers each took his turn in burying Elena's ashes. Their three cousins did the same with the ashes of their mother. For the older children this ceremony seems to have been helpful, but seven-year-old Carlos only partly understood what was going on. When the service was over, his older siblings and cousins said good-bye to their mothers and held and comforted each other; Carlos, however, could focus only on going out for pizza.

The memorial service seemed to mark another turn for the worse in Carlos's condition. Over the previous year his T cell count had continued to drop. He had lost a great deal of weight, partly because of huge ulcers in his mouth and throat that prevented him from eating, and he suffered from frequent high fevers. He came to the memorial service with a florid rash that had just been confirmed as caused by parvovirus. An uncle from New York who had come to Springtown for the service thought that the care Carlos was receiving at St. Luke's was not sufficiently aggressive and had him admitted to a big city hospital several hours away. Carlos was left there in a hospital bed, hooked up to a feeding tube and a morphine drip. His family did not visit; perhaps they lacked transportation. He was lonely and unhappy and after three days persuaded his family to take him home. They brought him back to St. Luke's and asked Dr. Bennett to remove the tubes and let happen whatever would come to pass. Dr. Bennett complied, prescribing a liquid morphine solution for his pain. Carlos was very thin, his skin was yellow, his cheeks were sunken, and his eyes shiny. He cried much of the time. Expecting Carlos to die, Dr. Bennett arranged for hospice care.

But Carlos hung on. The morphine saved his life, Dr. Bennett believes, because it permitted him to eat. And once he could eat, his condition slowly began to improve. But the pain continued, so Carlos remained on morphine long enough to become addicted. An even greater problem than his addiction was his family's inability to regulate the drug. It seemed to disappear faster than it should. Perhaps someone else was getting it. Or perhaps Carlos, who often gave himself his morphine, was taking too much. Indeed this seems likely. When the medicine dropper he was given to measure the drug disappeared—and this happened repeatedly—he would just use a kitchen spoon—sometimes a teaspoon, sometimes a tablespoon. Mrs. Alejandrez realized the need for more morphine only when Carlos was in pain and the bottle of Roxanol was empty. Then she would call Bill or Isabel and beg them to get more, somehow, often in the middle of the night. This continued for months.

To make sure Carlos was getting the pain medication he needed, Dr. Bennett prescribed Duragesic (fentanyl) patches. He gave Carlos as well as Mrs. Alejandrez written instructions—in Spanish and English—on how to use them. But Carlos would forget to change

his patches at the right time or would put them on the wrong way.
They would get lost or run out. Again, Isabel would receive frantic
phone calls from Mrs. Alejandrez asking for help in relieving his
pain. She could always hear Carlos crying miserably in the background.

School was another problem. Carlos had been open about his
HIV status, even using it to manipulate adults and other children
to get what he wanted. When he didn't feel like participating in
some classroom activity, he would complain to his teacher that he
felt tired and ask to go to the nurse's office, where he would sleep.
His habit of staying up until 1:00 or 2:00 A.M. watching television
made this a frequent strategy. He complained frequently of being in
terrible pain, though at least in school he was receiving the analgesics he needed. If he misbehaved and the teacher tried to discipline him, he would break into tears, saying that nothing mattered
because he would be dying soon anyway. Carlos was very good at
this, and on several occasions the teacher herself was reduced to
tears.

School administrators were uneasy about the presence of a student with HIV—especially one so vocal about his "having AIDS."
Isabel said to me, "The administrators were afraid there would be
this panic throughout the school because of a child with AIDS. Of
course Carlos is probably not the only one in that school with the
virus. My dad and I offered to come in and do AIDS education for
the school staff. But the principal said, 'His teacher just can't deal
with it. She gets too upset. And what if Carlos dies in her classroom?' I said to the principal, 'Well, big deal! She gets upset! She's
an adult, and this child has a right to be in school.' I found a lot of
unwillingness from the school to work with the situation."

Carlos was frequently absent since neither his grandmother nor
his uncle made him go to school if he didn't want to. When he did
attend, he was often tired or complained of aches and pains. School
officials suggested that he drop out of school, promising that he
would receive instruction at home. Isabel set up a meeting where
she, her father, and Mrs. Alejandrez (with the help of an inter-

preter) could discuss the issue. Two days before this meeting was to take place, a school official showed up at the Alejandrez home with papers granting permission for Carlos to be removed from the school. Mrs. Alejandrez was asked to sign them. She did not know what she was signing since the document was in English, a language she can neither read nor speak. The promised home instruction turned out to consist of one hour a week, between 6:00 and 7:00 P.M.

When Isabel found out about the document, and when she realized how the school was "fulfilling" the promise of homebound instruction, she contacted people at the state's AIDS Legal Services. They agreed to help, but Mrs. Alejandrez would not cooperate. Along with her unwillingness to face Carlos's HIV status, she believed — rightly, it seems — that the school didn't like having her grandson around. She would say to Isabel, crying, "Why would I want to send him to a place where they don't want him?" So Carlos stayed home watching television, or he called Isabel on the phone to chat or went over to her office to visit.

After Carlos had been on morphine for a year and his overall medical condition had improved, Dr. Bennett thought it was time to wean him from the drug. At first he tried to reduce the dosage, writing a prescription for 25 µg. rather than the 50 µg. Carlos had been getting. Isabel filled the prescription, then came to the house every three or four days to replace the patch. For several weeks all went well. Then one afternoon she found him with a 50 µg. patch on his back. Carlos told her that his grandmother put it on that morning and had put one on yesterday morning too. Isabel was discouraged.

Tapering off the drug was not working, so Carlos had to be weaned the hard way, "cold turkey." Isabel helped Carlos and his grandmother through this terrible process. "I spent quite a bit of time over there," she told me, "putting him in sitz baths, rubbing his legs, making heat wraps for them, and instructing Grandma on how to do all those things. I was angry because he had to go through all this because of the family's lack of supervision. I'd dealt with adult addicts, but never a child. He didn't understand what was happening; he was just in a lot of pain and didn't understand why. When I told him he wasn't going to have the morphine anymore, he cried for about a week, and he was so mad he wouldn't talk to me. But we worked through the situation together. It was hard. He'd call me on the phone screaming at the top of his lungs because he was in such pain. There was nothing I could do but go over there and hold him. He'd be crying, 'Why is this happening to me? Make it go away!' But there was nothing I could do. That was one of the hardest things I've ever had to do in my work with AIDS ministry."

Once past the awful experience of breaking his addiction, Carlos was able to go back to school. Isabel arranged for him to reenter after the Christmas holidays. This time, to avoid the problems caused when he used his disease status to manipulate teachers and schoolmates, she told him not to talk about having HIV, emphasizing that "it's private." This was difficult for her to do since she had always tried to make Carlos feel there was nothing wrong with having HIV. Dr. Bennett understood all this and, during a clinic visit just before Carlos was to start school, reinforced her advice. "I don't have problems with knowing you have HIV," he told Carlos. "Isabel doesn't have problems with it. And neither do Dr. Hawkins or Rachel or Ramona [the clinic nurse and the social worker]. But some people do. It's best not to talk about your having HIV. What Isabel has told you is right. It's private. You're doing well now. You look good; you've gained weight; you feel good; you're doing fine. You don't have to talk about it."

Carlos is now eleven and is thriving, though he occasionally has ear infections. With combination therapy, his T cell count has risen dramatically and his viral load is nearly undetectable. He is doing well in school, and he has friends. However, the difficulty in getting his grandmother or uncle to give him his medications persists. Dr. Bennett has at least partially solved this problem by having Carlos take some of his medications while at school. There has been discussion about whether Carlos would do better in foster care, where he would be properly medicated. But so far, given the help that L&F can provide, Dr. Bennett has been reluctant to suggest that Carlos be removed from his biological family.

Unlike some of the children in our clinic, Carlos has not sealed off his memories of those in his family who have died of AIDS. He tells me that he still thinks a lot about relatives who have died and is "sometimes very sad about this," especially at night when he can't get to sleep. I ask if he remembers his mother. He does, though he was only six years old when she died. "My momma was very pretty, and she had a dimple here [he points at his cheek], just like mine." His last memory of her is in a stuffy hospital room with all the windows closed. "She died of AIDS. She got it from sex and smoking a lot. She was havin' a lotta pain. She said she loved me, and she said to tell my dad to take care of me and Alonzo. And that was the last time I saw my mother."

Carlos is very open about memories of his family. But he no longer dwells on his own disease status. His having HIV is just a part of who he is. He is not particularly interested in knowing more about HIV; rather, he just wants to be as "normal" as possible. As his grandmother said to me, "He knows he has the virus, but he doesn't know what it means to have it. He's a little boy, and he just doesn't think about the virus."

Mrs. Alejandrez has recovered somewhat from her grief. She still avoids coming with Carlos to clinic appointments. But when she does come, she converses easily with Dr. Bennett and no longer dissolves into tears. During one of these visits (with Ramona translating), I explained my project to her and asked her to participate. She indicated that she would be happy do so, nodding to me in her dignified way as she emphasized that she wanted to do whatever she could "to help with this terrible virus."

So a few months later Ramona and I drove to Springtown to talk with Mrs. Alejandrez at her home. We found her reclining on a sofa in the sparsely furnished living room of a second-floor apartment. Despite our protests she sat up, wrapping a shawl around her shoulders even though it was a warm day. Below her long dress I could see that her feet and legs were swollen. She explained that she is tired much of the time and that her diabetes is "bothering" her legs and feet. Along with diabetes, Mrs. Alejandrez has severe arthritis and a heart condition. I was struck this time, as on previous occasions, by how sweet she looks—and how tired. A tiny, wizened, fragile-looking woman with light gray hair done up in a bun, she has always appeared much older than her sixty-four years.

Mrs. Alejandrez and I shook hands and exchanged greetings; she seemed pleased that I could do this in Spanish, though I explained apologetically that *Buenas dias, señora* was just about the limit of my Spanish. I conveyed to her the best wishes of Mrs. Blosser, a grandmother herself who had known the family through her work as an AIDS hospice nurse.[2] Mrs. Alejandrez remembered her well and asked me to send her love in return. Ramona then introduced the interview by explaining that I wanted to know more about Mrs. Alejandrez herself, about the family, and about Carlos.

She began by telling us she had given birth to fourteen children in Puerto Rico. When Ramona expressed her surprise, Mrs. Alejandrez responded, laughing, "You see, in Puerto Rico there isn't any television. So you just hang around, and you keep your eyes

---

[2] The relationship between these two women, both grandmothers who served as caregivers for children with HIV, seems to me very special. Though they have not seen each other for several years, it is clear that they remember each other with fondness. Mrs. Blosser became especially close to Mrs. Alejandrez during those painful days when so many in the family seemed to be dying of AIDS. She nursed one of the Alejandrez adult children during her last days and was holding Mrs. Alejandrez's seven-year-old grandson in her arms when he died. During this difficult time a wonderful relationship sprang up between these two grandmothers, though neither could speak the other's language. They communicated through hand gestures, hugs, facial expressions, and fragments of conversation. Mrs. Blosser remarks, "I'd say things to her like 'I'll be thinking of you and keeping you in my prayers,' and she'd nod. I'd say to her, 'You must really miss Helena [her daughter]. Are you still very sad?' And she'd say, nodding, '*Poco, a poco.*' We could understand each other because it was at an emotional level. When feelings go beyond what words can say, there's a connection. I think I have a grandmother's heart like she does, and that's why we could communicate." (Mrs. Blosser was Angelina Morales's foster grandmother. She and her husband are described more fully in chapter 3.)

closed, and that's how you get so many children!" She went on to tell us that she has lived in this country for twenty years and that her husband died nine years ago. She talked about her children who died of AIDS in their twenties, about how hard it has been for her to raise two active young boys (Carlos and his brother), and about her own ill health. "My life has been one of a lot of suffering," she said. "I've always worked hard. I've always taken care of children. And after all that, I'm still here. I'll keep on going as long as God allows me to." She attends church regularly, praying in the morning and the evening: "The thing I pray for the most is strength, strength to be able to take care of these children. I try to do it on my own, and then, when the children don't listen, I have to ask God for help."

One of my questions concerned her understanding of HIV and its treatment. I had worried that such a question might upset her and asked Ramona to be particularly careful in phrasing it. Apparently she succeeded, and to my great relief Mrs. Alejandrez talked easily about HIV. "The medicine and the food," she said, "are the two most important things because the virus goes through the body looking for something to eat. If that animal-virus has the food and the medicine, then it leaves the rest of the body okay. So you have to keep the child well fed. Then he doesn't have to think about it." I was struck by the ease with which she blended a grandmotherly concern for a child's eating habits, her own coping strategy (not thinking too much about HIV), and a logical, if not particularly accurate, explanation of the progression and treatment of the disease.

The rest of the interview was less colorful, as Mrs. Alejandrez talked about her physical ailments, how she managed to do laundry without a washer and a dryer, and her difficulties with the landlord. She apologized for the condition of her living room, where there were boxes piled in the corners, explaining that she had to move and was trying to find another apartment. When we rose to say our good-byes, Mrs. Alejandrez once more urged me to pass on her love to Mrs. Blosser, "*mi amiga* Lucinda."

I wondered how Mrs. Alejandrez, frail as she seemed that day, would withstand the rigors of moving. I also wondered what it would mean to Carlos and Alonzo to move to a different place. These questions were answered during one of Carlos's clinic visits, several months later.

Clinic Visit, February 1999

"Now squeeze my hand, Carlos," says Dr. Bennett. Carlos, who is sitting on the examination table, looks up at him and smiles as he complies with this request. "Squeeze harder!" Dr. Bennett says. "As hard as you can!" Carlos's smile widens into a grin as he tries to do this.

"Well, you have quite a grip," Dr. Bennett comments, picking up Carlos's chart. "Carlos, did you put rocks in your pockets? You must have hidden some rocks somewhere."

Carlos grins at him and says, "No. I don't got rocks anywhere!"

Rachel laughs. "Oh, you must have gained some weight, Carlos. That's great!"

"Yes, I do believe he did," says Dr. Bennett. "Or maybe it's those rocks he's got hidden! I'll bet that's what those big baggy jeans are for, so you can hide rocks in your pockets."

Carlos laughs.

At this clinic visit Carlos is accompanied not only by "Pastor Bill" (as the children call him) but also by a strikingly good-looking Hispanic youth who seems around eighteen years old. Pastor Bill introduces him as Juan, Carlos's older brother, and tells us that Carlos is now living with Juan's family. Dr. Bennett goes over and shakes Juan's hand, and Rachel and I do so too, introducing ourselves.

"Grandma was real tired," Bill explains. "So Carlos and Alonzo went to live with Juan. She's even more tired now that she's gone through moving to another place."

"Have you visited her there?" I ask Carlos.

"Yeah. I saw her on the weekend," he answers. "There was a big rat that came running out behind the stove! I was going to hit it with a broom, but when I got closer, it was so big that I just ran outside!"

Bill laughs and shakes his head. "It's a pretty lousy neighborhood. Her landlord convinced her she had to move. We tried to tell her she didn't really have to, but she thought she did."

"How are things going, Juan, with Carlos and Alonzo living with you?" asks Dr. Bennett.

"Fine," Juan replies, shuffling his feet and leaning back in the chair. His voice is very deep and thickly accented.

"Who else is living there in your house?" asks Dr. Bennett.

"My wife and her kids, they're four and seven, and we got a kid too—a baby."

"Sounds like a full house," says Dr. Bennett, smiling.

"Yeah," Juan says, smiling too.

"Who takes care of the kids?" asks Dr. Bennett.

"Me and my wife," he replies. "She works a day shift and I work the night shift at Norris Pipe Works. So there's always somebody there."

Dr. Bennett then turns back to face Carlos, who is still sitting on the examination table. "Do you have chores you have to do?" he asks.

"Oh, yeah," Carlos responds, suddenly very serious. "This week it's the bathroom and living room. And if I miss, I don't get no allowance. It's real important."

"Well, it's good to have chores at your age," says Dr. Bennett. He then launches into his usual questions about medications, which he directs both to Juan and to Carlos. Carlos is now on some seven different drugs, including Combivir, a nucleoside analog drug that combines AZT and Epivir, and the protease inhibitors Invirase and Norvir. Dr. Bennett wants to know when Carlos takes his medications and who supervises him at this task.

Juan replies that Carlos takes his pills before school and at bedtime. He assures Dr. Bennett that either he or his wife is always there.

"Good," says Dr. Bennett, nodding. "Making sure he takes his medications, and takes them like he's supposed to, this is really important. And he needs to take them whether he wants to or not."

"He don't like that liquid stuff," says Juan.

"That's the Norvir," says Dr. Bennett. "I've tried it, and I don't like it either. I know it tastes bad. He's telling you the truth, Juan; it's really awful."

Dr. Bennett turns back again to face Carlos. "Carlos," he says, "I can promise you that just as soon as we can get this medicine in a pill form, we will. What's important—and this is real important—is that you take it. *Are* you taking it?" he asks.

"Yes," Carlos replies.

"Every time and every day?"

"Yes."

"Who helps you when you take it?"

"My brother. He makes me do it."

"Well, that's good. Your brother is doing the right thing. Now Carlos, jump down off that table and come over here. I want to show you something."

Carlos complies. Dr. Bennett is sitting at a table, looking at Carlos's chart. "I want you to look at this," he says to him, pointing. "These are your viral load scores. See this one? It's 72,000. That's not good. Then this one, it's 41,000. That's better, but it's still not good. Then see this one here? It's your viral load for today. It's less than 500. That's really great! It's these medications, especially the one you don't like, that are reducing the amount of virus. Remember how sick you were several years ago? Those awful mouth sores that hurt so much? It's important that you take your medicines so we can keep you well." Dr. Bennett puts his arm around Carlos and draws him closer. "You really look good, Carlos. I'm just as pleased as punch. I'm pleased with you, and I'm pleased with Juan, and I know Pastor Bill is really pleased too."

"I sure am," says Bill, smiling broadly.

Loaves and Fishes

The story of Carlos and his grandmother would not be complete without some explanation of L&F, the AIDS service group that has provided for so many of this family's needs. Both Isabel and Bill know the Alejandrez family well. In recent years Isabel especially has been involved in caring for Carlos. This care has gone far beyond bringing him to clinic appointments. She went to the house at all hours when the family ran out of morphine, she fought with school administrators to provide him with the education he was entitled to as an American citizen, and she held him at his mother's funeral.

Isabel is very matter-of-fact about the services she provides AIDS patients, having been in this work since she was fourteen. Behind her professionalism is considerable pride in her parents for founding a ministry like L&F. "My parents started this when I was in high school," she tells me. "They named it Loaves and Fishes after that story in the Bible of how Jesus feeds the multitude. But from the very beginning everybody just called it L and F. At first it was scary because I really didn't understand what the virus was all about. But then we got to meet the people who had it, and that made HIV a different thing. You could see it was about people, not just this awful disease, and that put a lot of the fear I had aside. Then I went to college, and when I came back home, I knew that L and F was something that would always be a part of my life. Of course taking care of people is how my parents have always been. They always had foster kids and they took in Fresh Air Fund children. My brother and sister and I participated in all those things, so it just seemed like the way you should be."

A pretty twenty-seven-year-old with short dark hair framing her face, Isabel is married and just beginning to show that she is five months pregnant. This will be her first child. Like her parents, Isabel is direct and low-key about the remarkable work she does with HIV-infected persons and their families. Like them too, she has a wry sense of humor, which is most evident when she describes situations she can't change. Talking with Isabel, I am impressed by the energy and enthusiasm she brings to her involvement with L&F. "My work has focused on the kids," she tells me. "I do their case management, and I do various groups. I run a support group for children *affected* by AIDS. A lot of our kids fall into this category, over a hundred. . . . What I do has been a lot of fun. It's great being involved with the kids' lives in so many ways—school, family, friends, all these things—and having them know they can call you when something exciting happens, or something awful. My friends think it's amazing, the kind of work we do, but it really isn't. It's fun to show friends how practical this work really is, that caring and helping people are just not difficult, sacrificial things."

I ask Isabel what it was like to grow up in a home so devoted to serving others. "As long as I can remember," she replies, "my parents' home was a place where people gravitated. For some reason"—she laughs—"my sister and I always made friends with people with problems. So our home was like a haven even for our friends. At times it was, like, my mom and dad are pretty dorky because they want to be so involved with people's problems. But now, in retrospect, it's taught me a lot about patience, and mercy, and grace, and what really caring for people is all about."

The Hendersons get to know the families and their needs intimately because often they are actually present in the home (or prison or hospital or rehab center). What makes L&F distinctive from other AIDS organizations is that it is funded largely by individuals rather than federal and state programs, and thus it has more freedom to respond to whatever needs clients present, whether these be for food, clothing, transportation, medications, help with housing problems, school difficulties, drug addiction, AIDS education, or a myriad of other concerns. In addition to providing for such immediate needs, L&F runs a GED program,[3] various support groups, after-school programs for children, and classes in parenting skills, and Pastor Bill conducts church services, weddings, and funerals.

Loaves and Fishes began in 1987 by helping just one young man

---

[3] This program prepares adults for a high school equivalency exam that broadens their employment opportunities.

infected with HIV. Twelve years later clients included 186 infected persons as well as some 150 additional family members—spouses, siblings, children, and parents. I was astonished to learn that the staff of an organization that serves so many consists of only 5 people: Bill, his wife, Connie, their daughter Isabel, a friend whose specialty is drug and alcohol recovery, and a newly hired part-time secretary. I was also surprised to learn that with so many programs and activities L&F is able to function on a budget of only $260,000 per year. "In a faith-based ministry," Connie says, "you can do so much more for much less money because there isn't any bureaucracy behind you. And there's a minimum of paper work."

The more I learned about L&F, the more interested I became in getting to know the Henderson family. It is close to the Christmas holidays when I drive to Springtown to talk with Bill and Connie about their work. I arrive at a large warehouse in the slums. Bill, a trim man in his late forties with heavy dark eyebrows and a thick mustache, is waiting for me outside, despite the cold. "Just wanted to make sure you found the place!" he says. Bill tells me that L&F has moved here only recently and that they have chosen this location "as much for the neighborhood as for the low rent." They want their office to be situated among those they serve.

Before we sit down to talk, he gives me the "grand tour" of the building. It is very clean and somewhat bare, though a few framed inspirational mottoes of various kinds adorn the walls. There are several offices, small rooms for counseling, and a room that serves as a food bank. We pass a large room with cement walls that is partly fitted out as a church with pews and a simple altar with a cross at its center. Services are held here Sunday nights. The tour ends in a huge, unheated garage filled with furniture of all kinds. Bill explains that some of these items have been donated and will be given away to whoever needs them, while others are being stored for clients who are in prison or in residential rehabilitation centers. On one side of the room is a table overflowing with toys of all kinds, some colorfully wrapped. "Those are Christmas presents," he says, "for the kids we work with." Right next to the table are a rack of jackets and coats and boxes of more such outerwear "from our annual winter coat drive."

We retrace our steps to Bill's office, where we are joined by Connie, a warm and relaxed woman with a big smile. Her job with L&F, she explains, is doing paper work and keeping the books. Bill's office looks like any well-used work space, with a cluttered desk, overflowing file cabinets, and pictures of family members, friends, and clients. On the desk is a framed letter from a child who sent two pennies as a donation to Loaves and Fishes. Bill sees me reading the letter and laughs. "Yeah, this little girl, her grandmother had been supporting us and was invited to our banquet, so the little girl got dragged along to the banquet too. Poor kid. But I guess she must have picked up something from it, 'cause we got this letter and two pennies several days later!"

At my request Bill tells me how Loaves and Fishes came to be. "We always had a love for working with kids. So besides our own (we had three) we took in Fresh Air Fund kids. Then we started with Children and Youth Services as foster parents; we did that for about seven or eight years. Then—it was in 1987—we started teaching an evangelism course in our church. One of the girls taking this course was an ex-addict and was going to Narcotics Anonymous meetings. She had befriended this guy at NA who was sick and in the hospital, and she asked if we could go there and pray with him. We said we'd do that. So that's how we met our first guy with HIV. His name was Jim. Soon after he was out of the hospital, he went on a Spanish radio station to publicize that he had gotten HIV from drug addiction. He wanted to encourage teenagers to stay away from drugs. Then all his friends from NA didn't want anything to do with him any longer, after they found out he was HIV positive. That's when we stepped into his life. We tried to fill that gap and to befriend him. He kinda fell in love with us, and we fell in love with him. We took him to church and had him over for Thanksgiving dinner and those kind of things.

"Jim introduced us to a first and then a second and a third friend of his who were infected, and by the end of 1987 we were working with about twelve HIV-infected people, and we were still doing full-time jobs. That was hard. I did heavy construction, and Connie, she was an assistant to a school administrator."

During this early period whatever services Bill and Connie provided were paid for out of their own pockets or from contributions of friends. A turning point came in 1989, when Bill was ordained by their local church and formally recognized as an outreach minister. L&F acquired a board of directors as well as tax-exempt status as a charity. Thanks to the generosity of parishioners, donations increased, but so did the number of clients and the workload. Bill and Connie began to wish they could devote more time to working for L&F. "People were falling through the cracks," Connie observes. "Nights and weekends were when we were available, and people don't always get into trouble only on nights and weekends!"

One Monday morning in 1990 Bill was laid off from work. Nothing like this had ever happened to him before. Taking it as a divine message, Bill and Connie decided to make a leap of faith: He would not collect unemployment or look for another job but instead would work full-time for L&F. "From that moment on," says Bill, "it turned into a faith ministry. And it's that today. We just trust God to be our source, whether it be financial or whatever."

I ask them to tell me more about Jim, their first client.

"He was about twenty-eight, a heroin addict from a family with a lot of trouble," says Connie. "He had a brother who had already died of AIDS when we met him and a sister who was infected too. We knew him for only three years; he died in 1989. Jim was a sweet guy, always wanted to hug, and loved his kids. Drugs got the best of him, but inside, he was a great guy."

I begin to notice that when talking about a client, Bill and Connie will casually mention a host of problematic issues—drug addiction, difficulties with the law, noncompliance with HIV treatment—and then conclude that underneath these things, Jim or Ted or Luis is "a great guy" or "a wonderful person." Their compassion—and their patience—seem limitless.

The Hendersons go on to tell me more about individual clients and their problems. Most of the infected men they work with acquire the virus through injectable drugs. On the other hand, most of the women are infected by sexual contact with infected men— their husbands or boyfriends or, in the case of women who are prostitutes, their johns. Though drug addiction is also frequent among infected women, their drug of choice tends to be cocaine, and since cocaine is not injectable, it does not put them at risk for HIV infection. In recent years the number of infected women the Hendersons work with has risen dramatically. Almost all are young, and they are having babies. Luckily most of those babies have not been infected. L&F continues to grow, adding more and more infected men and women as clients each year, despite the fact that the rate of HIV infection nationwide has leveled off.

As they talk about themselves and their work, the Hendersons make it all seem very simple. They believe that God has given each person a particular gift, "a talent that He wants us to use." Once we discover what it is, we can develop that special talent. "You look at your gifts," Connie explains, "and you say to the Lord, 'This is what you've gifted me to do. How can I serve you?' Then, when the opportunity comes, you just step out and do it."

"In the job field," Bill adds, "I was a mechanic before I came out here and got into big construction work. I always had a very analytical mind. I could look at something and think, 'It's supposed to be doing this, and it's not, and I can fix that.' It's automatic, natural. We're doing the same thing today. You see a need; you just go and do it. You don't put together a committee to decide what to do; you just go and do it! That's where it started with us. You see a need, like there's this guy who needs food, so you just put him in your car and take him grocery shopping. Or he needs a friend, so you take him home. Or he needs some spiritual growth, so you take him to church. Of course we had to recognize how limited we are." He laughs and looks at Connie. "We had to see that there are things we're not capable of doing."

"Oh, yes." She nods. "There's so much we can't do. We see work-ers like us who really beat themselves up when clients don't change. But you have to accept that people make changes out of their own choices. Even if it's not the best for them, it's their choice. It's not that we don't grieve for them. If we could do something to make it different, we would—but we can't."

Bill remarks, "The only time I get close to feeling burned out, it's over issues, not with clients. It's the bureaucratic stuff. When some-body we work with falls—like a guy who goes back to doing drugs or an infected woman who has another baby—we don't know how many times they stood up to the Devil and told him to go to hell. We haven't the slightest idea. Somebody we've worked with for years suddenly shows up high as a kite. But I don't know how hard he's fought and how persistent the Devil was before he fell. I know the Devil's pushed my buttons, and I've sinned. How can I justify that I've fallen myself, but I'm going to complain about others when they fall?

"Anyway," Bill concludes, "Loaves and Fishes isn't about some-body's lifestyle or somebody's choices. And not everyone is a cute little kid like Carlos! We're doing what we do because we love peo-ple. And that's what it's all about."

IT is not uncommon in the AIDS epidemic for a grandmother to find herself thrust into the role of parenting young grandchildren. As physician Peter Selwyn puts it, these grandmothers "come for-ward like a line of weary angels, with great love and without hesi-tation," first to care for their dying children and then to take on full responsibility for their grandchildren. Mrs. Alejandrez has cer-tainly done this. Her contribution to Carlos's welfare is undeniable; she loves him, and she wants to take care of him. But for an elderly woman with health problems of her own who does not speak or read English, it can be very difficult to meet the needs of a young child with a fatal disease and elaborate medical regimens.

It is in such situations that community organizations like Loaves and Fishes or Faith-in-Action[4] can make a crucial difference. Their significance cannot be measured by their small size and local purview. They represent what is needed to bridge the gap between the intimate but often troubled world of home and family and the larger, often faceless world of institutions—hospitals, welfare agencies, governmental programs, charitable foundations. The job of driving sick children between home and clinic seems almost a symbol of this mediating role. They know much about the ways of institutions, and they know still more about the needs of children and families. When Isabel intervenes to help Carlos through withdrawal from morphine, she is doing what neither Dr. Bennett nor Carlos's grandmother could accomplish without her. Carlos's predicament typifies the problem of the disintegrated family: families fragmented by drug addiction or by jail sentences or, in this case, simply by the deaths of so many of its members. That Carlos seems so little scarred by the changes in his life and that he can remain with his biological family instead of entering the child welfare system are in large part due to L&F. Themselves a family, they give Carlos the help his own family cannot provide.

But the human meaning of an organization like L&F is no less important than its practical function. Both L&F and FIA are organizations that are nourished and directed by religious principle. But the activities of these groups seem to express a basic human instinct,

---

[4] Both groups are grass roots faith-based ministries serving people with AIDS. L&F has played a major role in the lives of the Alejandrez family, and FIA was involved in meeting the needs of the Morales children, as discussed in chapter 3. There are subtle differences between the two groups. L&F was begun by a minister ordained by an evangelical Christian church, whereas FIA was started by parishioners from more traditional churches who were trying to correct the indifference of their pastors and congregations. L&F is staffed by a single family and serves the community of Springtown. FIA, in Pittsford, was started by four persons, all volunteers, and now has a paid staff of five along with some thirty-two volunteers. L&F has always been funded primarily by private sources. Funding for FIA, on the other hand, has come largely from private foundations and government grants, though the local hospital and area businesses are also contributors. Local churches are now very supportive.

a response to others in need that seems rooted in human nature. It is as if we need to help those who need us to help them. I found the childhood recollections of Connie and Bill revealing. Bill remembers himself as a boy forever coming home with a lost kitten or a bird that had fallen from the nest; Connie recalls befriending kids who were poor and didn't wear nice clothes. They are doing today what they almost instinctively began doing as children.

Though there may be individuals who do not feel this impulse and societies that do not act on it, giving and helping are a widespread practice common to many cultures. Kathleen Norris in *Dakota* describes the ritual "giveaway" of Native American tribes in which everyone gives what they don't need and takes what they do. Originally this helped the whole tribe survive the winter, but even today, as Lakota artist Arthur Amiotte notes, the ceremonial giveaway is an important "reciprocal activity in which we are reminded of sacred principles," an act of giving that "enobles the human spirit."

More than a businesslike quid pro quo, reciprocal giving is grounded in kindness, affection, and generosity, not in calculations of gain and loss. The exchange of benefits freely offered and accepted takes place within the community it both creates and confirms. I am reminded again of the Greek ideal of *philia*, the communal bonding that connects family, friends, fellow citizens, and ultimately all members of the human race in mutual obligation. Reciprocity is basic to this paradigm, though what one gives may be disproportionate to what one receives.

What the Hendersons have to offer is not money but time, compassion, and energy. What do they get in return? Though they give with no expectation of anything coming back, there are obvious gratifications in the work of L&F: the friendships they form, the gratitude of those they help, the glow of satisfaction in doing good, and, given their religious orientation, some sense of divine approval. Philosophers have raised the question of whether any human act is finally and purely altruistic. Perhaps this is so, and people like Bill and Connie and Isabel would claim that they give less than they get back. Indeed it seems that truly generous people are able to receive as freely as they give.

I remember reading somewhere of a practice—from the Arab world, I think—whereby one who offers alms to a beggar thanks the beggar for the priceless opportunity to offer alms.

Both, it seems, are blessed.

PARTNERS FOREVER

Tommy Wheeler

Tommy is a shy, toffee-colored four-year-old. His father and mother are African-American. Both are infected. The father lost all paternal rights when it was discovered that he beat Tommy and even boasted about it. The mother was diagnosed with HIV while in prison, pregnant with Tommy. She has a long history of heroin and crack addiction, prostitution, and petty theft. Her present husband, Sam O'Brien, is Caucasian. With his help she became clean and found a good job with the city's Housing Department. Sam is a recovered addict with an extensive criminal record who now works hauling freight. He seems a good stepfather who cares a great deal for Tommy.

Tommy was first seen by Dr. Bennett when he was several weeks old. At six months he was diagnosed with HIV and put on AZT, Bactrim, and fluconazole. Videx was added when he was two years old. Medically Tommy has done well. Aside from thrush and ear infections, he has remained virtually symptom-free, with no serious opportunistic infections or hospitalizations. T4 counts have been relatively good, averaging 750, and his viral load has remained low after triple therapy was initiated when he was three and a half. Tommy seems unusually bright, but occasional violent behavior has caused him to be dismissed from day care programs more than once.

.   .   .

". . . AND the third little pig said, 'Not by the hair of my chinny-chin chin!'" Sam pauses in his story, turning his head to look at me as I come into the examining room. The ordinarily bright light has been turned way down, but it's not too dark for me to see him smiling broadly. Four-year-old Tommy is curled up on the examining table, lying on his side and facing the wall. Sam sits on a chair next to the table, lightly rubbing Tommy's back. Sam continues in a soft voice with his story. "This made the big bad wolf angry, and he said, 'Then I'll huff and I'll puff and I'll blow your house in!' So he huffed and he puffed, and he tried and he tried, but he couldn't blow that house down. And do you know why he couldn't?"

"No," says a small voice. "Why?"

"Because that third little pig's house was made of brick, and it was too strong for that big bad wolf to blow it down!"

Tommy turns over and notices I'm in the room. "Hi, Tommy," I say, then tell them both that Dr. Bennett is running late. I apologize for keeping them waiting, explaining that there are a lot of patients here today, and some have come in with serious problems.

Sam replies cordially, "Oh, that's all right. I know how it is." He adds, "I know that if Tommy were here sick, Dr. Bennett would take lots of time with him too." Sam is more forgiving than I would be about having to wait so long; he and Tommy have been here for more than an hour. I'm concerned about this, especially since Sam has told me on earlier occasions that it's hard for him to get off work to bring Tommy in for these appointments. To Dr. Bennett, it's very important that parents come to the HIV clinic with their children. Since Sam is trying hard to bring Tommy, it seems to me that we should do our part not to keep them waiting too long.

We're running behind, in part because there are more children than usual, add-ons with potentially serious problems. It is also true that Dr. Bennett takes the time he feels is needed for each patient and family. This can result in a long morning, one that extends right through the noon hour. But I know that there are other reasons behind the diminishing flexibility in the clinic schedule. Since the recent merger between St. Luke's and Heartland Health

System, a large HMO, there has been a gradual tendency to economize on time and staff wherever possible, often at the cost of patient comfort. The head nurse of outpatient pediatrics, who "subs" in our clinic when we are shorthanded or sharing nurses with another clinic, does her best.

But today someone in a position of authority has run the afternoon children's pulmonary clinic into the morning pediatric HIV clinic. This means that the same nurses and the same rooms are expected to serve two clinics simultaneously. It also means that the nurses work continuously from 8:00 to 4:30 or 5:00, with no time for lunch. It is now 11:45, and there are two more patients to be seen after Tommy. Dr. Bennett is performing a spinal tap on Mark, a seven-year-old who has been having severe headaches, to find out if his underlying HIV disease is affecting his brain. One of the nurses is helping him. The other is trying to find an examining room for a child from the afternoon clinic who was assigned an 11:30 A.M. slot. She stops by to ask me if I've seen Angelina's chart, but the phone starts ringing, and before I can respond, she runs to answer it.

The little examining room, dimly lit, is a quiet oasis in the midst of a chaos of jangling telephones, crying children, the buzz of adult conversation, and general busyness. I'm relieved to be there with Tommy and Sam. As my eyes adjust to the darkness, I notice that today Sam is wearing a black, sleeveless shirt bearing the inscription "You're only as sick as your secrets." He is a large, burly man of Irish descent whose long hair is pulled back in a ponytail. He looks like a biker. In fact he is a biker; his passion—other than Tommy and Tommy's mother—is his Harley. Sam's arms are covered with tattoos. His left arm bears an eagle with "NA" inscribed over it, letters that stand for Narcotics Anonymous. On the shoulder of his right arm is a sleeping monkey, also adorned with "NA." This, he has told me, is to remind him never to forget that he has a serious addiction problem. The same letters are mounted on a huge silver belt buckle that he always wears. On his wrist there is a strange tattoo, a bracelet of seven skulls. Each one represents an addict he has known who relapsed and died.

When I first met Sam, I was struck by the inconsistency between his tough appearance and his gentle attentiveness toward Tommy. When we see them for clinic appointments, Sam always seems eager to demonstrate, even show off, his parenting skills. He clearly wants to be seen as a good dad. By all accounts, he really does seem to be a good father to Tommy. It is Sam, rather than Tommy's mother, Marla, who makes sure he gets all his medications. It is Sam who regularly brings Tommy in for his appointments. It is Sam who tries to file a complaint when Tommy is turned away from a Christian day care center because he is HIV-infected.

I sit down next to Sam and urge him to go on with his story about the three little pigs. I'm struck by the appropriateness of this folktale for this particular child. There is a sense of menace in the story, with its threats of invasion, as well as a pervasive anxiety over having a safe home, one built so well and so solidly that the evils of the world can't knock it down. The wolf has easily blown down the first little pig's straw house and then the second little pig's house of sticks. Will a brick house be strong enough to keep out the wolf? For how long?

"I've been here a while now," says Sam, "and I'm all storied out!"

I ask him about his wife. Marla is a strikingly beautiful woman, poised, well dressed, with lovely skin and slick black hair. I don't know her nearly as well as I know Sam, since she has come with Tommy for his medical appointments only twice over the past two years.

"Marla's not doing so well," answers Sam. "She works full-time and comes home at the end of the day exhausted. She doesn't take AZT because it upsets her stomach. And she's not taking a protease inhibitor because we can't afford it. Since she works and brings in income, she can't get Medical Assistance. But she can't get insurance coverage through her job either, because she's been employed for only a year, and the Housing Department makes you work for the city for two years before you qualify for medical coverage. And my insurance won't cover her because her HIV infection is a pre-existing condition." He shakes his head.

I ask him if he has contacted the AIDS Support Network, a program with a site in West Hamlin, where Sam and Marla live. "They're working on it," he responds. "They say they're working on it."

At this point Dr. Bennett walks in, with Rachel, our head nurse, trailing him. "Well, hi there, Thomas," he says as he walks over and ruffles Tommy's hair. Then he turns to greet and shake hands with Sam. Dr. Bennett does this in a leisurely manner, as though he had all the time in the world. I'm always impressed with how unrushed Dr. Bennett appears, even on days as chaotic as this one. Rachel, however, is not so calm; her face is flushed, and she looks flustered. A woman with a contagious smile and a laugh that sounds like a chuckle, Rachel is the one who, from behind the scenes, makes the clinic work. She takes phone calls during the week between clinic sessions, handling some problems herself, sending others to the social worker or Central Scheduling, and reserving some for Dr. Bennett to deal with. She also takes on the responsibility of ensuring that he makes those calls.

"Let's see how you're doing, Thomas," remarks Dr. Bennett as he reaches in the pocket of his white jacket for the stethoscope that isn't there. As he does so, Rachel walks over and hands him her stethoscope. "Thanks, Rachel," he says, as though this were the first time this had happened. In fact Dr. Bennett routinely forgets his stethoscope as well as his prescription pad, and Rachel routinely just happens to have both with her.

After he has completed this part of the physical, Dr. Bennett has Tommy lie down on his back so that he can feel for lymph nodes and spleen. "You look pretty good today," he comments, smiling at him.

"I'm going to see Santa Claus!" announces Tommy in his husky voice as he looks up at Dr. Bennett. "I'm going to see Santa Claus soon!" He turns his head to the side to check this with Sam, who nods affirmatively.

"You are?" says Dr. Bennett. "Well, I think that's just great. Will you ask him to bring something to me too?"

"Oh yes, I will," responds Tommy. He reflects for a minute and then asks, "But what do you want him to bring you?"

"Oh, let me think. There's a lot of stuff I'd like. I guess I'll have to think about that for a while. You just tell him hello for me."

"Okay." Tommy smiles.

Dr. Bennett turns to Sam, his hand still resting on Tommy's leg, and asks, "How's he been doing?"

"He's doing just fine," Sam replies. "He eats lots—and all the time!" Sam laughs. "And he's very active, going here, going there, always in motion. And he has no problem with that new medication." Over the last two clinic visits Tommy's viral load has been rising, from an undetectable amount (less than 0.5) to 7,000, then to 132,000. Dr. Bennett changed his medications, adding the protease inhibitor Viracept.

"I put the Viracept in hot oatmeal or pudding," adds Sam, "and he just scarfs it right down."

"Well, that's good," says Dr. Bennett. Then, changing the subject for no apparent reason—and again, as though he had all the time in the world—he tells us all about a recent newspaper article indicating that heroin use is up in the area, especially among teens. He asks Sam, "What advice would you give to a parent about keeping their kids away from drugs?"

Sam answers simply and directly: "First, educate them early. Second, don't be naive! It used to be that kids started using when they were fourteen or fifteen, but now they're often younger. There are eleven- and twelve-year-old kids on their bikes going from door to door, transporting drugs."

"Do their parents know what they're doing?" I ask.

"A lot of these kids are from broken homes and live with a single mom who has other children too," replies Sam. "These mothers often know what their kids are doing. They'll say, 'We need the money.' They'll say, 'As long as my kid isn't using, it's okay.' But it's not okay."

Sam goes on to tell us how hard it is to break a habit of addiction, indicating that even now he still goes to meetings three times a week. "Drugs made me do terrible things," he observes. "I spent nine and a half years in prison: thirty-nine felonies, manslaughter, everything. I did terrible things. It was Narcotics Anonymous that turned me around."

As Sam talks to us so candidly about his past, Tommy is still lying on his back on the examining table, singing softly, with Dr. Bennett still stroking his leg. Sam has told me that Tommy often goes with him to these NA meetings, playing with toys and humming to himself in the back of the hall. The inscription on his shirt, "You're only as sick as your secrets," is a motto that Sam really lives, as I am to find out.

Thomas Wheeler was born at St. Luke's, addicted to crack and weighing under six pounds. Marla had been tested for HIV while in prison. She knew that she was infected and that Tommy could be too. She was allowed to spend an hour with him after he was born but was then returned to prison, where she had six more months to serve of an eight-month sentence for prostitution, passing bad checks, and forgery. It was Marla's grandmother, a reclusive woman who lives in a retirement home, who took him home from the hospital and who, with the help of a niece, cared for him during the first four months of his life. Dr. Bennett first saw Tommy at five weeks of age. Suspecting HIV, he ordered an antibody test, securing written consent from the grandmother. But Tommy was never taken to the lab for testing.

A month before Marla was to be released from prison, Tommy's father, Lester Wheeler, turned up one afternoon at the grandmother's apartment and took Tommy off to live with him. Lester had a full-time job, however, and Tommy spent days, and often nights as well, with Lester's mother. But this grandmother already had seven children of her own living with her, and their children as well. It was difficult for her to take on a five-month-old baby.

Tommy was next seen by Dr. Bennett when he was nearly six months old. It was Lester who brought him in. Tommy's lymph nodes and spleen were enlarged, and he had thrush. This time an HIV test was performed, and he tested positive. Lester was informed of this result, and Tommy was put on AZT, Bactrim, and fluconazole. Dr. Bennett remembers Lester, but with no fondness. "He alienated me early on, probably as much as any parent ever has. He was telling me how much he wanted a boy and that he has four children, all girls, and he never wanted them and still doesn't. He was so blatant about it. He told me that he really wanted a boy, and now that he's finally got a boy, the kid goes and gets HIV infection, and that makes him feel cheated!"

About this time Marla was released from prison. She moved in with Lester, who brought six-month-old Tommy back from his mother's house to live with them. For several weeks all went well; Lester worked during the day, and Marla stayed home and took care of Tommy. For a while Marla brought Tommy in for his medical appointments. Dr. Bennett remembers being impressed by her: "I thought then that she was a teenager (now I know she was older than that), and for a teenager she seemed really bright. She was articulate and well groomed, though maybe kind of hyper at times. I could tell that she liked to feel important. I have the sense now that when she's not on drugs, she'd be a good employee, very industrious and efficient."

After only two months Marla and Lester began doing drugs again. Marla was also back into prostitution, with Lester driving her to meet her tricks. Once again she was picked up by the police and sent back to prison, and once again Tommy had to be cared for by Lester's mother.

When Marla's second prison term was up and she was free, the same pattern repeated itself. Tommy came back to live with Marla and Lester, and within several months they began partying and doing drugs, often leaving Tommy home alone. Marla was again convicted of prostitution and forgery and, for the third time, sent to prison.

When she was released this time, Marla was serious about trying to break her drug habit. She went directly to a drug rehabilitation center and, after several weeks, graduated to a transitional housing unit for recovering addicts. It was here that she met Sam O'Brien. He had been attending Narcotics Anonymous meetings for some ten years, and he offered to take her with him. She began to go to meetings, though not as regularly as Sam. It was not long before Sam found out that Marla had a son, then a little more than a year old, who lived with his father and grandmother.

At first Tommy was leery of Sam and kept his distance. Sam has vivid memories of a picnic at a friend's house with Marla and Tommy. He thinks that this picnic marks the beginning of his relationship with the child. After a couple of hours playing with the other children, Tommy came up to Sam and to Sam's surprise confidently took his hand. They sat like that for a while side by side. Then Tommy got up, his hand still in Sam's, and they walked over to a hammock. Sam lifted Tommy up and put him in it, but Tommy didn't like the feel of the rope knots. So Sam got into the hammock himself, rested Tommy on top of him, and started rocking gently. Tommy fell asleep for about an hour. Sam remembers this incident with real pleasure. "I knew at that point that he trusted me. Every time I moved just the slightest, his little arms would grab hold around my neck and hold on to me. That was the beginning for us, for Tommy and me."

But Lester and Marla still had joint custody of fourteen-month-old Tommy. The child spent several weeks with Lester and Lester's mother, then several weeks with Marla and Sam. On one occasion Tommy was returned to them with filthy clothes, severe diaper rash, cradle scalp, and dirt encrusted in the creases in his legs and arms. Convinced that Lester wasn't taking care of him, they decided not to return him but just keep him. Lester seemed to accept this change. But he soon dropped his insurance coverage on Tommy, leaving Marla and Sam to pay for medical expenses out of pocket. After six months Marla petitioned the court to require that Lester provide child support. Lester also went to court, asking for custody. The judge ruled again that Lester and Marla should have joint custody, and thus Tommy, now a little over two years old, continued to go back and forth between his two biological parents.

This arrangement lasted for several months. Once, however, Lester brought Tommy back after a visit with two-inch strap marks across his back, his buttocks, and his legs. Sam got out a camera and took pictures, then drove Tommy to a local hospital's emergency room so that his condition could be verified and documented. Marla filed for custody, and Lester again filed a countersuit. These legal maneuvers came to an abrupt end, however, when Lester announced to a caseworker that he beat Tommy when the child didn't make it to the toilet and had an accident. Marla was given full custody, and Lester lost all parental rights. He was also directed to put Tommy back on his insurance policy.

For a year all went well. Sam hauled freight, and Marla had a full-time job working the desk at a home health agency. She had always been careless about taking her own medications as they were prescribed, and she tended to be careless about Tommy's medications too. Each time Marla or Sam called in for more AZT or Videx or Bactrim, Dr. Bennett insisted that Tommy come in for an appointment. But during this time Tommy was brought in for his regular monthly clinic appointments only once, by a volunteer from a local AIDS service organization.

Eventually Sam took responsibility for taking Tommy to medical appointments as well as for giving him his medications. Dr. Bennett remembers that "Sam was a little distant at first. He had a kind of cautiousness with the clinic staff that you might expect from a person who doesn't know whether we can be trusted and didn't know how we'd judge him. In those first visits Sam seemed even a little scary. He was long-haired; he was pretty loud at times; he was covered with those tattoos. There were a whole bunch of things about him that were foreign to us, and you know, he probably felt that about us too!"

On one occasion Tommy showed up with Sam after missing six months of appointments. Sam explained that he had been driving a truck and that he had just quit because the job required him to be away from home too much. This was my first encounter with both Sam and Tommy, who was now almost three and a half years old. Sam was friendly and willing, even eager, to give Dr. Bennett and me a full account of Tommy's situation: "It's been a year since we got full custody. Tommy and I, we've become real close during this year. Marla works a 2:00 to 10:00 P.M. shift. So Tommy and I spend a lot of time together—going to the park, walking the dog. I taught him how to ride a bicycle. When I work on my Harley, he helps me. He hands me my tools. We learned how to play catch together. His health has been getting better too. That's 'cause I'm constantly around to make sure he gets his medications! And I got him into Head Start. The one he was supposed to go to was in a township where there were all white kids, and I didn't want him being singled out for anything. So I went to the one in Springtown, and there were all kinds of kids there—white, Hispanic, black, Oriental—and I thought, 'This is the place.' He's been there now for about four months."

For a full year after this Sam brought Tommy to clinic appointments. During this year Tommy's viral load started to rise, and his medications were changed to include a protease inhibitor. It was now even more important that Tommy receive his medications regularly. Protease inhibitors, combined with reverse transcriptase inhibitors, are dramatically successful in reducing the amount of virus in the system. But if they are not taken regularly, the body can develop resistance to the drug. If this happens, the viral load is likely to rise, and the child will be vulnerable to life-threatening infections.

Thanks to Sam, Tommy received his medications regularly and throughout the year stayed well, with the exception of occasional middle ear infections and the usual childhood illnesses. One morning Tommy, then a little under four and a half years old, showed up for his clinic appointment with his mother. Marla was vague about the situation at home, mentioning "family problems." When Dr. Bennett asked her about Sam, she responded that she hadn't seen him for several days and that they were now living apart. Marla kept her distance. She seemed not to want to talk about whatever was going on between them, and we respected her need for privacy.

Five months elapsed until we saw Tommy again, this time with

Sam. But Sam's appearance and manner had changed: His long, curly hair, no longer in a ponytail, flowed loosely over his shoulders, and he seemed shaky and even tearful. Marla, he told us, had suffered a drastic relapse. She had gone back on drugs, kicked Sam out, abandoned Tommy, and returned to the streets, where she had been picked up for prostitution and sentenced to a month in jail. The court had given Sam temporary custody of Tommy.

Dr. Bennett was surprised by this turn of events. "I was inclined to believe that Marla would stay straight," he remarked to me afterward. "I sure wasn't expecting her to go off the wagon and then disappear. My impression of Marla has always been such a positive one. She was a person with whom I could identify much more than Sam, largely because of how she looked, how she talked, and the kinds of jobs she held. But now I think that even when she seemed to be doing well, she could have been drinking or doing drugs on the side. When she came in here, she wanted us to think well of her. And she's skilled at that."

It is not long after this clinic visit that I visit Sam and Tommy at their (and Marla's) home in West Hamlin and hear Sam's story about what has been happening over the past five months. They live in a very small two-story house in a run-down residential area of the city. There is a narrow porch in the front of the house, littered with toy trucks and cars and a beat-up bicycle with training wheels. It is summer, and it is hot. Sam welcomes me into the house and shows me into the kitchen, where we sit down at the table to talk. Tommy comes in and grins at me. He wants to know if I have any stickers for him today. I smile back, tell him that I only give out stickers at the clinic, but then hand him a toy I've brought for him, a Power Ranger action figure. "Cool!" Tommy says. Sam reminds him to say thank you, and he does, perfunctorily, like any four-year-old. He then trots off with his Power Ranger to watch television—public television, Sam emphasizes. From time to time he drifts back into the kitchen, either for a snack or for permission to watch the next show.

The kitchen is immaculate. The table and counters have been scrubbed. The refrigerator, which is opened on several occasions so that Tommy can have a snack or some juice, is very clean, quite unlike my own. School pictures of Tommy are taped to the upper part of the refrigerator door, as well as an official-looking document with heavy black lettering and a seal, Tommy's graduation diploma from Head Start. Magnetic letters cover the lower part of the door, some spelling out the words "cat," "dog," and "dad." Sam tells me proudly that this is Tommy's work.

Sam is quiet for a few moments, then begins to talk. Through much of his narrative he raps the knuckles of his right hand rhythmically on the table. It's as though he were pacing his feelings, not suppressing but controlling the emotions that lie behind the events he describes.

The recent trouble began when Marla took out a court-ordered protection from abuse against him. "What happened was that she wanted to go to Florida—her sister was paying, and her brother was invited too—and she wanted me to keep Tommy so she wouldn't have to take him with her. I said to her, 'Marla, your sister wants to take him along, so take him! He'll have a great time.' But she said no. And then I understood. I told her, 'Marla, I think I know why you don't want Tommy with you. You want to go and get high. You want to get messed up, and you don't want any witnesses.' That's when she took the PFA out against me and told me to move out.

"The day I moved out (I went and lived with my sponsee from NA) her brother moved in. I didn't want him here. He's an alcoholic, he's a crackhead, and he's a bum. The only thing Darrin did after he got here—and he was here for a month—was watch TV, lie on the couch, get drunk, and go up to Pittsford and do crack. And I found out he was physical with Tommy; he'd clip him alongside the head or knock him down if he didn't like what he was doing. When Tommy told me that over the phone, I was over here in a minute! But the locks had been changed, and I couldn't get in. I pounded on the door, and Darrin comes downstairs, wearing *my* bathrobe, and unlocks the door. I said to him, 'Tommy may be your nephew, but I'm his daddy! And don't tell me I'm not his father. I am his daddy. You lay a hand on him again, and it's just you and me!' Then Marla came downstairs and said to me, 'Either you watch Tommy while I go to Florida, or I'm going to have you arrested for violating the PFA, and you'll be in prison till I get back.' So I said, 'Fine, Marla, I'll watch Tommy. I was going to volunteer to do it anyway.' The fact that she used that PFA on me as blackmail so I'd watch Tommy told me she had probably started using again long before she went to Florida.

"So when she left, I came back here, to this house. Tommy and I spent the next two weeks together, and it was great. We had a blast. We were going everywhere. We went to meetings together. We'd do laundry together; there was a play area next to the laundromat, and we'd play while the laundry went through. I took Tommy fishing for the first time. He loved it! I went down to my sister's house to take him to her swimming pool. He's afraid of deep water, but he let me get him on one of those rafts. Then he dived off it—even went under the water—and I caught him, and when he came up again, he yelled, 'I was swimming! I was swimming!' During that two-week period is when Tommy went from the liquid medication to solid pills. Marla didn't think he was ready, but it turned out he had no problem at all.

"Marla stayed on in Florida for a week after her brother and sister came back home (they live in Cleveland). Then me and Tommy went to pick her up at the airport. He's real excited when we get to the airport. 'Mommy's coming home!' he keeps saying, over and over. Well, she comes walking off the plane and you can smell the alcohol five feet away from her. She reaches down and gives Tommy a big hug. 'Oh, I missed you, I missed you,' she says. And I looked at her and said, 'I guess your clean date's not good anymore.' She called me everything under the sun. Tommy is in tears. He's saying, 'Don't say that to Daddy, don't hurt Daddy, Daddy's not a #$%x!' Then she grabbed Tommy and shook him and said, 'Don't talk that way! Don't say that word!' But of course she'd just said it herself.

"Then she tells me that she wants to take the car and Tommy and drive to Columbus. She says, 'I have to go to Columbus; my medicine's up there.' She knows I'll fall for that. So I take her all the way to Columbus. When we're almost there, she calls and talks to Darrin, that's her brother, and tells him he should get his stuff ready. I said, 'Get his stuff ready! What are you talking about?'

"She says, 'Darrin's going back down to West Hamlin with me.'

"'Oh no he isn't!' I say.

"She goes, 'I still got a PFA out against you.'

"'I don't care,' I tell her. 'You're drunk. You're not driving. And *he*'s not going back to my house. He's been leeching off my money and living in my home for a month now while you've been keeping me away. It stops now, Marla. And if you continue to use, I'm going to take Tommy.'

"She says, 'You can't do that.'

"I told her, 'Okay, Marla, we'll see.'

"So we get to Cleveland, get to where her family lives, and we go up to their apartment. Darrin grabs his bag and goes to walk downstairs, and I say to him, 'Put it down. You ain't going nowhere.' He rips off his jacket and starts m——f——ing me. Tommy is standing right there. Darrin goes, 'I tried to be nice to you, but you m——f——ing white boys are all the same.'

"I don't remember taking my glasses off, throwing them across the room, and going after him, but I did. Marla's sister ended up between us. I said to Darrin, 'Don't you be nice to me. Let's go downstairs. Let's go someplace and have this out!'

"Her sister yells at me, 'No! Just leave! Get out!'

"So I leave. And on my way out the door I take Tommy by the hand. Marla says, 'No! You can't do that!'

"I say to her, 'He's staying with me. Right now I'm pissed at you and I'm pissed at your brother and I'm pissed at your sister. They know you're an addict, and they did nothing to make you get help. They just let it continue.' And I take Tommy and say to Marla's brother and sister, 'I don't want any part of you people right now,' and we go down to the car.

"Marla comes down in about ten minutes, and we drive off. Tommy is in total shock. He's afraid to speak. He's afraid to talk to me too! Which is a first, 'cause it's always 'Daddy this, Daddy that.' But he's not saying anything. Marla doesn't say a word either, until we hit the turnpike. Then she tells me, 'When we get home, I want you to pack your stuff and get out.'

"'That's not a problem, Marla,' I say. 'But I'm taking Tommy with me.'

"She says, 'No you're not!'

"And I go, 'Yes I am.'

"When we get back home, she calls the cops while I'm getting my stuff together. They come and arrest me, but they let me go on the spot. I go right over to my sponsee's house without my things—Tommy stays with his mother—and I stay there for a couple of nights. Then I have my mother call Marla and ask if I can come over and get my stuff. Marla tells her that I can come over and get it the next day if some of my family comes too. But that night at an NA meeting, I find out that Marla is dancing at Pete Warley's, a strip club just down the street. So when I come the next day with my family to get my things, I ask her, 'Are you going to get that job you talked about at the nursing home?'

"And she says, 'Nope. I got a job where I can make $50,000 a year.'

"I go, 'What, stripping at Pete Warley's?'

"She gets real mad. She picks up the phone and calls the cops again, and I'm arrested a second time. They take me down to the station, but they let me go right away.

"That same night she goes to a private strip party, a bachelor party, and puts on a show, does some other things too. She dropped Tommy over at my brother's house, saying she'd be back around 1:00 or 2:00 in the morning to pick him up."

At this point in his story Sam breaks down and starts crying. He pauses for a few minutes, then goes on, his voice choked. "Six days later—*six days later!*—I get this call from my brother. He says, 'Sam, what should I do? Tommy is out of medicine.'

"First I say, 'Well, call Marla and have her get more medicine.' Then I realize something's wrong, and I say, 'Hey, why's he over there without medicine?'

"'He's been here for six days. Marla never came back for him—' While my brother's in the middle of that sentence, I hang up the phone, jump in the car, and drive over to his house to pick up Tommy. I leave Tommy off at Richie's—he's my sponsee, and Tommy knows him and his wife really well, and they just love him—then I come back over here and find that the house is closed up tight. So I break into the house. The cat is dead. The dog's lying there, dehydrated. There's poop and pee all over the place. This was the time, you know, early in the summer when we had that hot spell. There was no water and no food for the animals. Marla had the house completely sealed up, and she was down in Harperville, doing crack.

"So I get Tommy's medicines, scoop up the cat and get rid of it, take the dog over to Richie's, then come back and clean up some more. Tommy and I stay at Richie's; because of the PFA, I still couldn't be at the house. I go to the PFA hearing, and they extend it two weeks because Marla doesn't show up. So we stay at Richie's another two weeks." At this point in his story Sam puts his hands behind his head, leans back expansively in his chair, and smiles, looking off into the distance. "During this time Tommy and I are sleeping in the same bed; he's going to church, going to meetings with me, going shopping with Aunt Karen, spending time with Uncle Richie and Aunt Karen (he calls them this because they're his godparents). He's spending a lot of time with good people who have a lot of good feelings about him!

"But for a week after I pick Tommy up at my brother's, it seems like he's afraid to say anything to anyone. It's like he wants to tell us, 'Stay away. Don't get too close to me.' It's like he's shut off from everyone again, even me. It reminds me of the first time we picked him up from Lester's house, when Lester still had partial custody. It was that bad. Finally Tommy tells Aunt Karen it's my fault that Mommy is doing bad things. Then Karen, Richie, and I sit down and talk to him. We tell him, 'It's not Daddy's fault. Mommy has a mind of her own. She chose to do what she did. It's not Daddy's fault that Mommy's not around. It's not Daddy's fault that Uncle Darrin came up to the house and stayed there.' We try to explain all this to him.

"It's because of this kind of thing and the nightmares he was having about 'the stranger' that I got me and Tommy into counseling. The counselor says that Tommy is looking for someone to blame for what happened. She says that he's only four and a half and it's too hard for him to be mad at his mother. He's looking for someone to blame, so he blames 'the stranger.' For him that's the crack dealer. He knows that strangers sometimes do bad things to people. And he knows that his mom is doing crack. Tommy knows all about drugs! He has to take medicines himself, and he goes to NA meetings with me. I tell him there's good medicine and there's bad drugs. . . .

"I tried to be with him whenever I could. Anytime he had a problem at Head Start, I took time off from work. When it came time for graduation from Head Start, I was there for the celebration. And now, when Tommy wants to go to his HIV children's support group, I take him there. And if they want to go somewhere as a group, I offer to go along and chaperon.

"Throughout this whole time Tommy was having nightmares. Still does. Last one was about a month and a half ago. This dream was about a stranger doing something bad to Mommy. I'm still not sure if it was a dream or if he saw something he wasn't supposed to see. In this dream the stranger was pushing Mommy down on the couch and pressing on her. Tommy said that the stranger was 'making Mommy kiss him everywhere' and that 'Mommy yelled at me to go to bed.'

"So I said to him, 'Was this a dream, or did you see something you weren't supposed to see?'

"And he tells me, 'It's a dream that I wasn't supposed to see.'

"'Tommy, did you see a stranger in the house for real?'

"'Oh, yes, there were strangers.'

"'Did you see a stranger doing something to Mommy?'

"And he goes, 'Every time! Every time I close my eyes to go to sleep!'"

Sam continues: "All this baffles the counselor we've been seeing. She says this kind of thing is not something you can get a child to talk about without projecting the answer you expect into his response. It's hard. Even your tone of voice and the look in your eye can cue him how to respond.

"Anyway, Tommy and I have become even closer since Marla's been gone. One time when she came back to the house, she detoxed for two days. She stayed in the bedroom all the time. Tommy was graduating from Head Start and she wanted to be there. So I took her. She stayed for half the graduation, then went out to smoke a cigarette and disappeared again. She was gone for six weeks.

"I remember trying to get her into rehab or into mental health. All the time I was trying to keep rapport going between the two of them, Marla and Tommy. Finally I gave up on this. I said, 'Enough. I'm drained out.' After a while Tommy started opening up; he started coming back from that dark side and talking about things. And he started to take care of me." Sam is crying again, silently, making no attempt to stop the tears that flow down his cheeks and onto his shirt. "That's when he started to take care of 'his partner for life'—that's the way Tommy puts it, 'his partner for life'—and that's me—" Sam's voice breaks, and he has to stop talking.

"His partner for life!" Sam continues, still crying, his voice pitched very high. "We made a promise to each other to be partners, to take care of each other . . . and Tommy is real needy right now. He needs a lot of reassurance, a lot of support, a lot of hugs and kisses. He likes to say prayers; he's always doing this when we drive someplace in the car. He'll tell me, 'I want to pray to God right now, Daddy.' So I'm driving along, and Tommy closes his eyes and says, 'Dear God, I love the things you do, but make Mommy quit doing bad things.' Or he'll say, 'Dear God, I love you and I love the things you do, and thank you for Daddy getting me the bunk beds.' Or he sometimes says, 'Dear God, I love you and I love the things you do, and thank you for putting Daddy in my life and me in Daddy's life. We're partners forever!'"

Sam says the last six months have been very hard. He has stayed away from drugs. "Using is not an option," he states assertively. "I go to a lot of NA meetings, pray a lot, look Tommy in the eye, do daily affirmations. And I stay away from women. Mostly I'm still with my wife in my fantasies. No matter how mad I am at her, it's Marla who's in my fantasies. But do I want this in reality? No. My faith and trust in her is blown. Regardless of everything else, I did not deserve to be treated the way I've been over the past year."

During the time Marla was on the streets, Sam was twice provoked to the point where he lost control. "I threw away seven and a half years of nonviolence. It was over Marla. These guys, they weren't really who I wanted to hurt. I wanted to hurt Marla's disease; I wanted to hurt Marla the prostitute and Marla the addict. But I couldn't do that without beating my wife, and I don't hit women. So I took it out on these men.

"What happened was that I walked up to this guy I know and asked him where Marla was. And he said, 'Don't worry about that whore bitch; she works for me.' I grabbed him and threw him up against this wall, and I started giving him rib shots. I could feel the ribs breaking underneath the impact I was using. And each one that would break, I'd move up to the next one and keep on jacking, keep on jacking, and I know I broke them clear up to here [Sam points to a place high up on his chest]. When I dropped him, he slumped down, and I just started kicking and kicking and kicking until I was exhausted. I walked back to my car and got in. I knew I had left him lying in a puddle of blood, and I didn't care. But fifteen seconds after getting in my car, I was flooded with shame, guilt, remorse, and fear that he was going to die. Fifteen seconds later I was no longer that enraged individual. My wife had torn my life apart, and this man had something to do with it . . . but she was my wife; regardless of what else she did out there, she's still my wife. I took everything out on him.

"A week later I'm driving a tow truck, and I hear this guy Jake say over the radio, 'When Sam comes in, tell him I rented his wife last night!' and then he laughs. So I ask, 'Where'd she go with you?' And he tells me. When I get back to the garage, I find him working on a car. He's crawling out from underneath it, and I jump out of my truck and run over, and I just start kicking him in the side of the head. Once I started, I couldn't stop."

I ask Sam about Marla's present situation. He takes a deep breath, looks out the window, then looks back at me. He tells me that after serving her most recent prison term, she was released to a halfway house but left after only ten days in residence. She is living now in an apartment in Harperville, trying to stay clean, "doing ninety and ninety" (attending ninety recovery meetings in ninety days), and trying to find a job. She very much wants to visit Tommy. Sam tells me that he could prevent such visits but doesn't know if he should.

He wonders how long Marla is likely to live. She has never taken her medications regularly, and she is now losing weight, fast. He knows that sudden weight loss is often a marker of end stage AIDS. "You know, I don't think anyone will see her in a year. I think she'll be gone. . . . Her losing so much weight, that scares me. What if she does have a limited time left and I'm denying Tommy the opportunity to get to know his mom when she's clean?"

On the other hand, visits with his mother are very difficult for Tommy. "I look at him after a visit with her. It's so hard on him. First comes the feeling of abandonment, and he gets real controlling. 'Daddy,' he says, 'go in there, get Mommy, and put her in the car. Make her come home, and we'll be a family.' I tell him, 'Tommy, that's not going to happen.' Then he wants to know why his mommy doesn't come to visit him, where is she, what she's doing. And I have to say, 'I just don't know. I don't know what to tell you, Tommy.' Then the next day, with all those feelings and emotions, he goes nuts. His anger at his mother comes out, but it comes out at other kids because he can't be angry at Mommy. He knows he's sad, and he knows he's mad. But he can't relate anger to Mommy. It's a boundary he won't cross. So he'll punch some kid and give him a bloody nose. This happened the first time his mother visited. The second time he went to day care the next day, tripped a little girl on purpose, and pushed her down on the ground on the sidewalk. She had to get seven stitches across her knee! I was told to find another day care. . . . I guess I'm going to have to find a special needs type of day care where they know that sometimes— on Monday, say—he might act out."

Marla wants to regain custody. Sam seems divided about what he should do. He'd like to "stick with guardianship, give Marla a year, and see what happens." He would set conditions for her: ask her to stay clean for a year and, if she can do so, allow her back. But the counselor he and Tommy have been seeing thinks this might not be such a good idea. "The counselor says that Tommy is adjusting well to the situation and that I should continue with custody. She tells me, 'Tommy has been through this pattern three times with Marla, and he's only four and a half. And before that he was abused by his father. I'm afraid Tommy is going to end up in the system. And if he ends up there, his health will deteriorate, his attitude will decline, and he'll have trust issues with everyone. If you let her have him, and he goes back and forth between you and Marla, the bond he's formed with you is going to be shredded.'"

It is late now and time for Tommy to go to bed. I set up another date for Sam and me to talk, telling him I'd like to know more about his background and Marla's too, so that I can better understand their present lives. Sam goes with me to my car, explaining, "This isn't a great neighborhood, you know, to walk around in." I get in the car, and as I back up, Sam waves and calls out, "God bless!"

The next time we meet, I begin by asking Sam about Marla's background. I have not been able to find a way to talk with her and must rely on his account. Sam tells me that Marla was molested for the first time when she was six or seven years old, either by her father or by one of several uncles. She does not remember who it was, and neither does her sister, who was also sexually abused. Her father was a heroin junkie, as were her paternal uncles and aunts. Her mother was a religious woman and disapproved of her husband's drug habit as well as his womanizing. When she left him, she took Marla and two other siblings with her. But Marla continued to see her father, and the sexual abuse continued as well. By the time she was eleven, she had been in several of the area juvenile detention centers or residential institutions. At twelve, she began prostituting herself. By the time she was fourteen, Marla was addicted to crack and on the street. At seventeen, she went to live with friends in New York City and vanished for about five years. When she returned to Springtown, she moved in with Lester. He had just been released from prison, where he had served time for manslaughter. Angry because a former girlfriend refused to let him into their apartment, he had opened the mail slot and shot her in the abdomen, killing both the woman and their unborn child.

Marla and Lester lived together off and on for several years. She continued with drugs, supporting her habit by prostitution. During one of her prison terms it was discovered that she was pregnant. She was released on bail to a rehabilitation center in Pittsford. Blood was drawn to perform an HIV test, but she left the rehab center before learning the results. After being on the streets for several months, she was picked up by the police and returned to prison, where she learned that her HIV test had been positive. A few months later Marla gave birth to Tommy at St. Luke's.

Since her marriage to Sam, Marla has held a good job with the city's Housing Department and has actually been promoted twice. But other aspects of her life are not as successful. She fills her prescriptions, takes them for several days, then forgets and gives up altogether. Sometimes she keeps her medical appointments at the adult HIV clinic and sometimes not. She has been taking large doses of Wellbutrin, far beyond what was prescribed to help her quit smoking. Though she has given up cigarettes, she has not stopped taking Wellbutrin, which, Sam observes, "puts her in a manic state where she feels invincible to everything." He blames her doctor, a general practitioner, for prescribing three or four refills at a time, while aware of her history of cocaine addiction.

Sam stops talking about Marla, pauses, and begins telling me about himself. "I was raised in a family I didn't want to be a part of. I come from a narrow-minded, bigoted, racist, sexist family of truck drivers, mechanics, and farmers. I get no support from my family. My sister to this day won't stay with Tommy. She and her husband are members of the United Knights of the Ku Klux Klan. There's a lot about AIDS in white supremacy literature. They say there's no telling how the virus gets passed. You can get it from kissing. You can get it from a spoon that's improperly washed. They say AIDS is a punishment sent down from God to get rid of the undesirables, but now Satan has taken control of the virus and is trying to kill everyone. It's really wild shit. But my sister and her husband read this stuff, and they believe it.

"I was using from the time I was thirteen. I was scooter trash when I was fifteen, and I was an outlaw biker by the time I was seventeen. I belonged to a real bad gang. I never could be a drug dealer because whether it was heroin, crack, whatever, I'd just use it. But I helped with drug deals. Like there was a drug deal down at the Redlight Inn with Puerto Ricans and bikers . . . I was expected to get there an hour or so early, find a position where I could have open access, a firing range on the Puerto Ricans, preferably in the back. I ran guns up here from Texas, Kentucky, Florida. I never had a legitimate job until I came into recovery.

"I stopped using when I was twenty-eight. That's fifteen years I was on drugs. I was in and out of prison this whole time, everything from manslaughter to armed robbery. I've got nine and a half years of prison time behind me. I stayed high the entire time I was in prison because as a gang member I had connections. It was easy to stay high in prison. Crack, heroin, crank, dilaudid, steroids. I was big into steroids. I liked getting all pumped up big.

"My whole life I've had this physical violence with men. I mean, I'd go toe to toe in a heartbeat, and I didn't care. Question my manhood in any way, and we'd go toe to toe. The last three years of my addiction I carried five guns on me all the time. I was a real dangerous individual. I carried a 357 double-shot derringer in the back of a black leather cap that folded down; I kept a .25 automatic in my right-hand back pocket. I carried a 9 mm here [he points to his chest]; another 357 here [he points under his arm]; and a .38 snub-nose in my boot. Under the seat of my motorcycle, I carried a Mac 10. I was no one to mess with.

"I think what broke the camel's back—hey, Anne, you know, I don't think I want what I'm about to tell you on tape." I turn off the tape recorder. Sam then tells me that at one point in the past there were some thirty-five people who had made him angry and whom he intended to kill. He lists the various weapons he had stashed away and the way he intended to use them. I'm astonished by this part of his story. The violent actions he actually carried out seem bad enough, but the violence he planned is truly frightening. When he's finished with this part of his story and I turn the tape recorder on again, I ask him, "What made you want to do these things? Why were you so angry?"

He sighs, pauses, and again starts rapping his knuckles on the table. "When I was thirteen, I was molested by my cousin and her husband over an entire summer. Here's what happened. I was sent for the summer to my cousin's house at Lake Erie. I was a farmer's kid. The only showers I knew about were at school. I get up there to their house on the lake; it was a beautiful place. They had two speedboats that they parked right under the house. Lizzie (that's my cousin) shows me the shower. It's glass-enclosed on three sides, and on the fourth side there's a full mirror. There's a Jacuzzi and a hot lamp area, and there's a mist room off to the one side of the bathroom. This bathroom was bigger than the whole downstairs of our house. I thought, 'Wow!'

"So I'm taking a shower, thinking that this is the first time I've really lived. I'm in there scrubbing myself, and I see someone walk by out of the corner of my eye. It's Lizzie, and she doesn't have anything on. She comes in and says, 'I want to have a shower too.' And then: 'Rub some soap on my back.' When I do this, she turns around. She reaches down, gets me excited, and then bends down and gives me oral sex. I knew it was wrong, but she was a beautiful woman. After she's done, she laughs real, real loud. Right then Max comes in and catches us. He says he has to punish me. I didn't know at first that I was set up; then I figured it out." Sam pauses; he is crying. "The only thing I wore that whole summer was a pair of BVD underwear. I was kept in this beautiful house all summer long. It was every day. Sodomy, giving him oral sex. He used vibrators both on me and on him and Lizzie."

"Did you ever tell anyone?" I ask.

"I told my dad, and he punched me in the face and broke my nose. I told my mom, and she said I had a vivid imagination. I told my sister, and she just out and out called me a liar.

"After that I was withdrawn, isolated, antisocial. I starting using as soon as I got back home. For years afterward—and I'm talking *years*—after what happened to me, I wanted to be a woman so I could make love to women. I thought that what happened to me was okay if I was a woman, but not okay for a man or a boy. I know that doesn't make sense. But I was thirteen, so what did I know? I'd never even heard the word 'rape.' I had no concept of what it was. Once my sexuality developed, I mean from age fifteen or so on, pain and pleasure were one and the same. This intensified as I got older. It became real extreme just before I got clean. Bondage, nipple rings that I'd yank until they'd bleed, my dick in one place and ramming a vibrator in the other, asphyxiation: I'd try anything. Pain and pleasure, both the same. There's lots of women that want this kind of relationship. Lots. Always the women have been willing. Sometimes they want to go further than I do. Celine—she's the ex who wanted to get back with me recently—she's the one who got me into asphyxiation and everything else. A real beautiful girl—to look at her and talk to her, you'd never expect it!

"After what happened to me, I became physically violent to men and sexually and emotionally abusive to women. I'd find a girl that came from a background of abuse, and I wouldn't physically abuse her, but I'd sexually abuse her and convince her that she wasn't worthy of anyone other than me. I'd belittle her. It would start off joking when we were with other people, like I'd say, 'How can you be so dense?' and then, when we were in the house and alone, I'd say, 'Do you realize how dense you are? How dumb you are?' It starts as a joke and then becomes a way of making her feel insecure and worthless and stupid. A lot of bikers do this."

I sit there for a moment, trying to process all this. "So how did you get to where you are now?" I ask.

"I committed my last crime nine months after I got clean. Well, I didn't actually commit it. I walked into this store — it was a Seven-Eleven — walked up the aisle, and headed toward the clerk as I pulled down this mask over my face with one hand and reached into my jacket with the other to grab the 9 mm. I came up behind the clerk — he was bending over, reaching under the counter for something — and I saw the reflection of myself in this mirror on the opposite wall, and I just knew I couldn't do this anymore. I put the gun away and was pulling the mask back up on my head — it was February, and it must have looked like one of those ski masks to keep out the cold — and he turns around and he goes, 'Can I help you?' I was all choked up. I said, 'You already did.' And I walked out of the store.

"But you were asking about what got me clean. For the last eighteen months of my active addiction I couldn't look myself in the eye. My mother had always said, 'You can read the soul in the eyes.' Well, I couldn't look myself in the eye. I was drinking about a half gallon of gin every other day, beer, doing anywhere between an eighth and a fourth of an ounce of crank every day, between fifteen and twenty-five number four dilaudid or a bundle of heroin a day. I wanted to get away from that plan I told you about, you know — where I was going to wipe out all those people. It took me ten days to get through withdrawal. I did it at a cousin's house.

"Then I rode my bike back to Springtown. And to prove that 'a power greater than myself' is a force in my life somehow, that same day my woman wanted me to take her to an Alcoholics Anonymous meeting. So I did. I walked into the meeting. I didn't trust anyone. I found the darkest corner, found a guy in a chair, and told him to get out. I sat back there, and when they asked if there were new-

comers, everyone turned and looked at me. I said, 'What the fuck
are you people looking at!' And they just said, 'We're glad you're
here. Keep coming back.'

"They were talking about God and spirituality and feelings and
emotions. I thought, 'God, do I have to sit through this whole thing
with her?' There was this old guy, smoking a cigar and wearing a
suit that looked too good for him. He had a scarred face and a really deep voice, and he looked like someone that used to rumble.
He had big hands, man-size hands. For a small guy, and being sixty-
five, he was extremely muscular. He started telling this story about
being on the docks in Chicago, making money with his gun. He did
enough opium, heroin, and alcohol to end up in the hospital piss-
ing, shitting, and throwing up blood. He hooked me with that story
about guns and violence and drugs. His voice, his personality, his
charm, his vulgarity, and his spirituality all grabbed something inside of me. For the next seven weeks I came to AA meetings just to
see if he would be there. And he was there, every meeting. That put
me on the way to recovery."

After nine months of AA meetings, Sam switched to Narcotics
Anonymous. NA not only helped him stay clean but liberated him
from the racism he thinks he acquired from his family. "When I
started to go to NA, I knew I had found a home. I was doing really
well, and I believed that I was finally on the road to becoming a
human being. Then, after I'd been clean for four years, I met this
guy named Hamad, a black guy. I walked into the meeting and took
a seat. I got up about five or six times to hug people I knew that
came into the meeting. Hamad was sitting across this table from
me, just glaring at me with contempt. I glared right back at him. He
took off his glasses, laid them on the table, cocked his head back,
and raised an eyebrow at me. I thought, 'Oh yeah? Well, two of us
can play that game.' So I leaned across the table and just looked at
him, bug-eyed. The chairperson called the meeting to order. Then
this black guy looks at me, winks, and blows me a kiss. I thought,
'Here's this guy—he's black, and he's a faggot!'

"The chairperson asked if there were any newcomers or visitors.

This black guy raises his hand and says, 'I'm Hamad, and I'm from Demmler.'

"Then the chairperson says, like he always does, 'Does anyone have a topic, or feel like using, or have a problem with recovery?'

"Hamad's hand goes up, and the chairperson calls on him. He goes, 'I want to talk about stupid ugly white boys, look something like *you*!' He says 'you' real deep and nasty, looking at me and pointing across the table at me. I can feel the vein in my neck start throbbing, and the one in my temple too. My knees start shaking from adrenaline, and my jaw starts flexing. All I hear is 'stupid ugly white boy, stupid ugly white boy.' It's just ringing in my ears.

"This guy goes on talking. 'Anytime I ever felt like using, anytime I ever felt like beating the shit out of my old lady, anytime I wanted to kick my boss's ass, anytime I wanted to stick a spoke in my arm, I'd go to my meeting in Demmler and find a stupid ugly white boy, looks something like *you*' — and he pointed at me across the table again — 'and I'd just wait there for him to say something stupid.'

"So I go, 'Talk about saying something stupid, you're doing a pretty good job of that right now!'

"And he goes, 'Hold on, hold on, I'm going to give you your turn. Eventually this stupid ugly white boy, looks something like you, would say something stupid. And when he did, I'd go up one side and down the other, and hope that stupid ugly white boy looks something like you would want to do something outside—'

"And I said, 'Let's go, now! Let's go! Right now!'

"Hamad said, 'Not yet. I'm not done talking. One day that stupid ugly white boy except he was Jewish, except he still looks something like you. . . .' People by now had moved away from that end of the table. They're sitting a table away. Hamad goes on, 'This stupid ugly white boy was sitting there glaring at me. And when he opened his mouth, I was waiting for something stupid. But instead he said that he's white, he's Jewish, he's gay, and he's at this meeting because he's afraid of black people. He said that he doesn't know how to have a black person as a friend, that he never called a black person for help. He said that if he shuts someone down because of their color, because of their sexuality, because of their religion, he cuts his support group by half, then by half again, then by half again. He said that he needed more support than just gay Jewish boys. He said he knows this disease of addiction has no prejudice, that his recovery can't go forward with prejudice, and that he needs help.'

"Then Hamad looked straight at me, and he says, 'I was like you, 'cause you're sitting there angry, with tears in your eyes.'

"And I started to bawl!

"Then he goes, 'That's what *I* did too. I sat there in that meeting and cried. I think you need to hear my message because I've seen you get up and hug just about every white man come into this meeting. But you didn't get up and hug one person of color — Spanish, black, or otherwise. And, you listen now, I want you to be my brother!'"

Sam is crying now and continues to cry throughout the rest of his story about Hamad. "For the next seven years Hamad and I got closer and closer. We were tighter than I've ever been with my own brothers. We went everywhere together. Hamad died three years ago from AIDS. He's Muslim, so he'd only take natural medications, herbal things. He didn't take any prescription drugs until the last few months, when he had a lot of pain. Just before he died, I went down to see him. His mom said to me, 'Sammy, he doesn't recognize anyone. He can't talk. But if you want to go in and see him, you surely can.' When I walked into that room, he turned his head and looked at me, and then he said, 'Hey, stupid ugly white boy!'"

While in AA and NA, Sam found that his habitual violence toward men began to taper off. His abusiveness toward women, however, did not diminish. "If anything, it became more intense. I tried not to manipulate women the way I used to, but sexually I was worse than ever before. Sexual abusiveness became my substitution for drugs. It became a substitute for my own feelings. After counseling for I'd say a year or a year and a half, I wouldn't play any sex games. . . . I was afraid to do mock rape, spanking, bondage, that kind of thing. Anything forceful or controlling, I wouldn't do any of that stuff. I was afraid I'd go to extremes again." He pauses, strokes his chin, then asks himself: "Have I gone too far since counseling? Yes. I've gone too far. It's like a relapse using drugs. I've gone too far. Even though it wasn't too far for her, it was for me, and I know that because afterward, I felt like shit."

Because of these problems with women, Sam started going to a Survivors of Incest group. "Meetings were held in this big room at Grinson Hall in Springtown, and they were really informal. The chairs were set up in a circle, but there were also chairs against the wall. I would sit way back against the wall. I'd never introduce myself. I'd never talk to anyone before or after. I'd always show up late, and I'd always break out early. Back then I had hair down to my ass, a beard down to my navel. I was real animal-looking. I was scary. I noticed that every time I showed up, a security guard would come to the door and look in four or five times. For three months I never said a word. I was still very angry. After three or four months they did a role playing that just kicked everything inside me. At first I didn't blubber or sob, though tears were just flowing out of my face. Then the people doing the role playing came over and hugged me. And then I bawled out loud for fifteen minutes straight. That role playing was just like what went on with me when I was thirteen. It was so close that I didn't actually hear what was going on out there because I was watching inside, watching what had happened to me. It took me a long time before I could really talk about that. But I stayed with it. And the group counselor helped me. I was with Survivors of Incest for three and a half years."

In listening to Sam's stories about AA and NA, I was struck by the fact that in both instances he mentioned a strong relationship he had developed with a particular person. Of course in each of these organizations the relationship between sponsor and sponsee is a powerful part of the recovery process. But the powerful relationships Sam talked about involved neither his sponsors or his sponsees. His ability to form and maintain close relationships seems to me an important aspect of Sam's personality. This is a man who as a child was cruelly abused. That he is so capable of establishing

trusting, intimate relationships bears directly on his appropriateness as a father for Tommy.

Sam has been attending Narcotics Anonymous meetings for
fourteen years. He has fourteen sponsees—as many as the years he
has stayed clean. He works hard to help them, though he estimates
that only half are really trying to stay off drugs. Still, he knows that
breaking a serious drug addiction is a major struggle, even with
help, so he does not lose hope when they relapse. Sam has himself
tested for HIV every six months, a habit he began years ago, before
he even met Marla. He is very busy now with his job, with involvement in NA, and with parenting Tommy.

Sam and Tommy both go to church on Sundays. Tommy attends
an evangelical church with "Uncle Richie and Aunt Karen," but
Sam likes a Unitarian church "where they talk about everything
from Allah to Valhalla!" I ask Sam why he doesn't take Tommy with
him. He replies, "They make me feel like an outsider, and I don't
want him to feel like that. Everybody there drives a car made in the
nineties; me, though, I drive either my Harley or my truck 'cause
that's what I've got! Everyone there dresses really well. I wear a
button-down shirt and my very best pair of blue jeans. I'm probably
the only one who doesn't wear a watch or a gold chain. I like to hear
their ideas, but they can be pretty snooty."

Sam doesn't know what to call his religious beliefs. Besides the
influence of the Unitarians, he does a lot of reading and has been
impressed by what he has learned about Eastern and Native American religions. "I believe that you get what you give; what goes
around comes around. We have to pay for the life we live. There's
the life I lived in the past. I consider my troubles with Marla the
consequences of that life. It's part of the price I'm paying for the life
I chose to live back then. Then I believe there's a positive force in
life and a negative force too. If you go around thinking negatively,
you'll attract negativity. If you give to the dark side, then you get
dark. If you give to the light side, you'll get light. But I also believe
that even if you give to the light, that doesn't mean darkness won't
overtake you at times. That's what I believe."

PERINATALLY acquired HIV infection nearly always involves a complex of biographical facts, psychological issues, and behavioral problems that go well beyond the disease itself. Preserving the health and well-being of an infected child often requires decisions about parents and potential caregivers. The parents not only are their children's past but can also be their future. In Tommy's case, the court will have to make a decision about guardianship; this involves making moral judgments about the child's mother, father, and stepfather, who collectively have a history of IV drug abuse, promiscuity, prostitution, forced incest, uncontrolled violence, and criminal behavior of all kinds, including murder.

Susan Sontag argues in *AIDS and Its Metaphors* that AIDS is a disease wrongly associated with moral transgression, that it tends to be considered, like syphilis or plague, either "punishment for an individual's transgression" or "retribution for the licentiousness of a community." When Sontag published her book in 1988, AIDS was a disease associated with homosexual practices. At that time in the United States, homosexuals were the dominant group of HIV-infected individuals. Now other minorities have also become "risk groups," and the moral stigma that cloaks this disease has been extended to them. Warnings like Sontag's are valuable and necessary, for history is full of savage examples of scapegoating. However, the capacity to pass moral judgments on ourselves as well as on others seems basic to human nature and an essential aspect of responsible societies. All cultures find ways to limit, contain, or punish individuals who harm others.

Moral issues that surface in connection with an infectious disease such as HIV should not be dismissed, but neither should they be simplified or exaggerated. The views of those on the religious right, who see AIDS as a divine punishment for sin, are as extreme as those of the radical left, who see all morality as relative and for whom moral categories exist only to be deconstructed. Behavior that harms a child—physical cruelty, sexual abuse, fatal infection—is simply wrong. Of course the same absolute judgment does not apply to the human beings who behave in this way. Sam, a former addict and killer, has turned his life around; Marla, still struggling with addiction and prostitution, may do so still. The drastic change that began when Sam, about to rob a convenience store, saw his own image in a mirror always remains a human possibility.

The themes of self-knowledge and moral judgment find literary expression in a genre that dates back to the Middle Ages, the morality play. These plays were overtly and often heavy-handedly moralistic, but they remained immensely popular well into the early Renaissance. They took as their subject the contest between forces of good and of evil—usually personified as angels and devils—for the soul of the protagonist, Mankind. Of course there is no evil angel, no mention of Satan or the Devil, in this contemporary story of Tommy, Sam, and Marla. Yet the allure of heroin and cocaine that ensnared Sam for so many years and brought about Marla's downfall seems as powerful and as demonic as any supernatural creature with horns and pitchfork. Today's real-life equivalent to the vices and tempters of medieval mythology are forces like drug addiction, pedophilia, violence, and uncontrolled promiscuity, compulsive behaviors that seem to drive people into states of being that are as destructive of others as of the self.

For Tommy, the struggles of good and evil that take place around and above him are beginning to go on inside him too. This young boy who prays so touchingly is the same boy who has been dismissed from a day care center for violence toward another child. He can go either way.

If these drives are potential or present in Tommy himself, they are also present in our society, reinforced and encouraged through our social structures. It is easy to condemn drug lords, gangs, pimps, and prostitutes, but violence and sexuality, which are often linked, are the mainstay of the entertainment industry and the media. The plight of Tommy and Sam and Marla may seem very distant from many of us, but the forces that threaten their lives— violence, abusive sexuality, and easy promiscuity—are pervasive in our society, and we ourselves are often complicitous. A society can tacitly encourage the forces that lead to actions it condemns while punishing those who succumb to them.

Tommy's story is incomplete. In the next few months there will be a court hearing; a ruling must be made on who can best serve as the child's guardian. This legal judgment is at the same time a moral judgment, for moral issues inevitably play a part in court rulings about guardianship of HIV-infected children. Tommy's well-being, both medically and psychologically, turns on the court's decision.

This decision is not, as in a morality play, the simple choice between Vice and Virtue, Good and Evil. Both Sam and Marla have been addicted to drugs in the past; both are presently clean. But the judge must guess their future. In this uncertain perspective it matters that Sam has been able to stay clean for fourteen years, very nearly as long as he was on drugs in the first place. The lurid and sensational past that he recounts with such amazing candor admittedly makes for colorful reading. But what most impresses me in Sam's story is how deeply he has changed and how far he has come—and how closely these ongoing changes are connected with Tommy. Any relapse on Sam's part now seems extremely unlikely. Marla, in contrast, has been free of drugs for only a few months, and such drug-free intervals in the past have always ended in relapse. Still, it will be important for the judge that Marla is Tommy's mother and that Sam is not even a blood relative. Our legal system privileges the rights of the biological parent, especially the mother. The judge may well decide in Marla's favor in order to give her the opportunity of demonstrating that she can stay clean and be a responsible parent. In such cases it almost seems that the child is used as a pawn in an attempt to rehabilitate the parent. Marla may be able to change, but what if she suffers another relapse? What will this mean for Tommy?

The real issue here, it seems to me, is not Marla's rights or Marla's rehabilitation but Tommy's future. Which option will be best for him? This is a child who is neither sick nor disabled by his HIV disease, yet is very much at risk. His well-being, happiness, and emotional stability turn on a decision that will be made not in a medical clinic but in a court of law.

ORDINARY GOODNESS

Alyssa and Marie

Eleven-year-old Alyssa and ten-year-old Marie live in the tiny rural town of Goshen, in Amish country, with their adoptive parents and two younger foster siblings.

Alyssa was born to parents who were both infected. Her mother, who is Caucasian, is still living; her Hispanic father died of complications from AIDS when Alyssa was an infant. She came to live with Esther and Jimmy Hammond, who are Caucasian, when she was six months old. She was adopted by them five years later. Alyssa has always been healthy. She is a serious, responsible child. Math gives her trouble, but she enjoys reading. She is very curious about the world and always full of questions.

Marie acts much younger than Alyssa, though there is only an eight-month difference in their age. Marie weighed less than five and a half pounds at birth. Her Caucasian mother, who died before Marie was a year old, was infected with HIV and syphilis and addicted to cocaine and methadone. Marie's Chicano father, Julio, is still living. Marie went to the Hammonds when five months old and has remained with them in foster care until her father permitted her to be adopted ten years later. When Marie was very young, her health was poor. Before the age of two she had been hospitalized twice for pneumonia, gastroenteritis, bacteremia, and otitis media. For several years she had severe leg pains that were thought to be transverse myelitis. Now, however, Marie is a playful, joyous child. She is out-going and social, and she sings beautifully.

For Alyssa and Marie, HIV is a manageable, chronic illness. In a sense life for these children is extraordinary by virtue of its very ordi-nariness. Both children have HIV yet are healthy. Both needed to be removed from their biological families and placed in foster care, but they are happy and well adjusted, and they retain good working re-lations with surviving members of their biological families.

.　　　.　　　.

Clinic Appointment, February 1999

COMING into the room, Dr. Bennett and I find Alyssa and Marie sitting side by side on the examining table, poring over a book. Alyssa is a thin, pretty eleven-year-old with long dark hair who today wears a purple shirt with ballet shoes on it and matching pants. She is shy, emotionally cautious, serious, and responsible. Her foster sis-ter Marie, younger by eight months, is a beautiful child: dark-haired, dark-skinned, with soft eyes. Marie is as outgoing, trusting, and voluble as Alyssa is withdrawn, reserved, and quiet. There is a third foster child, five-year-old Jackie, at the far end of the room busy opening and shutting any cabinets and drawers she can reach.

"Well, here's Alyssa and Marie, sitting here like two peas in a pod!" Dr. Bennett exclaims. "Who am I going to see first today?"

Alyssa looks up and shrugs. Marie also looks up, smiles at Dr. Bennett, then looks back down and goes on reading.

"Okay, girls," says Esther Hammond, their adoptive mother, "it's time to put down the book." Dutifully Alyssa closes the book and holds it on her lap. Esther speaks softly and rapidly, with a slight stutter. She is an attractive woman in her late fifties with a clean, scrubbed face and shoulder-length curly hair that is part gray, part sand-colored. She always dresses nicely but always seems a bit di-sheveled as well—no doubt because of the various demands for hugs, kisses, and lap sitting from the four children ranging from age

two to eleven that she brings to the clinic. Esther has infinite patience as well as infinite energy. With all those active children, her
world seems to me to border on pandemonium. But she has a
serenity at her center, a calming force that holds the incessant chatter and physical exuberance of these children within bounds.

"Hello, Esther," says Dr. Bennett, walking across the room to
where she sits. Esther, who is bouncing a fourth child, two-year-old
Nettie, on her knee, smiles back at him and frees one hand so that
she can shake hands. She seems very much at ease in the clinic. In
a sense Esther and Dr. Bennett are longtime friends, their relationship formed over ten years of medical appointments for her four
children, all of whom were born to mothers infected with HIV. Dr.
Bennett began seeing Marie and Alyssa during their infancy, and
the younger children, Jackie and Nettie, were also his patients until
it became certain, when each child reached fifteen months of age,
that they were not infected.

Dr. Bennett turns back to face Alyssa and Marie, who are still sitting side by side on the table. Marie swings her legs back and forth
while Alyssa has her legs neatly crossed in front of her.

"This nickel will tell us who gets seen first," says Dr. Bennett,
pulling a coin out of his pants pocket. He flips the coin from one
hand to the other, asking the girls to choose heads or tails. Alyssa
wins. Marie hops off the table and wanders over to Nettie, who
smiles broadly at her big sister.

"Alyssa, how are you doing today?" asks Dr. Bennett, standing
next to the examining table with one hand on her shoulder.

"Fine," Alyssa responds, somewhat mechanically. She has been
coming to Dr. Bennett's clinic monthly, ever since she was an infant, and every month she fields these same questions. Happily,
each time she has few health problems to report. From time to time
her viral load has risen slightly, but Dr. Bennett is quick to adjust
her medications so that it returns to an undetectable level. Otherwise Alyssa has always been very healthy.

"Are you gaining weight?"

She nods; then Dr. Bennett looks down at her chart. "Yes, I see that you've gained a half pound since last time. That's wonderful, Alyssa. I'm glad to see that.

"Any fever?" he asks, looking back up at her.

She shakes her head.

"Vomiting?"

"No."

"Diarrhea?"

"Nope."

"Well, that's good," says Dr. Bennett. "Let's talk about your medications."

"Two big horse pills . . ." Alyssa begins.

"Okay," says Dr. Bennett, "that's the Fortovase. How much?"

"Two, two times a day. Then there are the refrigerator pills . . . the blue ones."

"That's Viracept," interjects Esther from across the room.

"Yes, Viracept," repeats Alyssa. "I take three of those two times a day. Then there's a diamond one and a little orange one that I take at breakfast and at dinner and an antibiotic and a cold pill—"

"An antibiotic?" Dr. Bennett asks, turning to Esther. "What's that for?"

"Well," she replies, a little flustered, "Alyssa had a bad cold, and she says the kids always tease her when her nose is dripping, and so I gave her an antibiotic—her local doctor prescribed it—and a cold tablet too, one of those over-the-counter pills."

Dr. Bennett frowns.

"I gave her only one. I know you don't like cold medications," Esther adds, embarrassed. Then she says, with a short laugh, "I just didn't count on her remembering to tell you!"

"Oh, so you just weren't going to tell me!" he says jokingly.

"Well, I guess you caught me out!" Esther blushes, laughing again. This subject has come up before with Esther, as with most of the families in this clinic. Dr. Bennett is firmly opposed to cold medications for children—especially children with HIV—because of possible side effects. But he also knows that parents sometimes give children these medications anyway.

"Esther," he says, grinning at her, "have you heard about place-bos?"

Esther nods, laughing.

Dr. Bennett turns back to Alyssa. "Well, it looks like you've got all these medications just right. That's good."

During the exchange between Dr. Bennett and Esther, Alyssa has reached over to the equipment mounted on the wall next to her and taken the otoscope out of its holder. "Can I look in your ear?" she asks Dr. Bennett.

"Okay," he replies, bending down for her so that she can reach his ear. "See any potatoes in there?" he asks. Alyssa giggles, then replaces the otoscope in its holder.

"Okay, now that you're done with me, I'll go ahead with you. I'll bet I can find some potatoes in *your* ear," he remarks, looking first in one and then the other.

"Esther," he says, as he next examines Alyssa's throat, "her ears and throat look good. She just has an upper respiratory virus."

"You can lie down now," he tells Alyssa, "and . . . that's great, I was going to tell you to raise your knees, but you already know what you're supposed to do." Dr. Bennett feels for Alyssa's spleen as he asks her about school, after-school activities, and chores at home. He calls over this month's medical student, a shy young man with a crew cut, and shows him how to palpate the lymph nodes under the arm. As the student feels for axillary and cervical nodes, Dr. Bennett asks, "Alyssa, how many medical students have you taught over the years?"

She laughs. "I don't know . . . lots!"

"I'd expect that's right," says Dr. Bennett. "How long have you been coming here? Let's see, about ten years, I think. That's sure a lot of medical students!"

The student thanks Alyssa and steps back. "You're doing well, Alyssa," Dr. Bennett remarks. "Keep on taking your medications just like you're supposed to. Remember, they're keeping you healthy."

"Your turn now, Marie," he announces as Alyssa slides down from the examining table.

"Can I go now, Mom?" Alyssa asks Esther.

"You ask Dr. Bennett that," she replies.

"Yes, you can go. See you next time," he adds, and Alyssa smiles back at him as she leaves the room.

"Marie's been complaining of her legs hurting," Esther remarks.

"Tell me about your legs, Marie," says Dr. Bennett, lifting her up onto the examining table.

"They hurt a lot when I run, and they get really weak."

"Show me," he says. "Where do they hurt?"

"Well," she answers, "all over, not really one place."

"When do they hurt?"

"At school—well, maybe anytime."

"Okay. Let's get you back off this table," he says as he helps her down, "and now I want you to sit down on the floor, legs crossed and hands above your head." Marie complies easily; she's been through all this before. "You know what to do. I want you to stand up, Marie, and keep your hands up." Marie does this without effort. Dr. Bennett often asks the children in his HIV clinic to perform this simple exercise; he claims it gives him information about their musculature, nervous system, even problem-solving ability.

"Marie, I don't think there's anything wrong with your legs," says Dr. Bennett. "I don't mean to say you're not having these pains. I'm sure you are if you say you are, but you shouldn't worry about them. You can get back up on the table now," he adds, watching as she gets back up.

I notice that this time Marie gets onto the table without help. As Dr. Bennett examines her, he asks the same medical questions that he posed to her sister and goes on to inquire about after-school activities. Marie tries to answer, but she is ticklish, giggling and squirming constantly as he feels for her spleen, then her axillary lymph nodes.

"You're always tickling me!" she finally exclaims, still giggling.

As he bends over to look in her ear, Dr. Bennett asks, "Do you have chores after school, Marie? You have animals there at home, don't you?"

"Yes, we have two dogs, five cats with kittens coming . . . umm, let's see . . . a rooster and sheep—and the sheep, they're going to have babies too!"

"Do you take care of the animals?" he asks.

"No," she says, "my mother does. My cat is named Snowflake. She's going to have kittens soon. And Alyssa has a cat too, and her name is Sarah. But my cat's going to have kittens."

"Well, that's wonderful, Marie."

I listen with some amusement to Marie's account of all these multiplying pets and farm animals. The kids' HIV clinic—despite the fish painted in cheerful colors on the walls—is sterile and deliberately antiseptic. In contrast the Hammonds' farm, as I begin to picture it, is a place brimming with life, energetic and fertile. It is not until I visit the farm itself that I realize the extent to which this imaginary picture is both right and meaningful.

Esther and Jimmy Hammond

It is an hour-and-a-half drive from St. Luke's Hospital to Goshen, where Esther and Jimmy and their family live. Rarely have I encountered a place that so perfectly epitomizes the people living there. The trip to their home seems a journey back into time, as highways and cities yield to narrow country roads graced with an occasional Amish buggy and punctuated by signs proclaiming JESUS WILL COME AGAIN or, more simply and more starkly, REPENT! One sign that I always watch for because (in more than one sense) it marks an important turn, demands: WHERE WILL YOU / SPEND ETERNITY? / HEAVEN OR HELL? The landscape is also dotted with clusters of housing developments here and there, but these I try not to notice.

The rural background in which both Esther and Jimmy grew up is the America of small family farms, of country communities centered on churches, of a shared work ethic and shared religious faith, of a way of life rooted and grounded in nature. It is tempting to idealize this world as one that is simpler and somehow more natural than our own. But one must not overlook or minimize its pressures and restrictions, such as the rigid moral code that Esther calls "the law" and the racial bigotry that Jimmy had to outgrow. They knew, or soon discovered, how the church community that sustains and supports can become the community that condemns.

I turn off the road into the Hammonds' driveway and instantly feel as if I were in another, somewhat magical world. My thirteen-year-old son, who came with me on an earlier visit to pick up a free kitten, had much the same response. "This is a kids' paradise!" he exclaimed. The long driveway descends sharply into a stand of trees and then crosses a wooden bridge that opens out into a green, cup-shaped little valley. To my left a creek bubbles along beside the drive. In between creek and driveway are a playhouse and a wooden jungle gym. At the end of the drive, nestled against a big hill, is the house, a rambling yellow bungalow. Behind it I can see an old barn, a pen with two brown and white ponies, and a scattering of sheds for chickens and sheep. Beyond the little valley, woods and fields extend as far as I can see.

Esther has seen me drive up and comes out to meet me, Nettie in her arms. A shaggy, very overweight dog named Felix shambles along after them. As I catch sight of Esther, I realize how fond I've grown of her over two and a half years of clinic visits, picnics, and phone calls about the children. We are friends. Today, like all the times I've been with her, Esther is lively and animated. She has the high-energy level necessary for an older woman with four young children. Besides these, who are adopted or in foster care, she has an equal number of grown-up children from a previous marriage and no fewer than seventeen grandchildren. When she was young, Esther must have been strikingly beautiful. Now, at fifty-nine, she has the kind of beauty that reflects character: strength of mind and commitment to her beliefs, kindliness and generosity of spirit, patience and humility. Esther is certainly religious but "without being pious," as Dr. Bennett observes. Nor is she preachy or judgmental. She told me on one occasion that for her Christianity is "a relationship with the Lord." She explained: "To me it's not that you do something because there are laws set up about it. . . . It's a relationship, and in that relationship wherein you love the Lord, you want to do what He wants you to do because you love Him. And then they're no longer laws."

Today the three older children are in school, and Jimmy, her husband, is at work "hauling Amish." The Amish are a Christian sect with a strong work ethic who, on principle, do not use modern technology or drive automobiles. So four times a week Jimmy drives Amish farmers to market, where they sell their produce and meat. On market days he works hard, rising at 2:30 in the morning and often returning as late as 9:00 or 10:00 that night. I met Jimmy for the first time at the clinic picnic last fall. He is a few years younger than Esther, though he looks a good deal older. Like Esther, he was married before; he has three adult children and six or seven grandchildren. A heavyset man with a tan, deeply lined face, tobacco-stained teeth, and piercing blue eyes, Jimmy carries himself with the confident, earthy masculinity of a farmer. His deep, gravelly voice is slow and measured, but he has a surprisingly quick wit and a ready laugh. Though he seems easygoing and relaxed, he has already suffered four heart attacks and now has to limit strenuous physical work.

Esther and Jimmy have been formally married for twelve years. Esther comes from a devoutly religious farming family of German descent that has lived in the same part of the county for decades. She was raised in the Church of the Brethren, a conservative, fundamentalist, and community-oriented Christian denomination with affinities to the Mennonites and the Amish. Jimmy, on the other hand, was born and raised in Georgia; his southern heritage is perhaps most pronounced in his liberal use of "y'all." At seventeen he moved to southern Ohio, where he has lived for the past thirty years. Unlike Esther, he was never very religious. While still in his teens, he married a Mennonite girl. He spent nearly twenty years working on her father's farm, "practicing the Mennonite work ethic," as he puts it.

Esther and Jimmy bought this house and the fifteen acres surrounding it three years ago, using the money she inherited when her father died and the large and prosperous family farm was sold. The house itself is more modern than I would have expected, something between a farmhouse and a split-level built in the fifties. As Esther and I go inside and climb the stairs to the living room, I notice large portraits of her children, her grandchildren, and her foster children mounted on walls and propped up on the mantel. She pauses to show me a posed photograph of her parents in their later years. Her father is wearing the black suit of the plain people, and her mother, a lace prayer cap.

Her home is as comfortable as any I've ever been in. The living room is clean but cluttered, with children's toys underfoot and cats darting here and there. A big grandfather's clock stands in the corner, reminding us of its presence every quarter hour. There is an upright piano, its white keys marked with red lettering to identify the notes. As I discover during a later visit, when the girls play for me, it is badly out of tune. The sheet music on the piano stand is all hymns. We continue on into the kitchen, where Esther suggests we sit and talk. She returns to the living room with Nettie, plunks her down in front of the television, and feeds a children's video into the VCR. As she does so, I glance out the kitchen window, which looks onto a hill studded with trees. There are hundreds of birds flying through the branches. The stillness of this sunny but very cold February day is filled with their restlessness and energy.

The kitchen table is clean and bare, except for a Bible and a book of daily devotions. When Esther rejoins me, I ask about these books. She tells me that every morning before school the family sits around the table for devotions, which include prayer, a reading from the Bible, and a lesson for the day from the devotional manual. She adds, laughing, "'Course when I was little, we'd have a Bible reading at breakfast and then we'd get on our knees for prayer. I had to tell my friends when they'd visit for overnight, 'You have to know, in the morning we kneel for prayers!'"

Esther wants to read aloud an autobiographical narrative that she wrote three years ago, explaining that she thinks this will help her "get back into her feelings." Indeed it is clear that her background, both religious and familial, is very much a part of her present self. As I listen to Esther's account of her farm family, I am struck by the harmony between her heritage and her present devotion to Jimmy and these four children. The Esther of the past and the Esther of the present are linked by a religious ethos that is less conceptual and doctrinal than pragmatic and practical.

She begins: "I was reared on a farm in a hardworking family that was God-fearing and frugal. One big difference between then and now is that I made some bad choices along the way, and the consequences haunt me and make me feel unworthy. Though I have the 'head knowledge' of God's grace and have repented and accepted his forgiveness, the Devil uses my failures to keep me from fully using the gifts I think God has given me. However, God has blessed me with many children to love. My husband and I have had ten foster children, but the three we have now have been with us the longest. [Esther wrote this narrative before Nettie's arrival.] They came to us at six months, five months, and two weeks of age. They all were HIV positive at birth. One seroconverted to negative. We don't know what the future holds for the others, but we love them dearly. They are dedicated to the Lord."

Esther's narrative, which takes her about forty-five minutes to read, is shaped around the four seasons. Her remarks about spring planting and the fall harvest, in particular, strike me as suggestive of her present work in rearing foster children. "Spring makes me feel hope and joy as I see new life spring forth. It's the time of year I make a new partnership with the Lord. What I pray is, 'Lord, if you'll send the sunshine and the rain, I'll work the ground, sow the seed, keep out the weeds, and praise you as I harvest.'" Esther goes on to describe plowing and harrowing on cold spring days as she picked up stones: "I wondered if they grew there, because it seemed like the plow brought up more each year!" When she writes about the fall harvest and its labor, she is reminded of caring for children. She describes harvesting corn, digging for sweet potatoes, and blanching celery plants, then observes, "I think fall was my favorite season because I felt I was putting things to bed, or to rest, over the winter. I remember going to the barn at night to bed down the cows. It gave me warm feelings that all was well. Maybe I've carried that warm feeling to motherhood, as I tuck my children in at night."

Esther's story of life on a farm seems like something from a very faraway time. I comment on this, and she agrees. We both are quiet for a few minutes. Then I ask her about her life after this early period. She is embarrassed at first, referring again to "some choices I made," but then observes, "Well, God didn't keep people out of the Bible who made mistakes, did He!" I agree with her wholeheartedly.

Her upbringing was very strict. Girls did not wear jewelry or makeup. Clothing did not reveal the contours of the body, and dancing was out of the question. Though she knew her parents loved her, they did not display affection. The only physical contact with her mother she can recall is sitting on her lap for Bible stories every evening. Esther remembers meeting a boy in 4-H whom she liked, but her parents discouraged the relationship because they found out he was Presbyterian. At seventeen she married a Mennonite boy, also from a farming family. Marriage at such an early age was routine in this community, and both her family and her church encouraged the union. Each year afterward a child was born to the young couple, until there were four. Life was extremely arduous. Esther and her husband farmed in the summer, and in the winter they "hired out to do milking." This meant that they rose at four in the morning, took all the children to the milk house at a nearby farm—the milk house was always very warm—and milked some seventy cows. Esther observes, "It was hard, but we were young, and the Lord has always given me lots of energy."

Not long into their marriage Esther began noticing that when her husband was angry or irritated or just bothered by something, he would withdraw, sometimes for days at a time. At first she thought this was "just the way he was." But such episodes became more frequent and more prolonged, some requiring hospitalization. He was diagnosed as a paranoid schizophrenic. "It was awful," Esther remarks. "I never knew what to expect. I blamed myself. My mother used to say to me, 'If you make your husband happy, then you'll be happy.' But it didn't work out that way. What do I say to my family when he's not there for meals, and what do I say at church Sunday morning when people ask me where he is? I'd go out to the meadow, and I'd say, 'Lord, I know you don't like divorce, but what do I do?'" Esther is now crying softly. "The hardest part of it was that I was living under the law, and under the law you don't get divorced. But after years of not knowing what I would find when I came home and not knowing what would set him off, I finally left."

At the time of her divorce Esther's children ranged in age from nine to fifteen. The oldest son, who was critical of his mother's decision, chose to stay with his father. Esther moved with her three younger children to her parents' home. Though divorce is anathema for the Church of the Brethren, her parents were supportive, given the circumstances. For them, as Esther put it, "love dictated over law." After only a year she met the man who became her second husband. They married the following August. Her new husband became a good father to the children and took an active role in running the household and planning trips and vacations. "George was a good, kind man," she observes, "but he was also a perfectionist who lived according to the law." At this point in her story I begin to take notice of the frequent juxtaposition of "love" and "law." Under the law Esther accepts certain actions as sinful. But she also believes that law is superseded by love, since God's grace works through love, not law.

When she and George had been married for nearly ten years and only the youngest child remained at home, Esther earned a degree as a licensed practical nurse and began working as a private-duty nurse. One assignment took her to the home of a paralyzed girl. The girl's uncle was a frequent visitor. Esther grew to like him. Born and raised in Georgia, he was easygoing and relaxed, unlike most of her friends and relatives. He also had a wonderful sense of humor. "He would tell jokes," she remarks, "and he'd laugh so hard he couldn't get through the joke. I liked that. Not so straitlaced, like most of the people I knew. But he didn't know the Lord, and he was given to swearing." So Esther took it upon herself "to lead him to the Lord."

It is difficult for her to talk about what happened next. "One summer day when I was at the house taking care of this girl, he said something—I don't remember what—and I replied, 'Christians like to have fun too!' He took what I said the wrong way. When I left that evening to walk home, he was up at the end of the lane. And well, you know . . . that's when I got involved with Jimmy. As somebody said to me afterward, 'You had always been a good girl, and you must have decided that you didn't need to be a good girl anymore!' Anyhow, that's when it started with him.

"It just horrified the family. In the evening Jimmy used to come out near where I lived, to where I could see his car, and then I'd go out and meet him. My husband, George, and my youngest son, who was sixteen then, they decided they'd spy on Mom! Oh, boy. They did that a few evenings." Esther laughs nervously. "George was really angry, and he persuaded me to break it off.

"But I couldn't help looking out that window anyway. After about six weeks I spotted the car again, Jimmy's car." Esther is blushing now and laughs in embarrassment. "I didn't stay inside the house. I went on out to meet him. And after I did that, I just couldn't handle the pressure anymore of living with George but being together with Jimmy. So one night I packed up the car and thought I'd just leave. I moved out. I got an apartment in Springtown, and Jimmy came to me there, for one night. And then—oh, you'd think it would be so romantic; I could hardly wait to sleep with him—he snored so bad I couldn't sleep!" She laughs heartily. "Between his snoring and my conscience bothering me so bad, I couldn't sleep. So the next morning I got up and said to Jimmy, 'I can't do this. I just can't do it.'

"So I went back home. But when I came in the door, I really got it. George just yelled and yelled, and he dragged me over to my parents' house and yelled at me some more there. He told them I was sleeping around—'fucking around,' he said. He actually said that! When we got back home, I thought, 'I don't need this.' So off I went back to the apartment. Well, somebody told George where I was going. He came out to the apartment right away and took me by the arm and dragged me outside, and he was going to take me back to my parents again. I said to him, 'Please, don't take me to my parents again! Don't do that!' So we went home.

"As soon as we got inside, he said, 'You go upstairs and call your mom because I'm going to go get my gun and settle this once and for all!' I ran out of the house and down the steps. It was nighttime, so it was dark out. We were living in a development then, and I looked to see if anybody had any lights on. There was one house that did, so I ran there. He was coming after me, and I expected to be shot in the back anytime. When I got to the house with the light on, I knocked on the door and said, 'Please let me in!' and they did. Then I told them what it was all about. It was the last thing anybody in that neighborhood expected. George got there, and he knocked on the door, but they wouldn't let him in. He still had that rifle in his hand, so they called the police. When the police came, they took me back to the apartment in Springtown and said they'd keep their eyes on him. Oh, I get so nervous, just reliving this! There I was, running as fast as I could, expecting any minute to get shot in the back!"

Esther pauses, takes a deep breath, then asks me if I'd like something to drink, some tea maybe. I accept eagerly. We've been talking a long time, and the house is cold. These wooden stools also seem to become harder the longer we sit there at the table. When she gets up and makes tea for both of us, I can't help noticing that the same teabag serves, in addition to both hers and mine, two more teacups, which are kept in reserve, no doubt to be drunk later. I'm struck by the contrast between Esther's generosity of spirit and the parsimonious lifestyle that is a part of her heritage.

Esther goes on with her story. "After George and I were separated, I lived with a girlfriend for a while. I was working at the VA hospital. In a month or so Jimmy and I moved to a trailer court. We couldn't get married for a long time since neither of our partners would sign off on their marriage." Though Jimmy's family, including his wife, knew him to be a philanderer, they blamed Esther for what happened. Jimmy's wife believed that this was just one of his affairs and that he'd "get over it" and come back to her. Also, forcing Jimmy and Esther to live in sin in order to be together was a real punishment in this highly religious community. "We lived together for three years before we could get married," remarks Esther, beginning to cry again. "I hurt my family so bad. 'Mom,' my kids said, 'this is against everything you ever taught us.' And I'd pray: 'God, why am I doing this? I don't understand. I don't understand. What am I doing?' Yet there was something that drew me to Jimmy." Esther is now crying and laughing at the same time.

"It took a lot of healing on everybody's part. My dad was always there for me, and I'm so grateful for that. And Mother — oh, Mother was so angry at me! She was so ashamed of me! It took her several years before she could talk to me again without showing me her anger. And my children, they always loved me, but they couldn't understand. They were ashamed of me. One time, when Jimmy and I had just started living with each other, the kids invited me for a get-together. Everyone was there. They all had the purpose of getting Mom straightened out!" Esther laughs. "That was their plan. They said, 'Mom, we don't believe you'll be saved because the Bible says, "By their fruits ye shall know them," and we see what you're doing, how you're living.' I remember lashing back at them and saying, 'You just wait till you're eighty-five years old, and then you can come and talk to me!'" Esther speaks loudly and heatedly, then lowers her voice again. "I said that then because I was thinking of my dad. He was getting old then, but oh, how he was loving me through it all! I knew he didn't approve, but he was letting me find my own way.

"All that time, and afterward, I was struggling with my relationship with the Lord. Then one day I heard a radio preacher say, 'If you don't believe that God can forgive you, it's like you're slapping Him in the face!' That really got to me." Esther pauses for a minute and sighs deeply, gazing out the window, then turns and smiles at me. "And after I've said all these things to you about what I've done, oh, just look what the Lord has brought me to now! There are these children, there's this place where we live. . . .

"Anyway, to get back to what happened then, I wanted to take on foster children back when George and I were married. I had said to him, 'All we're doing is collecting money, accumulating things, and going on trips. I want more to my life than that. Let's take in foster children.' 'Nope,' he said, 'I've raised enough of kids.' I just could not persuade him. But there was such a void in my life that I made out an application anyway, on my own. When Jimmy and I got together, he said to me, 'If you want to take foster kids, fine, I'll help you.' So we reapplied together.

"The first child Children and Youth sent us was a teenage boy, but that wasn't so good." She laughs. "He'd swear terrible! And he and the neighbor kids didn't get along. We also had a couple of other ones, all for a short time. Then Jimmy had his heart attack, that was in 1985, and he asked me to wait for him to recover before bringing in more foster children.

"In 1987 someone called from Children and Youth and asked, 'How'd you like to take care of babies with AIDS?' Jimmy and I thought on it. And I did a lot of praying. There were three green lights. One was a series on AIDS just then at our church. The second was the Lord's promise to me that I would have enough energy. The third happened in our church group when a piece of paper was passed around with all our names on it and we were to write next to the person's name their spiritual gifts. What was written next to mine was 'compassion.' I think it was written five times, by five different people. 'Caring, compassion.' That was the third green light. So we called Children and Youth back, and we said yes.

"Alyssa came to us soon after that—it was the summer of 1988— and then Marie came next year, in March 1989. And now we have Jackie and Nettie too! I dearly love these children. Just look how the Lord has blessed me!" Esther is again laughing and crying at the same time.

As I listen to Esther's story, I am struck by the extent to which she has grown in her values, beliefs, and lifestyle beyond the community into which she was born. In her new family, rules are balanced with love and work alternates with play. The family prays together, but without kneeling on the floor. They live on a farm, and the children all have their assigned chores, but work does not dominate their lives. At a later visit with Jimmy I find that he too has moved beyond the moral value system he inherited. A native of the deep South, Jimmy grew up in a community where racist atitudes and practices seemed both natural and right. Now in his new family two of the children are Hispanic, and one is African-American.

Esther and Jimmy's new household seems to preserve what is best about the community values each grew up in, while dispensing with what is narrow-minded and limiting. What they have achieved is a creative freedom within an inherited traditional value system. Religion and work are still an important aspect of family life, but forgiveness is valued over judgment, play takes its place beside chores, and love is ranked highest of all.

Nevertheless, this new value system and lifestyle set them apart from their communities and even their families. Both Esther and Jimmy have been shunned for taking in children with HIV. Esther was surprised at the lack of support from people, some of them family members, in her church. "When Alyssa turned two, we wanted to put her in the Sunday school class for that age. But people were afraid. There were four sessions held after church where everybody discussed it. Jimmy and I didn't go, but we heard that my brother— my own brother!—stood up and said, 'Well, I'm afraid if we allow them in that class, we're going to lose other people.' So they made a separate Sunday school class for Alyssa and Marie.

"To this day I still can't take the girls to my oldest brother's house. They're still afraid. First he was afraid for his children and now that his children are grown, they're afraid for their children. My family—that's my brothers and sisters and their families—they have a reunion every year, and we're invited, but we're not allowed to take our foster children. So we don't go. My parents, though, were always very supportive, right from the beginning. In fact I think that was one of the things that brought Mother around after all those problems I had." Esther laughs. "I think she kinda saw that the Lord was going to make something out of me!"

Jimmy's problems were with his children, who were adults at this time. Esther describes several occasions when they invited his children, with their spouses, over for Sunday dinner, laying out a big meal "with all the fixings." Several times they came but would only pick at their food. One time a son and his wife didn't show up, later claiming they had forgotten about it. When I talked with Jimmy at another time about the way his children behaved, I found him still angry. He is even angrier when he talks about his daughter-in-law's refusal to bring the grandchildren for visits because she feared they would "get AIDS." Unfortunately Jimmy remains estranged from two of his three biological children and rarely sees his grandchildren.

Esther too had difficulties with her own children, also grown up and with youngsters of their own. "My own kids were 'hands off' at first. It was like 'We're glad you did it, but keep away from us!' They were afraid for their kids. It used to be that every Easter, or Thanksgiving, or Christmas, when we'd have everybody here—our kids and our grandchildren—we'd have to take Alyssa and Marie somewhere else, to a baby-sitter. One Easter I said to Jimmy, 'Let's just let the girls stay here for the Easter egg hunt; then we'll take them off.' So we did. I didn't call my kids or anything; we just went ahead and hid the eggs. So my son Peter pulled up in his car with his family. When he got out of the car and saw the girls, he pointed to them and said, 'Mom, how come they're still here?' And I told him, 'Well, we decided that we'd have the Easter egg hunt, and then they'd go off.' He said, 'Oh, if I'd known that, we'd have come later!' Well, Jimmy got angry, just like that. [Esther snaps her fingers.] He can get so angry. This really pushed his button! He said, 'Come on, girls, we're going now.' He left, and he didn't come back and he didn't come back." Esther is crying again.

"So on that Easter part of my family was here, but it wasn't my whole family. I said to my kids afterward, 'I won't do this anymore. You're all welcome to come, but I will not take the girls away anymore. I will not do that.' They do respect me, so I could talk like this. So they discussed it with each other and finally decided they would come, but they'd wait until their children were five years old to bring them too.

"Even now, with my kids I feel left out. Emotionally it's like I'm the child. There have been times that I've thought, 'Maybe they could just sin a little bit!'"—she laughs—"'so I wouldn't have to feel so alone?' Of course I've got Jimmy. He's so good to me, though I'd say about two percent of the time he loses his temper—"

Esther takes a deep breath, then goes on. "Besides, I do have a lot of energy. Two years ago I prayed about Nettie, about whether we should take her. When the phone call came from Children and Youth, she had just been born. The birth mother—she's black—had told her family that she'd had an abortion. She gave birth in secret and didn't want her family ever to know this. So we needed to make a decision right away. I prayed to the Lord. I said, 'Lord, I need an answer.' The answer that came to my mind was, 'Yes. Yes.' I had no mind-set of my own; it was just 'Whatever you want, Lord.' Then I practically argued with the Lord. I said, 'But how am I going to get the strength?' And he said, 'I will give it to you. I will give you strength.'"

Esther and I at the same time catch sight of five-year-old Jackie trudging up the driveway, coming back home from kindergarden for her lunch. We both realize that it is time to end our talking. As we get up from the kitchen table, Esther remarks, "After saying all that to you, you know, I feel good! There's part of it in there that I was not anxious to tell. But telling about it wasn't too bad after all. 'Cause when you look at the whole—and I have a tendency to separate that part and look just at that, and not the whole—when you look at the whole, it's like, well, maybe everything fits. This talking with you, it was good for me. It was almost like healing!"

I ask Esther on impulse, just before Jackie comes in the house, whether in some greater plan, maybe a divine plan, she is just "meant" to be with Jimmy. She smiles and there are tears in her eyes. "Sometimes I think about it all, and I say, 'Lord, is this what your plan was? And we had to go through all that, with adultery and hurting others, in order to get to your plan?' Then I say, 'No, no, You wouldn't want that, Lord, to get to your plan.' But maybe, maybe that was the only way it could happen. . . . Maybe . . . who knows?"

Alyssa, Marie, and Their Families

I drive out to Goshen again—also on a weekday, when the girls are in school—to talk with both Esther and Jimmy. I'm beginning to understand that at the heart of each successful foster family is something unique, something that evolves from particular backgrounds and values, from individual struggles, failures, and achievements. At my request, Jimmy describes his background and his life before meeting Esther, and then we move on to talk about the children. For the most part it is Esther who speaks. Jimmy, as he explains in his gravelly voice, is "not a man much for words." But despite his perceived discomfort with talking, he is very much a part of the conversation. From time to time he will interject a remark, usually to agree with Esther or correct some bit of information in her story. His sense of humor adds a wonderful perspective. For example, when he describes meeting Esther while she was caring for his crippled niece, he tells me that before the family hired Esther, he had checked out her credentials and told them, "She's too religious!"

Throughout our conversation he holds Nettie on his lap. His obvious affection for Nettie takes on added meaning when he describes growing up in the South of racial segregation, with cousins who were Klan members. I'm touched by the way this big, taciturn man bounces Nettie up and down, to her great delight, and sings snatches of songs to her during our conversation about Alyssa and Marie. As Esther goes back to when Alyssa and then Marie first entered their lives, Jimmy shows me, through his treatment of Nettie, the kind of love these children must have received from him over the past ten years.

In July 1988 Alyssa came to live with them as a foster child. She was six months old. The caseworker at Children and Youth Services told them that the child's mother, Monique, was fourteen, HIV positive, and moving around with the baby from place to place. "Monique was just a teenager then," recalls Esther. "And boy, did she ever have an attitude! No one told her what to do. She'd go to someone's home and then act up, so she'd stay only a little while before she'd be off. When I heard how young Monique was, I told Children and Youth that I'd be willing to take her too. But they decided against that."

However, Esther kept in touch with Monique. She frequently talked with her by phone or during Monique's visits with Alyssa. Esther learned that Monique's mother was an alcoholic who had for the most part let her daughter grow up on her own. Monique's father and brother both were addicted to cocaine. Monique herself was in foster care several times because her alcoholic mother often left her alone in the house. She began experimenting with drugs at the age of ten or eleven and was sexually active by the time she was twelve, when she had an abortion.

Alyssa was conceived when Monique was thirteen. Esther tells me that the father was Monique's mother's boyfriend, Manuel. Jimmy adds, "That's what you call sharin'!" Manuel was a slim, handsome Puerto Rican more than twice as old as Monique. He had already fathered four other children, who were living with their mother in Puerto Rico. He was involved with street drugs, and Monique's mother suspected that he contracted HIV by shooting coke. Not long after Monique gave birth to Alyssa, Manuel died of AIDS-related infections. On his deathbed he made Monique promise that she would not give Alyssa up for adoption but raise the child herself.

Monique received no prenatal care, and some of her boyfriends were abusive. She arrived at the hospital to deliver her baby with both eyes blackened and her body bruised. Nevertheless, she gave birth to a full-term, healthy baby. It is unclear whether Monique and Alyssa were diagnosed with HIV when Alyssa was born or several months later. When Alyssa's HIV antibody test was positive at four and a half months, she was assumed to be infected. It is now known, as I've pointed out earlier, that this test cannot detect perinatally acquired HIV infection in a child so young, but in 1988 there was much less information about HIV diagnosis for infants.

Dr. Bennett saw Monique only a few times, when she came along with Esther for Alyssa's clinic appointment. His memory of her is much less sympathetic than Esther's. He recalls "a large, heavyset fifteen-year-old Caucasian girl who was pretty arrogant and irresponsible, loud and kind of surly. We tried to counsel her on using contraceptives. I even tried to get her to have her tubes tied. But she declared that she was going to have another baby, and she did." Luckily this child, a boy, was not infected with the virus.

Some six months after the Hammonds took in Alyssa, Children and Youth Services called to ask if they would take another HIV-infected child. Marie came to live with them in March 1989. She was five months old. Unlike Alyssa, Marie already had an extensive medical history when she was remanded to foster care, and she was already under Dr. Bennett's care for her HIV infection.

Marie was born three weeks early to a twenty-eight-year-old Caucasian woman. Dora was addicted to cocaine and methadone, had syphilis and hepatitis, and admitted she was a prostitute. There is no evidence that Dora or her newborn daughter was suspected of having HIV infection. At birth Marie weighed five pounds and showed signs of tachypnea and tachycardia (rapid breathing and a rapid heart rate), probably caused by maternal drug addiction. She was sent to the hospital's neonatal intensive care unit for twenty-four-hour observation, then discharged home on a respiratory cardiac monitor. The plan was that Marie would be cared for by her mother, who in turn would be helped by daily visits from a home health nurse. This plan was at best minimally effective, and Marie spent only the first four months of her life with her mother. The nurses observed that though Dora was very loving and gentle with Marie, she was often sick herself and frequently depressed and lonely. She missed her husband, Julio, a young Chicano who was serving a one-year prison term for possessing and selling illegal drugs. She didn't get along with her mother-in-law, who spoke little English and was homesick for Mexico.

At some point during this early period, mother and child were tested and both found to be infected. Marie was referred to Dr. Bennett, who wanted to see her on a monthly basis. But Dora repeatedly failed to bring Marie to medical appointments both at the local hospital and at St. Luke's. Marie became very ill when she was four months old, but Dora refused to bring her to the hospital. It is unclear who reported the situation, but somehow a court order was obtained to force Dora to do this. When Marie arrived at St. Luke's, she was found to have pneumonia, gastroenteritis, and severe candidiasis, and Dora was nowhere to be found. She had apparently brought the child to the emergency room and then taken off. Since she could not be reached to give consent for tests and procedures, the hospital turned to Marie's father, Julio, even though he was still in jail.

Dora showed up at the hospital from time to time to see her baby and then would disappear again. The reason for this sporadic behavior became clear one night when Dora was sleeping on a waiting room couch and the police came for her. There had been a warrant out for her arrest. She was quickly arraigned and remanded to prison.

After a ten-day stay in the hospital Marie was ready to be discharged. With both parents in jail, custody was awarded to the child's paternal grandmother, who had been living with Dora and the baby. A tiny, wizened Mexican woman, she agreed to take off work for a month so that she could care for her granddaughter. Both then and for a long time afterward the grandmother refused to believe that Marie had any serious medical problem.

When this month drew to a close and it became clear that the grandmother would not be able to keep Marie any longer, the Hammonds were called by Children and Youth Services and asked to take her as a foster child. Esther remembers meeting the grandmother, who was holding Marie on her lap, in a room at Children and Youth headquarters. "We sat around a big conference table. She was at the end holding Marie, and I came up and sat right beside her. We couldn't really talk, since she didn't know English and I didn't know Spanish. Marie had those big brown eyes—just like she does now—and I just fell in love with her." It was difficult for the grandmother, who wanted to keep Marie in the family. But Marie's father was still in jail, her mother had disappeared while on parole, and the grandmother needed to go back to work. The Children and Youth caseworker arrived at a plan that was agreeable to all concerned. When Julio was released from prison six months later, Marie would be returned to his custody, and he would get a job and support the grandmother so that she could quit her job and take care of Marie. All this never happened. Julio had a serious drug problem and continued to be in and out of jail for years. Dora, Marie's mother, died of complications from end stage AIDS while still on the run. Marie just stayed on, year after year, with the Hammonds.

The Girls' Medical Histories

Marie was never as healthy as Alyssa when they were infants. Only a week after being placed with the Hammonds, Marie suddenly developed an earache and a high fever. By the time Esther arrived with her at the local hospital emergency room, her fever had climbed to 105. Marie was admitted with a diagnosis of bacteremia and otitis media. She was kept in the hospital for two weeks so that she could receive intravenous gamma globulin treatments.

Several weeks after she was discharged, Marie was brought in by Esther for an appointment with Dr. Bennett. He had been seeing her on a monthly basis since infancy. Esther remembers Dr. Bennett from this first visit as "professional but warm." She and Jimmy soon decided that Alyssa should also be seen by Dr. Bennett. Despite the fact that she seemed a healthy child, they thought she should be cared for by an HIV expert. So a month later, when Marie was seven months and Alyssa fifteen months old, Jimmy and Esther brought both girls for an appointment with Dr. Bennett.

Marie's condition seemed to have stabilized, and she required only a "checkup."

But Alyssa, at fifteen months, had reached the age when a definitive diagnosis of HIV could be made. Since her spleen and axillary lymph nodes were palpable and since the HIV antibody test he ordered was again positive, Dr. Bennett felt certain that she was infected. After consultations with the Hammonds as well as with Monique, who occasionally came along for a medical appointment, Dr. Bennett started Alyssa on AZT. At first Esther was apprehensive about side effects, but Alyssa tolerated the drug quite well. Getting her to take it, though, was another matter. Four times a day Esther fought with Alyssa over AZT. Finally, she appealed for help to the clinic nurses, who taught her to use her weight to hold the child down and then pinch her nose to encourage the swallowing reflex.

Esther's attention was soon diverted from Alyssa and AZT to Marie, now eleven months old, who again suddenly developed a painful earache and a fever. Despite medications, the earache persisted and her fever continued to rise. Marie was again admitted to the hospital. Once more after a two-week treatment of intravenous gamma globulin she improved and was sent home. Only a month after this episode Marie began to have difficulty standing. She was hyperreflexive, her legs were very weak, and movement was often painful. Dr. Bennett was worried that the virus had affected her spinal cord, causing transverse myelitis. When symptoms did not disappear, he decided to give her AZT, thinking that treatment of the virus might have a secondary effect on whatever was causing the problem with her legs. At the same time he enrolled Marie in a protocol designed to measure the effectiveness of intravenous injections of gamma globulin (ACTG 051).[1] Since prior ear infec-

---

[1] In the mid-eighties, an immunologist at Stanford reasoned that children with HIV who had a great deal of gamma globulin but minimal antibody production might be effectively treated as though they had hypergammaglobulinanemia, an antibody-deficiency syndrome. Physicians who treated HIV-infected children with intravenous gamma globulin reported success. Empirical success with IVIG resulted in ACTG 051, a double-blind study in which some children were given intravenous

tions had cleared up with treatments of gamma globulin, he reasoned that her leg pain might respond similarly. Marie's leg problems resolved around the time she turned two years old. Dr.
Bennett was greatly relieved when this happened but admits that he
does not know if the treatments he initiated actually helped produce this effect. The episode seemed to mark a turning point for
Marie and for her foster family. Since then neither she nor Alyssa
has had serious medical problems related to her HIV infection.

Adoption

Alyssa remained in foster care with the Hammonds until she was
five and a half years old, when they adopted her. During those early
years the court mandated that Monique be permitted to visit with
Alyssa every two weeks. The Hammonds complied, believing it in
a child's best interests to stay in contact with the biological parents.
But Monique often did not show up. One long absence followed a
suicide attempt soon after her sixteenth birthday. There were intervals when a boyfriend would discourage such visits. When Alyssa
turned five, Children and Youth Services put pressure on Monique
to allow Alyssa to be adopted by the Hammonds, even asking Esther
to persuade Monique to agree. Monique was willing.

Esther continues to take Alyssa to visit her mother since the
adoption, and sometimes she brings Alyssa's half brother back for
weekend visits at the Hammonds' farm. Alyssa is not enthusiastic
about visiting her birth family. There have been problems with her
grandmother, who, according to Alyssa, makes fun of her. There
have also been problems with her mother's boyfriends. Once when

---

gamma globulin, and some children received placebos. Marie was enrolled in this
study. Alyssa was not a candidate because she had received IVIG empirically prior to
the study. Results after the first year showed a decrease in the number and severity of
infections. But results after the second year indicated no difference between children
who underwent IVIG and those who did not. The reason was that Bactrim had been
introduced during this year as a preventative for pneumonia and, serendipitously, it
reduced the incidence of other infections as well.

Alyssa, then eight years old, was spending the night at Monique's house, she became frightened when she heard her mother fighting with her current boyfriend. Alyssa started crying. When Monique came into the bedroom and asked her what was wrong, Alyssa told her that she was scared and "wanted to go home to Mommy." Monique responded, "Well, I *am* your mommy." Alyssa then told her she wanted to go home "to my *other* mommy." Monique left the room to find the boyfriend mimicking Alyssa: "I want my mommy! I want my mommy!" When Monique returned to the bedroom, it was with the boyfriend. He announced to Alyssa, "This *is* your mommy. That other lady's not your mommy. Get that through your head!" Alyssa cried herself to sleep. She told Esther the whole story the next morning when she came to take her home and declared, "I never want to go back there again! Don't ever make me go there again!"

Esther still wants Alyssa to visit with her mother: "I think she needs to see her. I don't want there ever to come a time when Alyssa feels angry because I wouldn't let her see her mother. Another reason is the feeling I have about Monique: 'There but by the grace of God go I.' A third reason is the golden rule: 'Do unto others as you would have them do unto you.' I try to live by that." Thus at least twice a year Alyssa goes to her biological mother's house for visits. But there have been no further overnight stays, and Alyssa has asked that Esther and the other girls stay during the visit. Monique seems content with this arrangement.

Like Alyssa, Marie came to the Hammonds when she was an infant and remained with them in foster care until she was adopted much later, after nearly ten years. Esther made sure throughout this period that Marie visited with her father, Julio, as well as her paternal grandmother. Esther recalls, "One day Marie and I were in the car driving someplace and she asked if it was okay to love both Grandma and me. This was an easy question! I told her, 'Yes, that's fine.' Because I don't think we can have too many people that love us—in the right way, of course!" She laughs.

Relations between Julio and the Hammonds have always been

very good. From the beginning, and despite his frequent jail terms, Esther was extremely fond of him. "I've always liked Julio," she says. "I could take him as a son! I've always just appreciated him for who he is. And now, he and I are like kindred spirits. We both have a lot of the same values." Julio has continued over the years to visit regularly with Marie. He has watched her become more and more a member of the Hammond family, and he approves. Esther reports that he promised them several times, "I won't ever take her away. She's part of your family now." Julio has a steady job in a restaurant and has had no recent problems with the law. He has had numerous girlfriends but intends to marry the woman he now lives with.

Alyssa and Marie remained in foster care for a very long time before their original families agreed to adoption. A recent change in family law would prevent such extended foster care placement. Now permanent placement for a child must be arranged within a year. Either the birth family demonstrates it is capable of caring for the child, or the child becomes eligible for adoption. This new law unquestionably diminishes the rights of biological parents. But it also diminishes the limbo in which many children in foster care now find themselves, caught between their birth families and their foster families. Moreover, this law is likely to reduce costs of foster care, which are paid for by child welfare programs. Such cost reduction benefits the county, but this economy may restrict the number of families willing to take in children with serious problems. At first the Hammonds received $55 a day for each of their foster children, all of whom tested positive for HIV at birth. When the two younger children seroconverted a year later, this amount was reduced to $13.50 a day. When Alyssa was adopted, the county awarded the Hammonds $700 monthly toward her care, an arrangement that will terminate when she turns eighteen. She continues to receive an access card covering medical expenses and drugs. Marie's adoption, which is still in process, involves a different county. The Hammonds do not know to what extent the county will contribute to her support. For foster parents like the Hammonds, adoption represents not only a human commitment but also additional financial responsibility.

Difficult Questions; Difficult Answers

When and how to tell children they have HIV are questions that usually come up at some time or another. Even though their HIV status has never been concealed during clinic visits, they need to be told what it *means* to have HIV. Some parents and foster parents resist such conversations. I was at the clinic the day that Esther raised this issue with Dr. Bennett.

"Could I talk to you for a minute after the kids leave the room?" Esther asks Dr. Bennett, as he hands her prescriptions for Marie and Alyssa.

"Okay, girls, you can go now." Dr. Bennett has finished examining Alyssa and Marie and sends them off to find Nicole, one of the nurses, who they know has an Easter basket for them. He turns around to face Esther.

Esther begins talking as soon as the children close the door to the examining room, though Nettie is still struggling in her arms: "Alyssa's been asking questions lately about why she has to take so many medications. She's nine years old now, and I'm wondering if I should tell her she has HIV. I'm really not sure about this, and I want to know what you think."

"Is this the first time she's asked about it?" asks Dr. Bennett. Nettie has stopped struggling and gazes up at him solemnly, chewing a Gummi Bear.

"No," replies Esther. "Both girls have asked me why they have to take medicines, and I just said that they have a blood disease and they take these pills to keep them well. But the last time I said this to Alyssa, she looked at me and cocked her head to the side the way she does and said, 'Yeah, Mom, but other kids don't take this many.' So I'm wondering if it's time."

"Well, Esther," says Dr. Bennett, "it sounds to me like you're thinking it's time. There is no single answer to your question, but if *you* think it's time, then why not tell her?"

"I'm a little worried. . . . She sometimes has a problem with her attitude, and I'm afraid she'll just give up, like her mother did. Alyssa is the kind of person who says, 'I'll do it if I want to and not, if I don't.' She was that way about the pills. And she'll want to know how she got it. I'm waiting until she's old enough to tell her that."

"Who knows at school?" asks Dr. Bennett.

"The teacher, the superintendent, the nurse . . . and our school has AIDS education now so I know that the children have heard about it. . . ."

"Just tell her she has HIV infection."

"I'm worried that she'll translate 'HIV infection' into a fatal illness," replies Esther. "And then she'll get discouraged. It'll affect her attitude."

"Don't tell her she has AIDS because that's not an appropriate term. She's been infected with the HIV virus, so she has HIV infection." Dr. Bennett pauses, crossing his arms over his chest. "You know, Esther, there's a fine line here. If she hears about HIV or AIDS at school, and you wait to talk about it with her, she may feel that you've been lying to her when you eventually do tell her. I'd encourage you to tell Alyssa now."

Esther takes a deep breath. "What do I say if she asks me how she got it?"

"You just say, 'You got it from your mother.'"

"Well, then, what do I do about Marie?" Esther asks reflectively, looking off to the side, then answers her own question. "I guess I'll have to tell her too."

"Yes," says Dr. Bennett, nodding, "you will."

"Do you think the girls will talk to their friends about it? Won't it be a problem for them if they do?"

"Well, they might," Dr. Bennett concedes.

"I'll bet Marie is more likely to talk about it," Esther says, "because it will make her feel special, and you know she likes to feel special!" She laughs. "Won't it make them want to stay home from school more often?"

"Then you just don't go along with that," declares Dr. Bennett. "I'm sure you can be tough about that! Remember, even though they have HIV infection, when they're healthy, they're just like any other child. Esther, you want to know when is the right time to tell her. Well, the right time is when the child is asking. I know it seems hard, but it won't be. Answer their questions, but don't go beyond that. Let them ask; then you answer."

"Well," says Esther, "I guess it *is* time. I know I'll feel relieved once I tell them."

"Yes, you will," rejoins Dr. Bennett, placing his hands, palms down, on his thighs. "It's the right thing to do."

Esther told me about this conversation with the girls—briefly, right after it took place, and at greater length several years later during a taped interview.

"The way it happened," Esther says, "it wasn't a planned thing. We're all sitting around the kitchen table. You know that Alyssa has always been very outspoken about why she has to take so much medication. Well, one morning she starts again about how it's not fair, and that other kids don't have to take this many pills.' And I just answer her, 'Well, Alyssa, you're right. Life just isn't fair!' Then I tell them that they're both HIV positive. I don't mention that word 'AIDS.' I say again, 'The reason you have to take these medications is that you have a blood disease that's called HIV.' I don't go into a lot of detail. Marie hardly says anything; it's Alyssa who asks the questions. But that's the way they are about everything.

"Over the next few weeks Alyssa talks about it a lot. One time we're riding in the car someplace, and she says right out of the blue, 'Mommy, how did I get HIV?' I tell her, 'Well, you got it when you were born, from your mother.' Then Alyssa asks how her mother got it, and I say, 'She got it from having sex with a person who was infected with the virus or from using drugs.' I've always believed that you need to tell the truth, and I just don't know how to answer that question about how her mother got it without saying those things. I don't want in any way to put her parents down, but how can you tell a child how she got HIV without saying, 'This is the way it happened.' Alyssa went on thinking about these things for a long time. That summer she came to the conclusion that she wasn't going to get married and have children because she's not going to pass it on to her children. And she still says that.[2]

"It was a long time before Marie would talk about having HIV. It's different with her," remarks Esther. "Mostly her questions are about dying. I've talked oftentimes with all the children about death, how dying is just going on to be with the Lord, with Jesus, and that what we live in now is only our shell, but the part of us that really thinks and feels would be what goes on to Jesus. They accept that. But Marie's fear of death is even more a fear of *me* dying. She has often told me that she hopes she dies before I do. She lost her mother to HIV, and she knows I don't have HIV, but even so, she's afraid of losing me. I'm trying to help her work through these feelings now, but they're very strong in her. . . ."

Esther turns back to talk about that earlier conversation with both girls. "After that I was able to explain things that had happened in the past, things I couldn't explain when they actually happened because the girls were too young. I reminded Alyssa of that episode when Janet's parents wouldn't let them play together anymore once they found out Alyssa had HIV. What happened was that Alyssa—she was six then and had just finished first grade—had a very close friend whose parents invited her to go along with them to the shore for a weekend. I thought, 'How am I going to handle this?' Then I decided the best way to handle anything is to be right up front about it. So I went and talked to the parents and told them she was HIV positive. They were afraid. They didn't take her with them on their vacation, and they ended the whole relationship be-

[2] Several of the older children in our clinic have come to this conclusion. In most ways children with HIV are no different than any other children. But a child who grows up with a serious illness is often unusually mature, even wise, about certain issues relating to the illness, to suffering, and to death.

tween the girls. I just couldn't explain this to Alyssa then. But now I can tell her, 'That's why you and Janet couldn't play together. Some people are scared that it'll get passed on to their children, even though we tell them the way it's passed on. But they're still scared.'"

Alyssa and Marie both have been hurt on several occasions by the remarks or actions of people who knew they were infected. One such experience occurred after Esther had spoken about HIV at the church she presently attends. The grandmother and father of one of Marie's friends were in the congregation. When they found out that Marie had HIV, they became very distraught and refused to let the girls play together. In addition, the father asked the school principal to take Marie out of the class that included his daughter. Of course the principal refused. The father then asked that his daughter be put in a different class. Again the prinicipal refused. Esther remarks, "Eventually it all blew over. But it was very hard on Marie. Our pastor called us all in, both families, and Kim stood right there next to her father and said to Marie, 'My daddy says I can't play with you anymore.' Time healed this slowly and gradually. It's all right now. The grandmother and I are good friends—she'll bring me a chicken now and then.

"Alyssa had a bad experience around the same time. She got off the bus, and a little boy was standing there when she got off, and he said, 'Alyssa, you have AIDS! You have AIDS!' Then it just traveled down the line of children, each one saying to her, 'You have AIDS! You have AIDS!' She went through a couple of days of hurt feelings until it worked itself through. I met with the guidance counselor—she's been very helpful—and she said, 'We'll continue to keep our eyes and ears open and see how we can help.' I said, 'If it gets too bad for them emotionally, I'll just take them out and do home schooling.' And I'll do that if I have to. Alyssa and Marie and I had some really close times then. We sat down and cried together. I told them, 'We'll work with it, and we'll get through it.' It was a very close time.

"The next year was even harder for Alyssa. When she went back to school in September, there was a boy in her class who said, 'Well, at least my dad didn't die of AIDS. At least I don't have AIDS. At least my mom isn't gray-haired, and she can do things with me that your mom can't do.' I asked Alyssa, 'What did you say to him to make him say those things?' And she said, 'Mommy, I didn't say anything to him.' So I asked her, 'How did he know you were HIV positive?' She said, 'I told him last year. We were real good friends.' I talked with Alyssa's teacher about this, and she promised to work with Alyssa and help her to learn how to handle situations like this. She also promised that she'd find a way of working with the class. I sure appreciated that response." Esther sighs, then smiles at me. It seems very characteristic of Esther that she should conclude an anecdote about the ignorance of adults and cruelty of children with something positive.

A Home Visit with Alyssa and Marie

Arriving at the Hammonds' on a cold Saturday morning in early March, I find Esther and the four girls just returning from sledding on a nearby hill. "Seems the last of the snow, and we thought we'd do some sledding before it disappears," remarks Esther. We all go into the house together. The girls take off their boots and jackets downstairs, then look at the presents I've brought for them: a big container of Hershey kisses (I secured permission beforehand from Esther for these) and a box load of children's books that my youngest son has outgrown. Esther puts the candy up on a high shelf, leaving the books to them. When Esther and I go upstairs, they are deciding who will read which book first. If there are squabbles, they don't occur while I'm there.

The children soon join us upstairs. They all know that I have come to talk with Alyssa and Marie about HIV and that I've brought a tape recorder. Esther turns on the TV for Jackie, who sits down in front of it. Nettie joins her. Alyssa and Marie come into the kitchen and sit on stools around the counter. They are wary of a machine that will record whatever they say but curious about it at the same time. I encourage them to try it out, to say anything that comes to mind and then play it back. At first Alyssa will have nothing to do with any of this. Marie typically wants to jump right in. Esther suggests she sing something, and Marie readily agrees. With no trace of self-consciousness, she sings several verses of a lilting tune I have never heard before; it seems partly a children's hymn and partly country music. The words are variants on "Do unto others what you would have them do to you." Marie has an enchanting voice. I rewind the tape, then play it for them. Both girls listen attentively, giggling now and then.

We begin talking, leaving the tape recorder on. Marie wants to sing another song. "Wait a little bit," Esther tells her, but adds proudly that Marie was chosen to sing in the school play. She goes on to remark, "Alyssa is the reader in the family." Alyssa concurs, telling me that she loves reading diaries about children from older times and that Karen Hesse's *Out of the Dust* is her favorite. The girls chatter about TV programs, friends at school (giggling about the "boyfriends"), then talk about a reunion last weekend for children who attended last summer's camp for children with HIV.[3] I jump in at this point, indicating that other children from the clinic at St. Luke's went to this camp too and that they all had a great time. Then I ask the girls to tell me what they like least and like most about the clinic. Marie remarks, "What I really do *not* like is the shots. Especially the flu shot. I screamed. I hate that one worse than the lab work. The favorite thing I like is that they help us get well. Another thing I do not like is that they give us medicine."

"I like it when they give us presents," says Alyssa. "But I don't like

[3] Camp Dreamcatcher includes children affected by HIV through the illness of a close family member as well as infected children. Funded through grants and the contributions of businesses and individuals, it is a six-day overnight summer camp for children between the ages of five and fifteen. What makes attendance possible for many of these children is that it is free. The staff even arranges for transportation to and from camp for those who need it. The children from our clinic who have attended have had a wonderful time. For the older kids, besides the fun of any summer camp, it offers a setting to talk among themselves about the serious life and death issues that they face as children growing into adolescence with this disease.

the smell of the hospital. It smells bad. The hospital and Granma's nursing home both smell bad."

We talk about what they remember from when they were little children. I ask if they remember the mom and dad they were born to. Marie's response is typical: She answers the question, then rambles on about something only vaguely related. "I know about my dad. He's kind. He got married a lot, and he might get married again soon to Sally. That's not my *friend* Sally, 'cause she's too young to get married. But I'm not! I'm not too young to get married to Richie!"

"Oh, yes, you are!" exclaims Alyssa, her sense of outrage overcoming her uneasiness about the tape recorder.

"No, I'm not!" maintains Marie.

"Okay, girls," interjects Esther, "that's enough. Mind your manners."

"Do you remember your mom?" I ask Marie.

"All I know is that she ran away after she gave me to Grandma. My dad told me one time that my mom was really sad that she ran away and that she died a few weeks afterward. My dad said that when I was a baby, I used to punch him." Marie giggles. "It was when he would try and tickle me; then I'd get him in the nose!"

"How about you, Alyssa, what do you remember about your birth parents?" I ask.

"Um-um . . . my mom, well, she eats a lot. And my dad's dead. My mom has long brown hair, brown eyes, and brown eyebrows, and she's chubby. I don't like to go and visit her very much. And Esteban [her half brother], he pees in his pants." Alyssa makes a face. "He's eight. My mom doesn't teach him."

After more random conversation I ask the girls about the time, now several years earlier, that Esther told them they had HIV. Marie, the first to respond to my question, indicates that she doesn't remember. But Alyssa clearly does. "It was awful, because I didn't know, and I never knew, and then I found out that nobody else had the virus but me, and I felt left out."

"How old were you when your mom told you about this?" I ask.

"Seven," replies Alyssa.

"Then that means I was six," says Marie. "So I wouldn't have understood what HIV even is!"

In actuality Alyssa was nine and a half when this conversation took place, and Marie, nearly nine. It strikes me as significant that both girls remember themselves as much younger than they actually were. Perhaps this discrepancy reflects their vulnerability, or resistance, to knowing their HIV status. Indeed this "knowledge" involves a good many parameters: that they have an incurable and usually fatal disease; that they acquired HIV from their mothers, who in turn were infected from street drugs or through sexual relations; that they were put in foster care because their parents died or were unable or unwilling to care for them; and that they can't talk openly about HIV because of the risk of being stigmatized by others.

Alyssa goes on to say, "HIV is a disease that never goes away. And it gives you AIDS. AIDS is worse than HIV. My mom has it. She's really sick. You get a cough, and then you get really sick and you can die from it."

"Do you know how you got HIV?" I ask.

Again Marie is the first to answer. "My dad doesn't have it, and my mom does. She got it from smoking one cigarette after the other. And drinking . . . and that's how I got it."

Alyssa breaks in. "I got it from when I was in my mom's belly, and my mom was drinking alcohol, and my mouth was open and it went down my lungs, and she was smoking and she still does, and it went down my lungs and it makes fire so I can't breathe, so, um, so that when I come out, and I can't breathe and I want alcohol instead of milk, so then I have HIV."

Esther exclaims, "Well, this is sure an eye-opener!" She seems surprised and flustered. "I've wanted to be careful. I don't want them to learn too much too soon because I don't want them to have any negative feelings about . . . you know." She glances meaningfully toward me, and I realize that she's talking about the girls' biological mothers. The conversation changes, and we begin talking about Dr. Bennett.

"He's nice," remarks Alyssa. "Ever since I was born, he's been tickling me!"

"Yes," Marie chimes in, "he's nice, and he tickles me too. He's not mean, like that doctor you took me to for my eye," she says to Esther.

I ask the girls what they'd like to be when they grow up. Alyssa is the first to answer. "Somebody that helps other HIV kids. . . . I'd take care of them, like how Mommy does. I'd go to Africa and collect all the children and take them to my house so they would have shelter until somebody would want them. But I would make sure that they get a good family. And if they don't, I would keep them. If nobody wants them, I would just keep them."

"How about you, Marie?" I say to her.

"I want to be a veterinarian and a pound person that never puts any animals to sleep. I like it when my mommy prays out loud at night because I know she's there. So I know she's not leaving me."

"Marie," says Esther, "you're afraid that I'll leave you?"

Marie nods.

"That I'll die?"

Marie nods again.

"But you know there will always be somebody to take care of you, always . . ." she says, opening her arms.

Marie climbs up onto her lap. "I don't want anybody to take care of me but you."

"It might always be that way," says Esther. "I want always to be able to take care of you. It may be that the Lord will allow me to take care of you for a real long time —"

"But I still want you to live forever!" exclaims Marie, interrupting her mother.

"Oh, honey," replies Esther, "I'm not going to live forever." She laughs, rocking Marie back and forth. "Boy, the world would sure be full if everybody lived forever!"

"And then," interjects Alyssa, "there would be nobody to be with God!"

"I don't want to live forever either," says Esther, hugging Marie.

"I want to go home someday and be with Jesus. Your mother didn't take care of her body, but you do. Marie, the Lord will give you the grace to handle all this."

It is lunchtime, and I am invited to join them. The kitchen bustles as the older girls go about their tasks of setting the table, pouring the milk, getting Nettie strapped into her high chair. Then all of us sit on stools around the kitchen counter. "It's my turn to pray," Alyssa announces. She gives thanks for the food; asks God to take care of Nettie, Jackie, Marie, Mom and Dad, all their relatives, and all the animals; thanks God for bringing me to be with them that day; then concludes, "And please, God, make our HIV go away."

Clinic Appointment, December 1998

All of us—the nurses, the social worker, Dr. Bennett, and I—have heard about Alyssa's trip to Washington, D.C. Alyssa was chosen to travel with her family to Washington and, with the vice president and his family, hang the star at the top of the National Christmas Tree at the White House. Every year a child with some particular illness is asked to participate in this ceremony. Since this year the ceremony happened to fall on World AIDS Day, it seemed appropriate that a child with HIV be the "star child." Staff members at Dreamcatcher (the camp for children with HIV) were consulted. They chose Alyssa, who had attended for several years. Very soon she became a celebrity. She got to meet the vice president's wife, the family was given a special tour of the White House, and her picture was on the front page of all the local newspapers.

As the clinic staff gathers in the nurses' station before our young patients arrive, we pass around various newspaper photos of Alyssa. She looks like a modern-day princess. Her fine dark hair is pulled back from her face, and she is wearing a long Laura Ashley–like dress with a high collar and long sleeves with puffed shoulders.

Noticing that Esther has arrived with the children for their clinic visit, I wave to her, then walk down the hall to where the girls are being weighed and their blood pressure taken. Esther comes to meet me, Nettie in her arms.

"So you know about the Washington trip?" she asks.

"Oh, yes," I respond. "We've all seen the papers."

"Well, we've just got back," she says. "The kids are still really wound up. We all had a wonderful time, and Alyssa was the star of the show!"

I ask how Alyssa is handling all the publicity generated by the trip.

Esther replies, "The next morning after we came back, I told her, 'I don't know what you can expect in school today, but if they tease you and give you a hard time, all you need to do is say, "Hey, I didn't do anything to catch it," and just walk away.' When we had prayers that morning, we all prayed that she'd have an alright day. It seems our prayers were answered. When she came home after school, she said, 'Mom, kids played with me today that never played with me before!' It probably made a difference that when Alyssa's teacher heard about the trip, she thought it would be a good time to talk to the class about HIV and Alyssa's having it." Esther explains that the teacher thought this might help clear up misinformation for parents as well as students and prevent the kinds of painful incidents with their peers that both Marie and Alyssa suffered recently.

Esther and I walk over to where the children are being weighed. I congratulate Alyssa and tell her she looks beautiful in the newspaper photos. And she does. She is smiling and very talkative today, jumping up and down—in sharp contrast with Marie, who sits on a chair with her head down. I say hello to Marie, and she says hi in return, but without lifting her head. Esther whispers to me that "the green-eyed monster" has visited Marie. But, she adds, the whole experience has been wonderful for Alyssa, who has always lacked self-confidence.

I join Dr. Bennett with another patient while Nicole ushers the family into an examining room. About ten minutes later Dr. Bennett, Rachel, and I walk into the room. Alyssa and Marie seem in pretty much the same positions as they were out in the waiting room. Alyssa sits proudly on the examining table, beaming, and Marie sits quietly on a chair, her head lowered.

Dr. Bennett greets the family, commenting on their trip and asking Alyssa what it was like. "I've never been famous," he remarks as he looks in her ear. "How is it that you get to be famous and I'm not?"

Alyssa smiles as he says these things. She then goes on to describe what it was like to be raised up on a boom lift, accompanied by Tipper Gore, to where the star could be placed on top of the tree. "First there were lots of pictures. Then we went up real high. I could see the White House from up there."

"What was it like to be with Tipper Gore?" asks Rachel, handing Dr. Bennett a stethoscope.

"She's polite, and she's very busy," replies Alyssa.

When Dr. Bennett finishes examining her, she jumps off the table and goes out to chat with Nicole. As he sits down to write in Alyssa's chart, Esther says to Marie, "Okay, Marie, it's your turn now. You can get up on the table."

She does so obediently. Dr. Bennett finishes writing, puts his pen back in the breast pocket of his white coat, and swivels in his chair so that he faces Marie. She's now sitting on the examining table, swinging her legs back and forth, her head still down. He goes over to her and stands in front of her, taking her hands and entwining his fingers in hers. She raises her head to look at him.

"Did you go and visit the White House?" Dr. Bennett asks.

"Yes," replies Marie soberly.

"Did you have to stand in a long line to get in?" he asks.

"No, we didn't."

"Oh, so you were special!"

"Yes, we were special." She smiles just a little.

"You must be. Whenever *I* go to the White House, I always have to stand in a really long line."

Marie giggles.

"When you got in, what did you see?" he asks, feeling in her neck for enlarged lymph nodes.

"The Green Room and the Blue Room and the ballroom too," she replies.

"Did you dance?"

"No." She smiles, giggling.

"Well, if I had been there with you, we would have danced!"

"But there were ropes in front of the ballroom!" Marie protests, laughing.

"Then we would have gone and danced outside!"

Another Home Visit

In the spring I drove out to the Hammonds' farm again. This time the magic was partly that of springtime. Everything was green, the air was scented with flowering trees, and there were sheep grazing by the brook. It was lambing season, as Esther remarked. My tendency to slip into the sweet excesses of nostalgia for the pastoral life was sharply checked by what she told me had happened in the last few days. It had been a hard week. The newborn chicks had somehow escaped their pen and been eaten by the dog. One of the goats suddenly sickened and died within a few hours. A sheep, heavy with her lamb, developed a prolapsed uterus. The vet told Esther that this probably meant the lamb was dead, and that if she wanted to save the sheep, she would need to extract the dead lamb. Jimmy was not there to help, having driven the Amish to a weeklong market in Kentucky. So, following the vet's instructions, Esther severed the lamb's head with a kitchen knife, removed it, then pulled out the rest of the lamb's body. It took hours. Finally it was done, and Esther buried the lamb's head and torso. Two mornings later, going out early to check on the mother sheep, Esther found her in the act of expelling not only her uterus, but also her stomach and intestines. This time she called a neighbor, and asked him to come over and use his gun to put the sheep out of its pain. He did so, though it was several long hours before he could drive out to the farm. Esther decided to burn the carcass rather than bury it, since their dog had dug up the lamb's head the day before.

While I listened to this story, life in all its vitality kept insisting that I pay attention. A white cat with a very swollen belly was rubbing up against my legs. As we walked toward the house, Esther pointed out another cat, curled up in a box as she nursed her kittens. All around me the air was ringing with the high-pitched sound of children's voices. When we reached the house, Alyssa called out to me. I looked up to see her waving from the door of a little playhouse, tucked in the side of a hill. Marie stuck her head out of a window, and then four more curious little girls suddenly emerged from windows or doors of the playhouse.

I realized that Esther's story of suffering and death was not so much a contrast with the life around me as an integral part of it. If the Hammonds' place seems like such a haven for these children, a bucolic paradise, it is still the case that suffering, sickness, and even death remain very real possibilities in their lives. The future is uncertain. At present they are thriving because of powerful and effective medications and because they are in a loving foster home. But they still have HIV, and their bodies can eventually develop resistance to available medications. Esther seems healthy, but Jimmy's future is overshadowed by heart disease. He has already had four heart attacks, he is overweight, and he still smokes cigarettes. This family and the magical little glade in which they live seem to epitomize what one writer, in a very different context, calls "the special beauty of the contingent and the mutable."[4] As I drive away, I am struck by the radical contingency of this family's happiness, indeed of any happiness.

FOR me, this last visit to the Hammonds' farm recalls a passage from *Tales of Good and Evil* by the contemporary American philosopher Philip Hallie, a passage that I use as the epigraph for

---

[4] The quotation is from Martha Nussbaum's book about ancient Greek literature and philosophy, *The Fragility of Goodness: Luck and Ethics in Greek Tragedy and Philosophy.*

this book: "In the eye of a hurricane the sky is blue and birds can fly there without suffering harm. The eye of the hurricane is in the very middle of destructive power, and that power is always near, surrounding that blue beauty and threatening to invade it. . . ." He goes on to observe: "In a world of moral hurricanes some people can and do carve out rather large ethical spaces. In a natural world and a social world swirling in cruelty and love we can make room." It is possible, Hallie argues, to push back the hurricane, though not perhaps to push it very far, and thus create "a blue peace that the storm does not know." Those who do this, Hallie insists, are not heroes who are outside our "moral sphere" and whom we cannot imitate, but people like us.

It was Hannah Arendt in her remarks about Nazi Germany who taught us to see the banality of evil. From people like Esther and Jimmy I've learned about the ordinariness of the good. Certainly the act of taking in four children with HIV seems an extraordinary action, but Jimmy and Esther are just ordinary human beings, as ordinary, and as flawed, as you or I. No one in this chapter, or this book, wears a halo.

As I ponder the story of this family, I find myself thinking not of the Christian teachings so important to Esther but of Albert Camus—the thinker who was important to Hallie—and, in particular, of Camus's great work of moral fiction *The Plague*. The religious faith that Esther lives by is, at least in one way, very close to Camus's humanism. For Camus, to live, fight, or even die for what one believes is not a matter of heroism or sainthood but simply doing one's job. In the words of Dr. Rieux, the story's narrator, "the only means of fighting a plague is common decency . . . doing my job." For Esther and Jimmy the act of taking in these children is the most ordinary thing in the world. They do not think of themselves as special in any way. They simply feel they are just doing something that needs doing. Like any of the foster parents in our clinic, they have love to give, and these children need love. Any of them might say, as Rieux does, "there's no question of heroism in all this. It's a matter of common decency."

The ancient Greeks, wise about so many things, understood the intricacy of the relation between good and evil. Homer and the great Athenian tragedians Aeschylus, Euripides, and Sophocles knew that what is best in each of us is inextricably bound up with the particular way in which each of us is flawed. To use the Greek concepts, they understood that an individual's *hamartia*, which means "wrongdoing" or "error," is intimately connected with that person's *arete*, or "excellence." This understanding was reflected in the characterizations of Achilles, whose heroic valor is hardly to be distinguished from his fiery wrath, and Oedipus, whose overriding urge for knowledge brings about his downfall.

It is the same with more ordinary mortals like ourselves. As Hallie writes, "So many of us—perhaps all of us—are moral mixtures, impure. . . .Those we most deeply love and admire are loved and admired by us not in spite of their faults, but because their faults are somehow a facet of their virtues, if only a dark facet." Esther's and Jimmy's wrongdoings, their shared *hamartia*, are linked with the *arete* that they also share. The same life force that drove them out of their homes and into each other's arms is linked with their ability to love and nurture these children.

I wonder if the paradoxical connection of *hamartia* and *arete* may not apply to a whole society as well as to an individual. The culture that produces the drug abuse and sexual irresponsibility that give rise to AIDS also produces dedicated caregivers, volunteer foster parents, and humanitarian organizations like Loaves and Fishes or Faith-in-Action. The logic of this connection is responsive, even causal: As social evils lead to disease, the disease calls forth the individual and collective powers that seek to cure it and counteract its effects.

Here again *The Plague* proves enlightening. On one level the epidemic that overwhelms the town of Oran symbolizes the Nazi occupation of France. But the German invasion that brought France to its knees also inspired the Resistance, in which Camus himself took part. Like the Resistance, the loosely organized team that fights the plague in Oran gathers to itself all sorts of people, all of whom are motivated by what Camus calls "common decency." And it is quite literally "common," for what unites them against the plague is the shared humanity that is at once their lowest and their highest common denominator. The "job" they all undertake, whatever their personal agendas or ideals, is simply to do what "being human" seems to demand. But this is no light task. As Tarrou and Rieux agree, it is harder to be a man than to be a saint.

Of course not all the citizens of Oran fight the plague, as not all citizens of France resisted the Nazi occupation. Goodness is "ordinary" not because it is universal, average, or even typical, but because it expresses a basic humanity found in all walks of life. Hence it makes for community. Rieux and the rest do indeed form a team, an alliance that cooperates against the plague but at the same time develops deeper human ties among its members. Rieux and Tarrou, for example, are coworkers who take time out to become friends; this too is part of a humanity that is communal as well as individual. If plague divides and isolates, what resists it is a life force that connects and unifies.

In these respects Camus's novel translates directly into what I have witnessed while observing the HIV clinic at St. Luke's. It matches my sense of the ordinariness of goodness in the clinic staff and in family caregivers like the Hammonds, and of the extraordinary things they do that seem so ordinary to them. It explains the way these individuals, seemingly connected only by a disease, form themselves into moral communities: the interracial families created by Esther and Jimmy and by other foster parents; the medical clinic that becomes, for those who work there as well as those they treat, an extended family; or service organizations like Loaves and Fishes and Faith-in-Action. Paradoxically these moral communities have been brought into being by a disease—moreover, an infectious disease.

In Camus's novel the plague passes from the town of Oran. In life, at the moment when I write, HIV in this country appears to have reached a point of stasis: The rate of infection has slowed; the risk of transmission from mother to infant has been drastically lowered; transmission of the virus from blood transfusions is nearly eliminated. What was a terminal disease seems nearly controllable, at least for some. But this remission is only for this place and perhaps only for this time. Elsewhere in the world AIDS continues its ravages. Furthermore, in this country, as Dr. Rieux warns about Oran, the plague that so mysteriously ebbs and vanishes is not eradicated. Its remarkable capacity to mutate may someday defy our drugs and therapies.

Like Camus's plague, HIV infection in America is both a real disease and a symbol of larger and even darker realities: drug abuse, sexual irresponsibility, prostitution, and patterns of child abuse or neglect that are associated with most cases of perinatally acquired HIV infection. For such systemic cultural ills we have yet no cure. But in the tiny microcosm of a single pediatric clinic and the community it serves we can see the forces of ordinary goodness that rally to help children with HIV and their families. As Camus's narrator in *The Plague* observes, "what we learn in a time of pestilence [is] that there are more things to admire in men than to despise."

AFTERWORD

NONE of the stories in the five preceding chapters really has an ending. Happily none of the children I write about has yet died. But none is cured of HIV. This open-endedness can frustrate our almost instinctive hunger for closure, our assumption that any good story should end, like a musical composition, with a resonant final chord—major or minor, as the case may be.

However, since one purpose of this book has been to show, in a small but detailed sample, just how HIV-infected children are cared for in this country at the turn of the century, then this inconclusiveness is not only justified but necessary. Medical research and treatment of HIV, the dynamics of family relationships, the foster care and welfare systems, and the structure of the medical system itself are all changing even as I write. The fact that each of these stories does not really end is thus consistent with the ongoingness of the world around them. The following postscripts, completed just before the book goes to press, report on further developments in the lives of these children and their families.

Maria and C.J. Montalvo

I have kept in touch with Cesar and his family by phone. They have moved yet again and are now living on a farm in Tennessee.

Cesar has stayed with Penny, the woman whom he introduced as his new landlady that last day we saw the family in the clinic. They were married in the spring of 1999. He sent me a wedding picture of his bride and himself leaning against a fountain. Cesar is smiling. His face is now heavily lined, making him look much older. His hair is short. Penny is squinting against the sun. She looks beautiful in a full-length bridal gown, her blond hair intertwined with the folds of a lacy veil. They are surrounded by children. Avricita and Maria are wearing fancy long dresses and carrying flowers. C.J., his hair slicked back, is dressed neatly in a formal black suit and white shirt. He proudly holds a small white pillow with the ring on top. Two other youngsters, about five or six years old, are standing to one side, holding the bride's long wedding train. The inscription on the back of the picture tells me they are Cesar's nephew and niece.

The family also sent me pictures of C.J. and Maria. Nine-year-old C.J. sports long, wavy hair and an impish grin. He stands leaning back a little, his shoulders raised and his thumbs hooked into the pockets of his jeans. Maria, now ten years old, is smiling the way children do when a photographer has said or done something silly. Her face still looks pinched. The pupils of her eyes are white, rather than black; Dr. Bennett tells me this is probably an indication of cataracts.

C.J. has continued to be asymptomatic, but Maria has been sick a great deal. On several occasions her weight loss was so severe that she was put on gastrostomy feedings. A tube was inserted through her nose and a liquid food supplement drained through the tube into her stomach. After an hour or so the process was reversed, and the liquid not absorbed was pumped out though the same tube. Not surprisingly, Maria hated this. Her most recent medications include some of the very latest antiretroval drugs available: Norvir and Fortovase (both protease inhibitors), Combivir and Abacavir (NRTIs), and Sustiva (an NNRTI). But her viral load has continued to rise. The last time I spoke with Penny, she reported that Maria's viral load has climbed to 520,000, and that her doctors have taken her off all medications. It seems that in this race between the ever-mutating HIV virus and new, effective medications, the virus is finally winning.

Joey and the Riley Family

Joey remains a happy, active child, thriving in every way. His health has stabilized, and he loves school. Melissa too is doing well—especially in sports, at which she excels. She plays baseball and soccer and is the manager of the basketball team.

In other ways, however, the family is in serious trouble. Loretta's treatments for cervical cancer, though successful in eradicating the cancer cells, resulted in large-scale radiation burns. Ever since, she has been in considerable pain. The codeine-based analgesics have been only partially successful. Her doctors knew this but were reluctant to start her on morphine because they feared she would become addicted. After Loretta had gone through some six months of unremitting and increasing pain, her doctors suggested she undergo a colostomy (the surgical creation of an artificial anus), which they planned to reverse some nine months later after the tissue damaged by the radiation burns had healed. The colostomy did provide some relief from pain, but it also brought a new set of problems. The incision continued to open and needed to be resewn every month.

Unfortunately Loretta's radiation burns did not heal. Nine months after the colostomy, exploratory surgery revealed damage so extensive that her doctors advised immediate surgery to remove the burned tissue. Loretta agreed. She said to me, "I had no choice. The doctors told me that if I didn't have the surgery, I'd die, and that was it." Her bladder, uterus, ovaries, rectum, vagina, and part of her colon were removed in a risky and lengthy procedure with the curious name of "pelvic exoneration." Loretta survived this radical surgery, recuperated during a two-week hospitalization, and then went home. But while she was gone, conditions at home had deteriorated: The house had not been kept clean and had become infested with fleas. Loretta soon developed a fever that sent her back to the hospital. Not only did her doctors find that her surgical incision was infected, but they discovered lice and fleas around and even within the site of the wound. This time she was discharged to a nursing home, and various attempts were launched to have the Rileys' trailer cleaned, repainted, and fumigated.

The clinic staff stayed in close contact with the family while all this was happening. There were now two social workers trying to help them: Ramona from our clinic and the social worker for gynecology/oncology patients. The more involved the social workers became in setting up support services, the more difficulties they seemed to encounter. The Rileys accepted services but frequently "fired" people sent to their home to help. They took money but did not always use it to pay for necessities. Bills were left unpaid. Despite food stamps and aid from a local food bank, food remained a problem for them.

I have learned that "helping" in such a situation—even with the best intentions—is not easy. It is not enough simply to write a check. What had appeared to us as simply a problem of not having enough money now seemed a problem of not spending money sensibly. In the past Loretta was somehow able to balance their income and their expenses. Perhaps she will recover and be able to do so again. She is hopeful. Follow-up pap smears have been encouraging. She says her doctor assures her, "There's no more cancer." But over the past year Loretta has lost more than 130 pounds, and her health continues to deteriorate.

It is hard to see what the future holds for the Rileys. Community groups and national charities have rallied around this family. Gas money was provided by a cancer foundation. The Rileys' church took up a contribution and gave them $600 to buy school clothes for the children. Mike stayed at the hospital's Ronald McDonald House, and a foster family was found to care for Joey and Melissa during Loretta's hospitalization. Of course all medical expenses were covered. But there is a danger that the individuals, groups, and agencies that have been trying to help this family could become impatient or exhausted. It may be necessary now to assign the family a caseworker who would take over management of their finances. So far both Loretta and Mike vigorously resist this intrusion into their lives.

Felicity and the Dawsons

Felicity turned out not to be infected. The Dawsons were relieved, though not as much as we expected them to be. When they learned the good news, Sarah said simply, "Well, we took her not knowing, and we would have loved her either way."

Sarah gave birth to a healthy baby girl. The two babies—only four months apart—seem to relate well to each other. They also have doting grandparents in the foster mother and father whom Sarah calls her parents.

Ellie, thought to be pregnant with her third child, moved to another state where she worked as a security guard. There was some speculation that the move might have been motivated in part by her wish to keep this baby. Whatever may have happened, she returned to Harperville a year later—alone.

Angelina Morales

Angelina looks wonderful. Though still shy, she smiles a good deal and interacts with us easily. Her skin is now completely smooth. It is hard to remember her appearance only a few years ago, when her face was mottled with molluscum lesions, and, once those were surgically removed, with scars from the lesions. Though she is in good health, there have been occasional behavioral difficulties. As Mrs. Fanthorpe says, "Angelina can be so difficult sometimes. She can get moody, and she can be so mad about things!" The Fanthorpe household is run on strict lines, and Angelina is punished when she breaks the rules or is disrespectful to her foster parents.

The family has moved to a better neighborhood, where the children (there are now four, three of them foster children) can safely play outside. The Fanthorpes remain very religious. At first Angelina participated in religious observances because she had to, but now, at eleven years of age, she is beginning to find religion personally helpful. She now likes to go to church and enjoys its youth activities.

At present Angelina has no contact with her biological family. Her brother Roberto, with whom she was so close, continues to have trouble with the law and is now in reform school.

Most important, the Fanthorpes decided they want to adopt Angelina, and adoption proceedings are already under way. But several months into adoption proceedings, Mr. Fanthorpe, who had never been sick a day in his life, became suddenly ill with severe headaches and incapacitating dizziness. A CT scan revealed there was fluid on the brain, and surgery was scheduled as soon as possible to insert a shunt that would drain off the fluid.

With the sudden drop in income that came about as a result of Mr. Fanthorpe's inability to work, all unnecessary expenses were eliminated. Even food was a problem for a while. Mrs. Fanthorpe, on her part, interpreted everything as a trial of faith. She would conclude our conversations by assuring me, "I just know that God is with us through all this."

Angelina came through this difficult time with flying colors: She kept complaints to a minimum, did not throw tantrums, and was supportive and helpful around the house. But she paid a price for this success. First, cold sores appeared around her nose and mouth; then she developed pneumonia. Though she was not hospitalized, she did have to be brought to St. Luke's weekly for treatments with intravenous antibiotics. Eventually she recovered from her pneumonia and went back to school, about the same time that Mr. Fanthorpe got better and returned to work.

It remains a struggle for Angelina to control her temper. Recently, when Angelina had misbehaved, Mrs. Fanthorpe sent her out to the back porch for some "time out." Angelina threw a tantrum and screamed so loud that a neighbor called the police. Children and Youth Services was notified, and adoption proceedings halted "to assess the situation." The Fanthorpes have never wavered in their decision to adopt Angelina, which they believe is God's will, and consider this only a temporary setback.

Tommy Wheeler

Tommy is still living with his stepfather, Sam. Marla has moved in with a man who, according to Sam, is an "ex-trick." The court has directed that Sam remain legal guardian and that Tommy spend every other weekend with his mother. But Marla wants him back permanently and is working hard to make this happen. Lester, Tommy's biological father, is also back in the picture. He wants Tommy returned to Marla or to the custody of his own mother. According to Sam, "He just doesn't want a white guy bringing up his kid."

At Marla's instigation, there was a court hearing in the spring of 1999. She wanted her custody rights extended so that she could see Tommy more often. I was asked to attend the hearing as a character witness for Sam. The atmosphere in the court hallway was heavy. Sam, Marla, Marla's present boyfriend, Tommy's father, other relatives, and character witnesses all were waiting outside, some singly and some in small groups, to be admitted to the courtroom. I could easily identify Lester, since Tommy looks so much like him. There was little interaction among all these people. When the doors to the courtroom opened, the judge called only the "principals," along with their lawyers, into his chambers. The hearing lasted only fifteen or twenty minutes. Apparently the judge dismissed Marla's request for extended custody rights, indicating that she needed to have a fixed place of residence and to remain drug-free for longer than a few months. He also ordered counseling sessions, one series for Tommy and Marla and another for Tommy and Sam, to investigate the actual relations between the child and each caregiver.

Six months have elapsed since then. Tommy's living arrangements remain unchanged: He lives with Sam but stays with his mother and her boyfriend every other weekend. Sam and Tommy have kept up with their counseling sessions. It is unclear whether Marla and Tommy have done likewise. But she is determined to have Tommy returned to her custody, and she wants Sam out of her and Tommy's lives.

Sam's lawyer has told him, "Prepare yourself to give Tommy up," warning him that if Marla makes a good-faith effort to comply with the court's directives, she is likely to regain custody. In fact her lawyers—who are representing her pro bono—are petitioning the court that the order for psychological counseling be waived and that Marla be permitted to have Tommy back, since she can prove she has remained clean and lived at the same place for more than six months. Sam feels that he can no longer turn to his lawyer for help since his debt is so high. Sam does not think that Marla will be able to keep clean. He thinks that she is able to do so now because she has a strong motive—to have her son returned to her— and that once this happens and Sam is out of the picture, she is likely to relapse. "And then," he asks, "what will happen to Tommy?"

Carlos and His Grandmother

Carlos has returned to his grandmother's. The arrangement by which Carlos and his brother Alonso lived with their older brother Juan, his wife, and their three children lasted only a few months. From the beginning Alonzo was a problem, since he refused to obey Juan and encouraged the other children to misbehave, and so he was sent to Chicago to live with Carlos's father and another sibling. Carlos missed him. When he would come in for his clinic appointments during this interval, he looked sad and didn't talk much. On one occasion he told me he wished he could move to Chicago too "so we could all be a family." He also told me that he missed his grandmother, but that "she don't want me. She's said she'd send me away before, every time I'm bad."

Nonetheless, at the end of a few months Carlos was returned to his grandmother. He seemed much happier the next time we saw him, when Pastor Bill brought him for a clinic visit. But Bill's report was discouraging. He told us that he was concerned because, once again, it seemed that Carlos was not taking his medications as he should. Bill always checks Carlos's HIV medications when he picks him up to take him to see Dr. Bennett. From the number of pills in each bottle, it became apparent that Carlos was taking twice the prescribed amount of one drug and not enough of the other. When Dr. Bennett asked Carlos who supervised him when he took his medications, he admitted that no one did—not his grandmother now, and not Juan before that.

Carlos has missed several of his clinic appointments. We know that Loaves and Fishes, the community AIDS group that has been so helpful to Carlos, is going through difficulties: Isabel's time with clients is restricted because of a new baby (her first), and Pastor Bill's work has been drastically curtailed because of heart problems. Besides the loss of virtually half the work force of this little family organization, they have acquired eighty new clients over only a few months.

The clinic staff is concerned about Carlos. We all know that the alternative to living with his grandmother is foster care. But twelve-year-old boys with HIV are hard to place; furthermore, we know that his grandmother loves him and tries hard, and he loves his grandmother. I've found a student at a nearby college who is willing to serve as a kind of "Big Brother" to Carlos. This young man is willing to visit with Carlos, take him to basketball games, help him with his homework, drive him to his clinic appointments, and see that his prescriptions are filled. Perhaps this arrangement will tide things over, at least for a while.

Alyssa, Marie, and the Hammond Family

The Hammond family keeps growing. There are more animals: Four heifers graze "out in the meadow," and there is another litter of tiny kittens. And there is another foster child too. For several months during the summer Alyssa's nine-year-old half brother lived with the Hammonds. It seems that his mother went back on drugs, and Children and Youth Services had to find foster placement for the child.

Soon after this boy went back to live with his mother, the Hammonds took in yet another foster child, eight-year-old Micky. A little boy with HIV who has been coming to St. Luke's clinic for years, Micky is a shy, sweet-tempered, somewhat passive child. He has not seen his father, who lives in Puerto Rico, for a very long time. Most of his life he has lived either with his mother, who has a serious drug problem, or, during the frequent intervals when she is in jail, with his grandmother. Over the past year he has been in several different foster placements and is just beginning to display the kind of emotional outbursts that became such a problem for Angelina and her caregivers. But Esther and Jimmy, after much prayer, have decided to keep Micky as long as he needs foster care. "He fits in so well with the rest of the family," Esther explains. "And you know, I have a feeling that they're going to send him back to his mom. Maybe I can help make that work! I'd sure like to try."

GLOSSARY OF MEDICAL

TERMS AND ACRONYMS

Abacavir (Ziagen). A reverse transcriptase inhibitor approved in December 1999.

ADD (attention deficit disorder). Children with this disorder have difficulty concentrating, are easily distracted, and are often hyperactive. ADD is often identified when a child starts school and learning problems are identified. HIV does not cause or contribute to ADD. However, children born addicted to drugs like morphine and heroin are at risk for this disorder. ADD in children is often controlled with medications.

AIDS (acquired immunodeficiency syndrome). HIV disease in an advanced stage.

AIDS cocktail. See **Triple therapy.**

Antibody. A protein that circulates in the blood. Antibodies bind to invading organisms, neutralizing their pathologic effects and enhancing other components of the immune system that might help destroy them.

Antigen. A protein that, when introduced into the body, stimulates the production of an antibody specific to that particular antigen.

Antiretrovirals. Drugs that interfere with HIV replication. These include nucleoside reverse transcriptase inhibitors, non-nucleoside reverse transcriptase inhibitors, protease inhibitors, and other pharmaceutical compounds to come.

Aspiration pneumonia. A kind of pneumonia caused by bacteria that live in the mouth but are somehow aspirated into the lung.

Asymptomatic HIV. A condition in which the disease is present in the body but has not produced symptoms.

AZT (Retrovir, zidovudine, ZDV). AZT is probably the most intensively studied as well as widely used antiretroviral drug in both children and adults. It was the first reverse transcriptase inhibitor to be licensed, in March 1987, for the treatment of HIV.

Bacteremia. Bacterial infection in the bloodstream.

Bactrim (trimethoprim-sulfamethoxazole). A widely used drug used to treat and to prevent PCP in children.

Biaxin (clarithromycin). A drug commonly used to treat MAI in children.

Candidiasis. An infection with *Candida albicans*, a fungus that affects the mucous membranes. In HIV-infected persons candidiasis usually occurs in the mouth, but it may also infect the lungs and blood.

CD4 count. See **T cell**.

Children and Youth Services. The state agency responsible for children's welfare programs.

Clinical drug trial. A series of steps that must be completed before a particular drug can gain FDA approval. Usually a clinical trial takes about twelve years to complete. It includes three and a half years of preclinical testing, six years of studies in humans, and about eighteen months for the FDA review process. Clinical drug trials in humans involve three phases. The first tests the drug's safety; the second examines the drug's effectiveness and side effects; the third verifies effectiveness and identifies adverse reactions. The HIV epidemic has resulted in accelerated programs for drug development and review.

CMV. See **Cytomegalovirus.**

Combination therapy. See **Triple therapy.**

Combivir. A combination of AZT and Epivir. Combivir is particularly helpful for children who need to reduce the number of medications they take.

Crixivan. See **Indinavir.**

Cytomegalovirus (CMV). A herpes virus that usually leads to mild flulike symptoms in most people but to severe multiorgan disease in those who are immunocompromised.

ddC (Hivid). See **Zalcitabine.**

DdI. See **Didanosine.**

d4T (Zerit). See **Stavudine.**

Didanosine (ddI; Videx). A reverse transcriptase inhibitor approved in October 1991. Didanosine was first evaluated as a monotherapy and was found to be as or more effective than AZT.

Diflucan. See **Fluconazole.**

DNR (do not resuscitate). In the case of terminal and irreversible illness or injury, a physician's written order (based on the patient's or parents' wishes) not to begin such lifesaving measures as mechanical breathing devices.

Duragesic. See **Fentanyl.**

Efavirenz (Sustiva). A non-nucleoside reverse transcriptase inhibitor that became available in September 1998.

ELISA test. A blood test that is used to indicate the presence of antibodies to HIV. ELISA testing was used primarily in large-scale screening of blood products. Mandated testing of the nation's blood supply by ELISA testing began in March 1985. The ELISA test is used often to detect HIV in individuals because it is inexpensive (about seven dollars in state-sponsored labs) compared to other such tests and has a high rate of reproducibility as well as rapid results.

Encephalopathy. A generic term referring to any malfunction of the brain. HIV encephalopathy is a viral inflammation of the brain cells.

Epivir (3TC). See **Lamivudine.**

Epogen (erythropoietin). A factor given by injection that stimulates red blood cell production. Epogen is sometimes used in patients with HIV to counteract the side effects of AZT, which can reduce red blood cells and thus cause anemia.

Fentanyl (Duragesic). A morphine-like drug available in a timed-release transdermal patch and effective for chronic pain over time.

Fluconazole (Diflucan). An antifungal drug effective in treating thrush.

Fortovase. A more easily absorbed form of saquinavir that received FDA approval in November 1997.

Gamma globulin (IVIG). A class of blood proteins that contain antibodies to fight infection.

Gancyclovir. An antiviral drug used primarily to treat CMV retinitis.

Gastroenteritis. Inflammation of the stomach and intestine.

Hemoglobin. The protein in red blood cells that carries oxygen.

HIV (human immunodeficiency virus). A retrovirus that targets the T lymphocytes, particularly the T4 subset, which regulate the immune system.

Hivid (ddC). See **Zalcitabine.**

Hospice. A kind of care offered patients when death seems inevitable. Comfort is emphasized more than treatment, tests, or procedures. In the United States hospice is most often not a place but an approach to care that can be administered in the patient's home. In the early years of the AIDS epidemic, however, there were a number of AIDS hospice centers intended to house such persons in the final stages of disease.

IgG. A class of immunoglobulins. An individual's IgG, determined by a blood test, gives information about his or her immune status.

Immunocompromised. Term to describe persons whose immune system is not functioning properly, thus rendering them more susceptible to infection.

Immunodeficiency syndrome. A generic term for all forms of immune deficiency, whether related to antibodies, white cells, or cell-mediated immunity.

Immunoglobulin (Ig). Gamma globulin that has been extracted from plasma and contains specific antibodies to a variety of infectious organisms. At one point in the history of HIV treatment, patients were given IVIG (intravenous immunoglobulin) in an effort to prevent or treat infection.

Impetigo. A contagious bacterial infection of the skin consisting of red, itchy patches and small blisters. In children, impetigo usually occurs around the nose and mouth.

Indinavir (Crixivan). A protease inhibitor with poor palatability that was approved in March 1996.

Invirase. See **Saquinavir.**

IVIG. Intravenous immunoglobulin.

Lamivudine (3TC; Epivir). A reverse transcriptase inhibitor approved in November 1995. In treating children, it is often used with AZT.

Lymph nodes. Glandlike structures that help prevent the spread of infection. Palpating the lymph nodes in the neck, in the armpits, and in the groin is standard procedure in the routine physical examination of an HIV-infected person. Enlarged lymph nodes often indicate that the virus is circulating actively in the body.

Lymphocyte. A specialized white blood cell in the immune system.

MAI. See *Mycobacterium avium–intracellulare.*

Make-a-Wish Foundation. An organization that arranges for special gifts for children with terminal illness.

Medical Assistance. The federally funded welfare program that covers the cost of medical care for the very poor.

Molluscum contagiosum. A viral infection of the skin characterized by smooth, waxy, raised lesions. In young children, areas of eczematous dermatitis frequently surround a cluster of mollusca.

Myambutol. A drug used in conjunction with other drugs to treat tuberculosis.

***Mycobacterium avium–intracellulare* (MAI).** An infection, very rare before the AIDS epidemic, caused by a bacterium. MAI can occur anywhere in the body. It is called disseminated MAI when it is present in the body but not localized. MAI is often difficult to isolate through blood tests and is sometimes treated empirically. There are now prophylactic drugs that can prevent MAI in many infected persons, though their effectiveness becomes limited the longer they are used.

Nelfinavir. See **Viracept.**

Nevirapine. See **Viramune.**

Non-nucleoside reverse transcriptase inhibitors (NNRTI). A group of antiretroviral drugs that are structurally and chemically different from NRTIs, but that also inhibit HIV replication. NNRTIs are useful in combination therapies.

Norvir. See **Ritonavir.**

NRTI. See **Nucleoside reverse transcriptase inhibitor.**

Nucleoside analog. Shorthand for nucleoside analog reverse transcriptase inhibitor. A drug that, when entering an HIV-infected cell, interferes with the virus's ability to replicate itself. Nucleoside analog drugs do this by preventing reverse transcriptase, an HIV enzyme, from further synthesis into the DNA chain.

Nucleoside reverse transcriptase inhibitor (NRTI). See **Nucleoside analog.**

Opportunistic infection (OI). An infection caused by a microorganism that is usually present, though benign, in persons with intact immune systems but becomes pathogenic in persons whose immune systems are damaged.

Otitis media. Middle ear infection. A common problem for children with HIV.

Pancreatitis. Inflammation of the pancreas that may cause severe abdominal pain. Acute pancreatitis is not uncommon in children with HIV. It is sometimes caused by certain antiretroviral medications, such as ddI and ddC.

Parvovirus (fifth disease). An acute viral disease that occurs most often in children and is caused by human parvovirus B19. The typical manifestations of the disease include a low fever, malaise, and a blotchy rash on the cheeks. Children who are immunodeficient can develop long-lasting infections accompanied by severe anemia.

PCP. See *Pneumocystis carinii* pneumonia.

PCR (polymerase chain reaction) test. A highly sensitive way to detect HIV infection. PCR is a technique by which any fragment of proviral DNA (DNA sequences in which HIV is already present) can be multiplied to an amount large enough to be measured. PCR testing is especially valuable in early diagnosis of HIV in infants. Viral load is an indirect result of PCR testing.

Pediatric AIDS Clinical Trials (PACT). Drug trials for pediatric AIDS funded by the government and sponsored by the FDA.

Perinatally acquired HIV. Infection of the fetus or infant by the mother near or at the time of delivery.

Placebo. An inactive substance in a controlled drug trial against which an experimental drug can be compared.

Pneumococcal meningitis. An inflammation of the meninges (membranes) covering the brain and spinal cord caused by the pneumococcus bacterium.

***Pneumocystis carinii* pneumonia (PCP).** A kind of pneumonia caused by a fungus. PCP is one of the most common opportunistic infections in children with HIV. It can be prevented in many infected persons by giving Bactrim prophylactically.

Prednisone. A steroid used to diminish inflammation.

Protease inhibitor. A kind of drug that is effective, when combined with nucleoside analogs, in reducing replication of the virus. As its name suggests, this drug inhibits the function of the protease enzyme to interrupt HIV replication. Protease inhibitors differ from nucleoside analog drugs in that they interfere late in the reproductive cycle of HIV, whereas nucleoside analog drugs interfere early on.

Retrovir. See **AZT.**

Rifampin. A drug that is used to treat various forms of tuberculosis.

Ritonavir (Norvir). A protease inhibitor commonly used in children.

Roxanol. A morphine-based drug used to ameliorate severe pain.

Saquinavir (Invirase). The first protease inhibitor approved for use in adults, in December 1995. This drug has largely been replaced by Fortovase, a more rapidly digested version.

Seroconversion. The point at which an individual exposed to HIV has antibodies to HIV present in the blood serum. Children born to HIV-infected mothers have HIV antibodies and, if they are not infected, after a year become seronegative.

Stavudine (d4T; Zerit). A reverse transcriptase inhibitor that won FDA approval in June 1994. It has been used effectively in combination with either 3TC or ddC.

Sustiva. See **Efavirenz.**

T cell count (also called T4 count or CD4 count). T cells are lymphocytes that help in the production of antibodies necessary for cell-mediated immunity. As "helper cells," they are vital components of the immune system. A drop in T cell count is usually associated with lessened immunity and an increased risk of acquiring opportunistic infections. Until viral load testing became available, the T cell count provided a way to measure the clinical efficacy of anti-HIV therapies. The T cell count in infants and young children is normally higher than in adults.

3TC. See **Lamivudine.**

Thrush. A *Candida* infection of the mouth. It is one of the most common opportunistic infections in children with HIV. Thrush is easily detected, appearing as white splotches in the mouth. It can cause no discomfort at all; however, if widespread and not treated, thrush can be painful, making it difficult to eat or swallow.

Transverse myelitis. Inflammation of the spinal cord. Symptoms most often include sudden back pain and weakness in the legs. Treatment in most cases is nonspecific and symptomatic.

Triple therapy. A combination of anti-HIV drugs that includes two reverse transcriptase inhibitors and one protease inhibitor.

Vertically transmitted HIV. Infection directly from mother to fetus during pregnancy.

Videx (ddI). See **Didanosine.**

Viracept (Nelfinavir). A protease inhibitor that won FDA approval in March 1997. Viracept was one of the first protease inhibitors licensed for use in children.

Viral load. A measure of the amount of virus in the body. The viral load test (costing one to two hundred dollars), developed around 1994, measures the number of HIV RNA strands in blood plasma. It is important in determining whether anti-HIV medications are effective.

Viramune (Nevirapine). A non-nucleoside reverse transcriptase inhibitor that, in early 2000, shows great promise in diminishing perinatally acquired HIV in poor countries.

Western Blot assay (p24 antigen test). More specific and more expensive than the ELISA test, the Western Blot (about sixty dollars) is used in testing an individual only after there has been a positive ELISA test to confirm its accuracy. Combined ELISA and Western Blot testing is 99 percent accurate.

Zalcitabine (ddC; Hivid). A reverse transcriptase inhibitor approved for adults in June 1994. Zalcitabine has not been approved for use in children as a monotherapy. However, the combination of ddC and AZT appears to be well tolerated.

Zerit (d4T). See **Stavudine.**

Ziagen. See **Abacavir.**

Zidovudine. See **AZT.**

BIBLIOGRAPHY

Arendt, Hannah. *Eichmann in Jerusalem: A Report on the Banality of Evil.* New York: Viking, 1963.

Baxter, Daniel J. *The Least of These My Brethren: A Doctor's Story of Hope and Miracles on an Inner-City AIDS Ward.* New York: Harmony/Crown/Random House, 1997.

Camus, *The Plague*, tr. Stuart Gilbert. New York: Modern Library, 1948.

Centers for Disease Control and Prevention. *HIV/AIDS Surveillance Report*, 10:1 (1998), 1–40.

Coles, Robert. *The Call of Service: A Witness to Idealism.* Boston: Houghton Mifflin, 1993.

Dickens, Charles. *The Adventures of Oliver Twist.* Oxford Illustrated Dickens. Oxford, England: Oxford University Press, 1949.

———. *Bleak House.* The Oxford Illustrated Dickens. Oxford, England: Oxford University Press, 1948.

———. *David Copperfield.* The Clarendon Dickens. Oxford, England: Clarendon Press, 1981.

———. *Little Dorrit.* London: Collins, 1954.

———. *The Life and Adventures of Nicholas Nickleby*. New York: Heritage, 1940.

———. *The Old Curiosity Shop*. New York: Dodd Mead, 1943.

Dostoevsky, Fyodor. *The Brothers Karamazov*, tr. Constance Garnett, rev. and ed. Ralph E. Matlaw. Norton Critical Edition. New York: W. W. Norton & Co., 1976.

Glaser, Elizabeth, and Laura Palmer. *In the Absence of Angels: A Hollywood Family's Courageous Story*. New York: G. P. Putnam's Sons, 1991.

Hallie, Philip. *Tales of Good and Evil, Help and Harm*. New York: HarperCollins, 1997.

Mohrmann, Margaret. *Medicine as Ministry: Reflections on Suffering, Ethics, and Hope*. Cleveland: Pilgrim, 1995.

Norris, Kathleen. *Dakota: A Spiritual Geography*. Boston: Houghton Mifflin, 1993.

Nussbaum, Martha C. *The Fragility of Goodness: Luck and Ethics in Greek Tragedy and Philosophy*. Cambridge, England: Cambridge University Press, 1986.

Oleske, James. "Antiretroviral Therapy and Medical Management of Pediatric HIV Infection," *Pediatrics* 102: 4 (October 1998), supplement, 1005–62.

Pizzo, Philip A., and Catherine M. Wilfert. *Pediatric HIV: The Challenge of HIV Infection in Infants, Children, and Adolescents*, 2d ed. Baltimore: Williams & Wilkins, 1994.

Selwyn, Peter A. *Surviving the Fall: The Personal Journal of an AIDS Doctor*. New Haven: Yale University Press, 1998.

Sontag, Susan. *AIDS and Its Metaphors*. New York: Farrar, Straus, Giroux, 1988.

Sophocles. *Oedipus Tyrannos*, tr. David Grene. *Sophocles I. The Complete Greek Tragedies*, ed. David Grene and Richmond Lattimore. Chicago: University of Chicago Press, 1954.

——. *Philoctetes*, tr. David Grene. *Sophocles II. The Complete Greek Tragedies*, ed. David Grene and Richmond Lattimore. Chicago: University of Chicago Press, 1954.

Stine, Gerald J. *AIDS Update 1999: An Annual Overview of Acquired Immune Deficiency Syndrome*. Upper Saddle River, N.J.: Prentice Hall, 1999.

Verghese, Abraham. *My Own Country: A Doctor's Story*. New York: Vintage/Random House, 1994.

White, Ryan, with Ann Marie Cunningham. *Ryan White: My Own Story*. New York: Dial, 1991.

Wiener, Lori, Aprille Best, and Philip A. Pizzo. *Be a Friend: Children Who Live with HIV Speak*. Morton Grove, Ill.: Albert Whitman & Co., 1994.

Wiznia, Andrew A., Genevieve Lambert, and Steven Pavlakis. "Pediatric HIV Infection." *The Medical Clinics of North America. Management of the HIV-Infected Patient, Part I*, 80: 6 (November, 1996), 1309–36. Philadelphia: W. B. Saunders, 1996.

Zuger, Abigail. *Strong Shadows: Scenes from an Inner City AIDS Clinic*. New York: W. H. Freeman & Co., 1995.

RESOURCES

National Nonprofit Organizations Concerned Specifically with HIV in Children

The Elizabeth Glaser Pediatric AIDS Foundation began in 1988 with the efforts of Elizabeth Glaser, Susan DeLaurentis, and Susie Zeegan to direct funds toward research on effective treatments for children with HIV. The impetus for the foundation was the struggle of the Glaser family after Elizabeth and her husband, Paul, discovered that not only had she contracted HIV during a blood transfusion, but she had unknowingly passed on the virus to her daughter in utero and to her son during breast-feeding.

The mission of the foundation is to support basic pediatric HIV/AIDS research. Its goals include reducing HIV transmission from an infected mother to her newborn, prolonging and improving the lives of children with HIV, eliminating HIV in infected children, and promoting awareness and compassion about HIV/AIDS worldwide.

Website: www.pedaids.org

Main office (in California)

Elizabeth Glaser Pediatric AIDS Foundation
2950 31st St., Suite 125

Santa Monica, CA 90405
phone: 310-314-1459
e-mail: info@pedaids.org

In New York

Elizabeth Glaser Pediatric AIDS Foundation
225 West 34th St., Suite 1606
New York, NY 10122
phone: 212-947-7511
e-mail: ny@pedaids.org

In Washington, D.C.

Elizabeth Glaser Pediatric AIDS Foundation
805 15th St. NW, Suite 500
Washington, DC 20005
phone: 202-371-0099

Community-Based AIDS Service Organizations

Under the Ryan White Act of 1990, states are allocated funds for a
variety of direct care services for persons with HIV/AIDS. The Ryan
White Act mandates that states develop multicounty consortia, or
coalitions, that will be responsible for the distribution of government
money allocated for this purpose. The Ryan White Foundation itself
closed in 1999 because of a lack of funds. It was established in 1991
in memory of Ryan White, a child with hemophilia who contracted
HIV through a blood transfusion. Ryan became a spokesperson for
the need for education about HIV and tolerance toward those afflicted, especially children. He died in 1990.

For information about community-based AIDS service organizations supported by Ryan White Title II funds, contact the Health Department of individual states and ask for the list of Ryan White
consortia in that particular state.

General Resources

For Information About Treatment

The American Foundation for AIDS Research:
  800-39AMFAR (392-6237)
  or 323-857-5900 (Los Angeles)
  or 212-806-1600 (New York City)
AIDS Treatment News: 800-TREAT 12 (873-2812)
PROJECT Inform, National HIV/AIDS Treatment Hotline:
800-822-7422

For General Information About HIV/AIDS in Children

CDC National AIDS Hotline: 800-342-AIDS (342-2437)
CDC National AIDS Hotline (Spanish service): 800-344-7432
CDC National Prevention Information Network: 800-458-5231
National Pediatric and Family HIV Resource Center: 800-362-0071
PKIDS (Parents of Kids with Infectious Diseases): 877-SSPKIDS, or
pkids@pkids.org

For Information About Clinical Trials

AIDS Clinical Trials Information Service (ACTIS): 800-874-2572

*For Information About HIV Legal and Policy Issues Regarding
Children and Families*

AIDS Alliance for Children, Youth, and Families: 202-785-3564